Trail Gimp

SELF DISCOVERY AND EMPOWERMENT ON THE APPALACHIAN TRAIL

APRIL WEYGAND

APRIL WEYGAND

Trail Gimp: *Self Discovery and Empowerment on The Appalachian Trail*

Copyright ©2023 by April Weygand

All rights reserved. No part of this publication may be reproduced, stored in a retrieval system, or transmitted, in any form or by any means without the prior written permission of the publisher, nor be otherwise circulated in any form of binding or cover other than that in which it is published and without a similar condition being imposed on the subsequent purchaser.

First Printing, 2023

ISBN : 978-0-6456902-5-5 (Print)

Published by Change Empire Books

Cover design by: Matt Davies, Very Much So Agency | matt@verymuchso.com
Book Interior and E-book Design by Amit Dey | amitdey2528@gmail.com

To Madison and Tyler
May you forever follow your dreams.

And for Brian
Who helps me to fulfill my own.

TABLE OF CONTENTS

Acknowledgments. vii

Disclaimer ix

Prologue xi

Chapter 1: Greg. 1

Chapter 2: The First Attempt. 9

Chapter 3: Coed Naked Bridge Jumping. 27

Chapter 4: Adjusting. 39

Chapter 5: North Carolina 53

Chapter 6: The Dream Job 63

Chapter 7: A New Dream. 73

Chapter 8: The Second Attempt 87

Chapter 9: Nightgrumbler. 99

Chapter 10: The Haven Farm. 107

Chapter 11: Chasing Little Bus 119

Chapter 12: Still Chasing Little Bus 131
Chapter 13: Keeping up 139
Chapter 14: Missing 151
Chapter 15: Making Miles. 163
Chapter 16: April, Meet Trail Gimp 175
Chapter 17: Conquering Fear 187
Chapter 18: The Beginning of the End. 195
Chapter 19: Mount Katahdin 213
Epilogue 219

ACKNOWLEDGMENTS

This book could not have been written without the help and encouragement of many people.

With the help of the International Women's Writing Guild, I wrote an initial manuscript in 2007. Laurie Harper read the oversized and unmanageable composition and gave me her expert opinion and advice. It needed work, but there was a definite possibility for future publishing. Life got busy, and I put it on a shelf. Thank you, Laurie, for taking the time to help me.

I am also indebted to dozens of others for their help, feedback, and encouragement.

Cathryn Mora of Change Empire Books and fellow writers Charlie Giles, Kathy McKenzie, and Irene Salter for the advice and encouragement in writing this.

My family, Madison, Tyler, and Brian, who made dinner and did all the other things which enabled me to write until the wee hours of the morning.

The staff of April Fresh Cleaning, who allowed me to come in late after an epic night of writing or leave early for the same reason. Teamwork makes the dream work, and I couldn't do this without all of you.

Tom Stock, Katherine Girdich, Kelly Colburn Bienick, Karen Charbonneau, Melissa Ward, Suzanne Edson, Michelle Raynor, Gail Cangiano, and Tonya Yasenchak, thank you for your time as readers. Your ideas and suggestions have been invaluable.

Many friends from the trail who verified information, relived scenarios with me, and hiked with me. I can't possibly list the hundreds of people, but includes Gina Varrichio, Whitney Allgood LaRuffa, Sean McGahee, Eric Northcutt, Haley Pepper, Darius Kavaliunas, Hilary Lang, Andrew Long, Deborah Brown, Mike Dubin, Karen Borski, Ipo Salcedo, and Bruce Heine. Bo Smolka deserves an extra thanks for taking the time to read and give me a ton of feedback on this manuscript. You have been too kind. Darrin Kimbler deserves a shoutout for putting the idea of a 1998 thru-hike into my head in the first place. I'll be eternally grateful.

I'm most grateful to Roxanne Whitworth, Eva Rosamofsky, and Rob Vojtko, and the rest of the crew in Charlotte, who supported my hike and always accepted the phone charges. Your friendship and support mean the world to me, then and now.

And to my longtime friend Matt Campbell, who suggested a few years ago that I start writing again, thank you for believing in and encouraging me.

And, of course, thank you to my extended family at home: sisters, aunts, uncles, cousins, and especially my Mom and late Dad.

DISCLAIMER

This is a memoir of my hikes on The Appalachian Trail in 1996 and 1998. All information is true to my knowledge and memory, supported by trail journals, photos, guidebooks, and maps. I apologize in advance if someone has a memory that differs from mine.

In some cases, I have changed someone's real name or trail name to protect their privacy. Although trail names aren't common knowledge to the general public, hikers know each other by trail names. I've tried to provide anonymity to some by changing their name or using a lesser-known trail name.

PROLOGUE

December 2006

The phone rings at seven in the morning. Nothing good comes from a phone call this early.

"April," my aunt says, "You might want to get to the hospital right away. Your mom is on her way. Your dad took a turn for the worse, and we're not sure how he's doing."

Dammit. I know he's not at his best, but I hoped that getting him to the hospital yesterday would prolong his health a little more. I jump into clean clothes and rush to get ready. I drop my two-year-old at daycare and run to the hospital with my newborn son as fast as I can drive. I call my husband to update him and tell him to get to the hospital as soon as possible. Dad has been fighting cancer for a few years. He's fought hard with chemotherapy, but his tumor is non-surgical, and he's had complications. He never complains. He never shows if he gets down and depressed. He wants to live to see his grandchildren grow.

I want that for him too. I want my kids to know their grandpa. As much as I try to remain positive, I have a sinking feeling that today might be the day. I try to ignore the feeling and keep pushing it out of my thoughts.

I find my mom at the hospital, and within moments, my older sister and several aunts and uncles arrive. We take over the lounge on the floor, just outside my dad's room. It's noisy and busy, with doctors and nurses running around while alarms sound and codes are being called over the intercom. It helps that family is here. Aunts and uncles are like extra parents - we see each other through everything and support each other. We try to remain upbeat, discussing everyday life, passing my son around, and celebrating new life in our family. Nobody cries. Nobody discusses the elephant in the room.

Dad's room is busy. He's in and out, going for x-rays and tests. We take turns in his room, talking to him, though he doesn't respond much. Everyone talks of miracles, but I'm prepared. I know he won't make it through the day, and I quietly accept it. While I'm talking to my uncle, my sister races into the lounge, waving her hand frantically in front of her throat. I hear alarms coming from my dad's room. We race in to see the nurse leaning over him with her stethoscope. "He's in cardiac arrest. He can probably hear you, but only for another minute or so." Various relatives call out between tears.

"We love you, Wayne!"

"Don't worry; we'll take care of Lil for you. She'll be fine."

"You can rest now, Wayne."

"Bye, Dad. See you soon. Tell everyone in heaven I said hi," I whisper.

My mother leans down and throws her arms across him, sobbing uncontrollably, begging him not to leave. "I'm not ready! I can't do this without you," she wails. We all stand by, motionless, unable to help. It's heart-wrenching to watch. How do you watch someone lose their spouse, their life partner of 40 years? Someone must do something. Someone has to say something. Why is nobody moving? Finally, I kneel and whisper to her.

"You need to let him go," I say gently.

"I can't," she cried. "I'm scared. I don't know how!"

"Yes, you do. You knew this day would come. You're ready."

And then he is gone. Muffled cries and the silence of tears fill the room. I see my Godmother enter the room, and I meet her near the door to quietly break the news. I catch her as she collapses into my arms. My husband silently leaves the room a few minutes later, fighting back his tears. He wipes his red eyes and stares past me when I try to console him.

"I hate this disease," he cries. "Cancer is the worst thing in the world."

"I know."

"How can you just stand there?" he asks, this time looking directly at me. "Why aren't you crying? Your father just died, and you don't shed a tear?" He bellows incredulously. "Where do you get your strength?"

Images of rocks and mountains, streams and trees, and white blazes come to mind. I wasn't always this strong - stubborn, yes; willful, absolutely. But inner strength, well, that's often hard to come by.

Once upon a time, I thought I was strong. At least that's the image I portrayed – quick to laugh, make jokes, and agree with others. I thought if I laughed first, they would laugh with me, not at me.

That strength my husband asked about? I found some on a mountainside in North Carolina, in a shelter in Pennsylvania, and climbing the White Mountains in New Hampshire.

Where did I find my strength?

I found it on The Appalachian Trail.

― CHAPTER ONE ―

GREG

August 1995

I hate to admit it, but life is not going well. My plan to become an elementary school teacher, be happily married, and have a mortgage, is not working. I'm a substitute teacher because there aren't any jobs available. I don't have a boyfriend, and I'm still living with my parents. I'm 25 years old. It's pathetic.

I'm driving home after visiting some friends in Boston, three hours away. I had a good time laughing and joking, going out to dinner, and taking in the sights. And now, I'm going home to my miserable life.

What's wrong with me?

When I arrive home, I walk into an empty house.

"Mom? Dad? Anyone around?" It's silent, except for the incessant beep of the answering machine. I press the button.

"Hi, this is Sally, Arlene's neighbor. I can't get in touch with Arlene, so I thought I'd call you to see what's going on with Greg. Can you give me a call when you get a chance?"

Greg? What's going on with my cousin? I push the button again.

"Hi Lil, it's Nancy. We're leaving now; we'll meet you at the hospital."

Hospital?

I press the button repeatedly, listening to message after message about my cousin, an accident, and heading down to the burn center. I have no idea what's going on. I call my Aunt Nancy. I get an answering machine. I call my Aunt June. Answering machine. I call my sisters. Answering machines. Frustrated and without answers, I call my Aunt Arlene's neighbor, Sally. I listen in disbelief as she tells me that my cousin was in a house fire, is in critical condition, and is being airlifted to the regional burn center, two hours away. Apparently, the rest of my family is on their way to the hospital.

An hour later, my dad calls home.

"Hey, Dad, what's going on?"

"There was a fire at Aunt Arlene's house – Greg got caught in the middle of it, and he's burned pretty badly. They airlifted him to the Westchester Burn Unit – the rest of the family is here, too."

I look at the phone in disbelief. *Did I hear my dad right? Greg was burned in a fire? How did my 21-year-old cousin get burned in a fire?* I snap back to reality, and the practical side of me answers. "Okay. Well, I just got back from Boston, and I can jump in the car and head down."

"Really, April, there's nothing you can do here. We're just sitting around in the waiting room."

My mind races back to Valentine's Day, 1977. I'm seven years old. Dad is working out of town, and Mom is outside walking the dog. She had put the tea kettle on the stove to have hot tea when she returns because it's so cold outside. My sisters and I are unloading the dishes from the dishwasher. I stop to go to the bathroom, and when I finish washing my hands, I hear screaming from the kitchen. I race around the corner to see my older sister standing behind my younger sister, holding her dress out from her body to prevent the flames from burning her. My younger sister had leaned over the stove to turn off the burner to silence the whistling kettle, and her fluffy dress caught fire after touching the red-hot burner. My sisters are screaming and crying. We just went over fire safety at school. What are you supposed to do when you see a fire in a house? The first step is to get out. So, I turn around and run down the steps into a foot of snow.

My uncle Ted was living with us for a while, and he knew something was wrong when he saw his niece run outside mid-winter without a coat. He ran upstairs, saw my sister in flames, threw her on the floor, and rolled her until he extinguished the fire. In the end, the scars on her arm and torso slowly faded, and eventually, she was fine.

I know Greg will be fine, too, eventually.

I decide to stay home, knowing I'll see Greg in a few days, and I set about to be helpful. I call some neighbors to update them, and since Greg is supposed to be heading back to college next week, I reach out to his school.

"Hi, my name is April. I am Greg's cousin. I wanted to call and let you know that he was injured in a fire today. I don't know how serious yet, but he won't be at school next week as scheduled. I'm sure he'll be fine, and we'll keep you updated as he recovers."

I unpack my suitcase, clean up the house, play with the cats, and do anything to keep busy and my mind occupied, wondering when Greg will be home.

I'm sitting on the couch, watching TV the next day, when my dad comes into the house.

"Hey, Dad, I'm downstairs," I holler.

He comes downstairs and stands awkwardly, shifting his weight from one foot to the other. He looks down at the floor.

"Um, Greg didn't make it," he says quietly.

I'm sure I misunderstood what he said. "Didn't make it?" I say after a minute, trying to process his words. "You mean he died?"

"Yes, he died this morning."

Greg's an athlete. Healthy. Hard working. Good person. Smart. Kind of goofy. All my thoughts about Greg swirl through my brain. I just saw him a few days ago. He's almost like my brother. How could he possibly be dead?

"April, he was burned so badly. His organs just started shutting down one by one."

Dad went upstairs while I sat slumped on the couch, numb. Nobody has died in our family except my grandfather a few years ago, and grandparents are supposed to die when they get older; 21-year-old track stars are not supposed to die. My aunts and uncles are like extra parents, and my cousins are like brothers and sisters.

The next few weeks drag by. My family is a mess. My mom and aunts cry all the time, and we even attend giant family group therapy sessions. Greg is the closest thing my mom had to a son. He even lived with us as his parents moved up from the city. I move right into logistics mode. I help return phone calls, notify the college of Greg's death, update friends, cook dinners, and clean the house. Someone has to do it. I'm the dutiful one.

A month later, school starts back up, and once again, I substitute teach during the days, work nights and weekends at the mall, go out with friends, dance, party, and watch football. Repeat. It's the same old routine. I'm bored. I'm stuck.

I wander into a used bookstore in town and discover *A Walk Across America* by Peter Jenkins. It was published in 1979. I read the back cover and realize the author started walking across the country from Alfred, NY. Funny, Geneseo, my alma mater, is about an hour away from Alfred, and I've been there a few times to visit friends. I feel an instant connection to the author, and I picture some random guy donning a backpack and just walking wherever he feels like walking. I buy the book, and I can't wait to get home to start reading.

Why would some guy just walk across America? Why not? It seems intriguing. In the book, he mentions that he crosses the Appalachian Trail a few times. What is that? I've been day hiking with some friends from work. I like it. It's freeing. No time schedules and customer service are required – just laughing with friends and enjoying the breezes and wildlife. I learn that the Appalachian Trail is a footpath through the Appalachian Mountains, over 2,000 miles long, stretching from Georgia to Maine.

It was meant to be a short wilderness escape for people living along the East Coast. But a guy named Earl Shaffer returned from World War II and decided to hike the whole trail, end to end, in one year. He wrote a book about his hike called *Walking With Spring* and the idea of a thru-hike was born. What is it like to thru-hike the Appalachian Trail?

I stalk my local library to research the Appalachian Trail. I find a two-volume book called *Hiking The Appalachian Trail*. It's essentially a collection of stories of the first 50 people to thru-hike The Appalachian Trail. I read at any opportunity I can find, including the time I should be sleeping, and I devour the 2,000 pages within a few weeks.

I love to travel, and the idea of putting on a backpack and walking where the wind takes me sounds exciting. It brings life to my daily thoughts. What would it be like to hike through the mountains instead of teaching every day? Instead of working in a mall? I imagine the freedom that hiking every day would bring. I picture pretty trails under stately trees, ending at picturesque lean-tos and relaxing by campfires while gazing at the stars. Oh, how relaxing and magical that would be.

One day, I am going to hike this thing.

Weeks later, I answer the phone to hear my newly married, 22-year-old sister crying. She has been complaining of headaches for a while, which everyone assumed was stress, dealing with college graduation, the death of our cousin, and her wedding, all within a few months of each other.

"April, my headaches..... sent me for a CT scan... they can't determine.... MRI... tumor..."

What?

I piece together what she's trying to say. My sister has a brain tumor. She had a CT scan that showed something...but they couldn't figure out what it was. An MRI showed it was a brain tumor. Surgery is scheduled in a few days.

Once again, my extended family gathers in the waiting room of a hospital. The idea of losing my sister is not an option we entertain, but Greg's death taught me that nothing is guaranteed. Bad things can happen to good people. Still, I refuse to acknowledge that anything bad could happen. We know nothing about brain tumors. Cancerous? Benign? Surgery? Does she need chemotherapy? Will she need radiation? Will her speech or memory be affected? What does all this mean?

The doctor comes out earlier than expected. Is that good or bad? We hold our breath. Is he smiling? Is he coming to tell us about complications?

"Everything is fine, surgery is finished," he says. We finally exhale. "It was a low-grade, very slow-growing tumor, and we removed it entirely. She won't need radiation or chemotherapy. She should be just fine, but we'll follow up as a precaution."

Our prayers are answered, and everyone hugs everyone, crying joyfully and thanking God.

Thank you, Greg. I'm sure you probably want some company up there. Thank you for not taking my sister. Thank you for letting her live her life.

My sister is recovering, and I am restless. I'm still in the same routine. I go to work in the morning to teach someone else's lesson plans. I come home to eat dinner, read the newspaper, then head to work again at the mall. On the weekends, I go to work at the mall, come home to change, and head downtown to meet up with friends. It's routine, and I'm finally sick of it. I need a change.

But how am I going to make a change? I can't find a teaching job. Everything requires money, and I don't have much of that. I remember that guy who walked across America. He didn't have a lot of money. It doesn't take a lot of money to hike The Appalachian Trail. Once you buy your gear, you just need a little spending money. But how does one go about hiking The Appalachian Trail? How do you get there? Can I hike alone? I'm a young woman – my parents won't like me hiking alone. How on earth do I quit my job?

The idea of hiking The Appalachian Trail fills me with curiosity and excitement I didn't know was still within me. I wake up excited about the possibility of hiking mountains I've never seen, living in places I've never heard of, and doing something vastly different from anything I've ever done. It's exhilarating, intriguing, and maybe slightly dangerous, and the entire idea intoxicates me.

I contact the Appalachian Trail Conference and request some information. I devour any book I can find about the AT. I learn that there are trail towns where you can buy supplies and food, and I begin to research gear. I purchase gear guides to research backpacks, boots, water filters, tents, clothing, and pots and pans. One night at dinner, I abruptly tell my parents my plan.

"Um, I've decided that I'm going to hike the Appalachian Trail starting in April."

They look at each other, knowing I must be joking because April is only two months away.

"I have it figured out. I'm buying all my gear with the money I have saved and the money I'll make from teaching. The Appalachian Trail Conference will help me find a female hiking partner. The trail starts in Georgia and finishes in Maine. It should take me about six months. I promise I'll be safe."

From the comments I've been making and the books I've left around the house, my parents know a little about the Appalachian Trail. So little, though, that my mother asks, "Is it paved the whole way?"

Paved? I look at her as if she has three heads. *What kind of wilderness trail is paved?* I decide not to worry her, and I gather some of my books to show her the nice, wide trails and the clearly marked white blazes to mark the way. I don't show her pictures of the rocks, the "bridges" over rivers made from wire and rope, and I certainly don't mention that there have been a few murders along the AT either. Instead, I tell my parents that hundreds, if not thousands, of people attempt to hike the entire Appalachian Trail every year. So there will be plenty of people. I'll be safe. I promise.

I save as much money as possible and go on a shopping spree to buy all the equipment I've been researching. Once home and in my room, I set my tent up and take it down, then do it again, practicing until it becomes second nature. I take out my stove, put it together, boil water, let it cool, and put it away. Although I nearly set fire to the picnic table the first time, I repeat this until I can do it in my sleep. I learn to use my water filter, practicing until it seems I've done it millions of times. I pack everything into my backpack and unpack it. I wear my backpacking boots everywhere, hoping to break them in and loosen the leather a bit. Repeat, repeat, repeat. I'm ready. I give my notice to all my jobs.

The Appalachian Trail Conference connects me to a few people looking for female hiking partners. After talking to a few of them, a young woman from Canada, Melissa, agrees to be my hiking partner. She's about my age and seems nice. Her dad is driving her to the trailhead in Georgia, and they offer to stop by to pick me up. My parents invite them to stay the night, probably so they can be sure I'm not hiking with a lunatic. All parents agree that their mid-20-something daughters have rocks in their brains, and they're crazy to attempt this hike, of which only 10% actually finish. Girls aren't supposed to hike long-distance trails. Girls are supposed to have nice jobs and take care of houses and kids. They aren't supposed to be traipsing through the wilderness. But what can they do? Our minds are made up, and off we go.

CHAPTER TWO

THE FIRST ATTEMPT

April 1996

April 13, 1996 arrives, and I step on the approach trail for the first time. I try to jump up and down with excitement, but my pack is too heavy. I never weighed it at the visitor center, insisting it was 40 pounds, although I'm pretty sure it weighs much more. If I knew it weighed too much, I would probably quit before I started. So, I'm hiking in ignorant bliss. I look for the next blue blaze, a two-by-six-inch rectangle painted on a tree that indicates the trail. White blazes indicate the actual Appalachian Trail. Blue blazes represent a side trail. My excitement is tempered a bit because we still need to hike seven miles just to *get to* the beginning of the Appalachian Trail. I had read that the approach trail is some of the hardest hiking in the beginning. I believe it. I think the trail is a 45-degree angle all the way up, if not more. And to make matters worse, it's been raining on and off. What kind of idiot begins a six-month hike in the rain?

It's one thing to practice hiking around town, wearing my hiking boots everywhere I go. It is something entirely different to be hiking on the actual

Appalachian Trail. My boots, which were comfortable at home, already feel entirely too tight, and they are extremely heavy; it takes all my energy just to lift my foot and move it a few inches up the trail. I maneuver around wet rocks and slippery tree roots; I'm certain I will slip and fall at any moment.

Melissa and I continue walking, with her leading the way because she has a bum ankle. The problem is, I still can't keep up with her. I stop every couple of feet to catch my breath, trying to remember what my high school track coaches taught us about breathing properly – in through the mouth and out through the nose? Or is it the other way around? Oh my God, I don't even know how to breathe anymore! I knew I shouldn't have quit the track team. Melissa turns around to wait for me, and when I catch up, she asks, "April, are you okay? Your face is all red."

Of course, my face is red! I can't breathe; this mountain is almost vertical, and I'm sure my heart will explode any minute.

"I'm fine, thanks," I manage to respond, huffing and puffing. I'm suddenly aware that all the rollerblading and exercising I've done recently has prepared me for absolutely nothing on this trail. I am woefully out of shape.

I'm also learning that one can't learn how to hike the Appalachian Trail by reading a book. I thought I had prepared well. I've been hiking for all of 30 minutes, and I am entirely too hot. I know it's rainy today, so I put my Gore-Tex jacket on. They say Gore-Tex is breathable. I disagree. We stop every few minutes to take off our rain gear and then stop again a few minutes later to put it back on. Finally, we realize that we're getting wet anyway, either from rain or sweat, and we just decide to hike in our shorts and T-shirt and accept the weather thrown at us.

I'm hot and sweaty; a few minutes later, when the wind blows, I'm cold again. My legs are muddy from the wet trail splattering every time I step, and I'm soaking wet from rain or sweat. And this backpack is really heavy. We see a lightning bolt hit the mountain too close to us and hear a giant KABOOM that shakes our feet. We scream at the top of our lungs, drop our packs in the middle of the trail, and run a few feet to hide under a small tree. We cower like children for a few minutes until the storm seems to pass, and we gather our packs to continue. This is turning out to be a rough start to my fantasy. I was expecting to glide effortlessly through the trees like an ethereal fairy. I was expecting rain and mud at some point, but not *this*.

Melissa yells, "Plaque!" at the top of her lungs, indicating she's reached the summit. The plaque is the beginning of the Appalachian Trail, which I've been dreaming about seeing for months. I stumble and dig deep within myself to push myself up the mountain, and when the trail becomes less steep, I'm too tired to be very excited.

I walk over to where Melissa is standing as another loud clap of thunder makes me question my sanity. The rain falls from the sky in buckets. "I'm headed to the shelter!" I yell. I barely glance at the plaque as I pass, not even bothering to take a picture of it with the camera hanging around my neck. Did I really think I would be a National Geographic photographer documenting every step I take?

The shelter is exactly what I expected. It's a three-sided wooden structure with an additional sleeping loft upstairs, rebuilt only a few years ago. It can easily sleep 15 or more people, which is good because there are about that many people here already, either in tents or set up in the shelter. There are nails in the walls upon which to hang packs and several tuna fish cans hanging from the ceiling by strings. The idea is to hang your food bag from a hook beneath the tuna fish cans, so when the mice come out in the evening, they can crawl down the string, but the tuna cans prevent them from getting to your food bag and eating your provisions. *Mice?* I've only spent one night camping in a shelter before, and I didn't see or hear of any mice. I'm sure they're exaggerating.

There is a shelter register – a notebook that hikers sign into when they arrive at a shelter. It's also a way of leaving notes for other hikers behind you. I don't know anyone on the trail except Melissa, so I simply sign my name with a message: "Glad to be out here, finally."

The practice of assembling my Whisperlite International 600 stove at home was a good idea because I can make dinner without setting the picnic table on fire. My stove is collapsed inside my pot. I pull out my stuff sack, position the legs to make a tripod, hook up the hose to my bottle of

Coleman Fuel, prime the stove by opening the valve to allow a little gas to fill a cup and close the valve, light the gas with a lighter, and then open the valve again to allow a hot, blue flame to build. I fill my pot with water and place it on top of the stove. Voila.

After eating, I start my chores: – washing my pot and pan in biodegradable soap, disassembling my stove, and filtering water. This is not like turning on a faucet at home, no siree. A two-foot-long hose is attached to the bottom of my filter. I put this hose, which has a pre-filter at the end to prevent any larger debris from entering the filter, into a puddle of water or a stream. Then I push and pull a lever up and down about a thousand times, and clean, fresh water comes out of a tube at the top, filling my water bottle. It's eleven ounces of luxury for me. It's important to filter water to remove contaminants and parasites and to prevent waterborne illnesses such as giardia. Other people carry iodine tablets to save weight, but I don't like the taste of that. A filter is heavier, but I like the taste of fresh, clean water better.

After chores are finished, I set up my sleeping pad and bag, and lie down in the shelter to rest, relax, and write in my journal. I hear someone casually mention the bear tracks in the area. *Bear tracks?* We collectively decide that hanging our food bags from trees is the safest thing to do. At home, I did not practice hanging my food from a tree.

Thankfully, about a dozen others can help me because I'm not used to throwing a rope over a tree branch to hoist my food 20 feet into the air. I did learn that half of my pack weight is food, and I hope my food bag doesn't break the tree limb that it's hanging from. I need to eat more food to lighten my load.

I spend the next few hours talking to all the guys at the shelter here. Melissa and I are the only women. People are here from all walks of life – professionals taking time off from a busy career or just retired from one, someone newly divorced who needs to get his head together, several guys in the construction or service fields who just wanted to hike the trail, and one guy just out of college. We are from all areas of the country. Some people are thru-hikers, intending to get all the way to Maine this season, some are section hikers, hiking for a pre-determined number of days or miles, and the day hikers, out for a few hours, have already gone home.

After a while, talk turns to gear.

"April, how do you like your external frame pack? What made you buy a Gregory pack instead of a Kelty or a Jansport?"

"Why do you have a stainless-steel pot instead of an aluminum one? Aluminum is much lighter, you know."

"Hey, how do you like that water filter? I'm using iodine tablets, but I don't like the taste. I'm considering switching to a filter, but I'm concerned about weight. How much does yours weigh?"

"How are those boots? I know that's a good brand – I thought they were a little expensive, though."

And so it goes for an hour.

I finally collapse into my sleeping bag at the incredibly late hour of 8:40 pm. I am spending my first night as a thru-hiker on the Appalachian Trail, and I smile with pride as I fall asleep.

I wake up in the morning groggy and grumpy. It turns out that nobody was exaggerating about the mice in the shelter. I didn't sleep very well, constantly being woken up by them or the fear of them in the shelter. I'm not used to wild creatures running around in the middle of the night.

Melissa and I pack up and head to the Hawk Mountain shelter, seven and a half miles away. After about half an hour, we come to a parking lot of a forest service road and see Melissa's dad sitting there.

"What are you doing here, Dad?" Melissa asks.

"I just wanted to be sure you girls were okay and double check that you really want to be out here. I'm heading home if you want to go home."

"Dad, we'll be fine. We're having a good time. Right, April?"

"Yep - having a great time," I respond flatly, with all the excitement I can muster. I mean, I am excited to be out here, but I didn't get much sleep. I'm tired, and my pack seems heavier than it did yesterday.

Melissa hugs him and says, "Have a safe drive home, Dad!"

The trail is flat or slightly downhill, so I enjoy myself now. It's warm and sunny with blue skies, the birds are chirping, and the views through the trees are pretty. But my feet begin to hurt after a few miles. My toes slam into the front of my boots every time I walk downhill, and my heels jam into the back of my boots every time I walk uphill. I feel sharp pain coming from my feet and wince in agony with every step I take.

Melissa has already gone ahead to get to the shelter, and I drag myself slowly up the mountain. I can barely breathe, and now I can barely walk. I come across a small stream and collapse on the edge of it. I filter a quart of water and guzzle it. My feet are screaming, so I remove my boots and peel off my socks to see why. I cringe in horror at my feet. My heels have so many blisters that they look like raw hamburger meat, and large blisters have formed on every one of my toes. I shove my feet into the stream, hoping the icy, cold water will help the swelling. I rummage around my pack for Advil and pop a few like candy. The suffering is too much, and I can't stop the tears from spilling from my eyes. I just can't help it.

Neither the stream nor the Advil help very much. What am I doing out here? Why the heck am I enduring this? I'm 1000 miles from home, in the middle of the north Georgia woods. I'm sure there are better things I could be doing with my life. I should be teaching. I should be hanging out with friends in my apartment. I should be traveling, staying in hotels, and having fun.

The problem is I can't find a full-time teaching job, I can't find a boyfriend, I don't have enough money to get an apartment, and I don't have any friends who want a roommate. I suck it up, put my socks and boots back on, and hike toward the shelter.

I arrive at the shelter 30 minutes later and feel foolish that I have just spent an hour crying my eyes out at a creek that was only a mile back. Over a dozen people are here at the shelter, some of whom stayed at Springer last night, and everyone is busy in their own way. They are cleaning equipment, writing in their journals, filtering water, cooking dinner, or just chatting with other hikers. As soon as I walk in, I hear a bunch of people say, "Hey, April, glad you made it. Come on in and get comfortable." I instantly feel better. We have a good time talking with each other while we do our chores, and I beam with pride as I hang my food bag all by myself.

The skies are gray in the morning, and it's cold; someone tells me my hike to Gooch Gap Shelter will be rough. She wasn't lying. It's a horrible, muddy hike. Every step is either uphill or downhill; there isn't a single, flat stretch of trail in the entire eight-mile section. My legs throb with every step. I can't breathe or walk, and I try to hold them in, but I can't prevent the tears from falling again.

I can't walk anymore, so I collapse in the middle of the muddy trail and have a pity party. I blubber like a child for 15 minutes and suddenly remember how I might be able to escape from this horrible idea of mine. My college roommate lives near Atlanta, and if I can figure out how to get to town, I might be able to get a bus to her house. Right now, I need friends and comfort, and I just want someone to take care of me because I'm a pathetic mess.

Then, reality strikes. I realize that I need to get up and move to get anywhere. I either die right here on the trail or move forward. These are my options. I suck it up, put my big girl pants on, and move forward. I trudge through the mud, the muck, the rain, uphill, downhill, around trees, over rocks, across streams, and finally, *finally*, I see the shelter.

My heart falters, and I let out an audible whine as I realize the shelter is full. It's not nearly as large as the last two have been, only fitting about six to eight people, and now I know why. Many people quit by this point, realizing it's ridiculous to hike 2,000 miles in the woods. I've hiked all of 23 miles, and I realize how stupid this is.

Once again, some people from last night recognize me and welcome me to the shelter. There are some new faces as well. They look warm, dry, comfortable, and happy. I'm sure I look like a filthy, wimpy, blonde mess. I set up my tent nearby and collapse inside.

I wake up 45 minutes later, starving like I haven't eaten in days. I rummage through my food bag and pull out Lipton noodles, tuna fish, a candy bar, and trail mix. A memory of one special date comes to mind when an old boyfriend and I were eating lobster in a nice restaurant. There were tablecloths and cloth napkins, real dishes, and glasses. I hoped to eat in nice restaurants like that when I got older.

But here I am, in the middle of the woods, putting together a stove to boil water to make instant noodles. I shake my head as I wonder how my life has gotten so far off track.

Once again, the other hikers and I chat before bed, sharing stories, discussing gear, and making plans for the next day. Nobody seems to care that I can't find a teaching job. Most people here are single, and not everybody owns a house or has their own apartment. Nobody thinks it odd that I'm still living with my parents. Some applaud me, telling me it's a great way to save money. I go to bed with a smile, realizing that maybe things aren't as bad as I think they are, and I plan to hike on, putting away the thought of surprising my old roommate.

We arrive at The Walasi-Yi Center, a trail store with an attached hostel. The coolest thing is that it's the only building on the entire Appalachian Trail that the trail *actually passes through*. I've hiked five days and 31 miles, plus that dreadful approach trail. People don't add the approach trail in their mileage – so it's like a free day of hell that doesn't count. Many of us spend time at the store, and I learn the root cause of my blisters: boots that are entirely too small for my feet. I bought my street size, and apparently, you're supposed to be fitted for boots, and they should be bigger than your street size to allow your feet to swell. The owners of the center tell me I should buy new boots. The idea of spending another $300 on new boots is not appealing, and they try to hide their amusement when I ask if there is any way of stretching the leather. It's possible to stretch boots perhaps a quarter of a size, but not two sizes like I need. I forego the new boots, deciding to hike with thin sock liners instead of my soft and bulky socks.

A few hikers and I eat a nice dinner at a local restaurant and relax with new friends at the hostel. About a dozen of us are staying here, laughing, and sharing stories and generally getting to know a little more about each other.

In the morning, Melissa says, "April, how far do you want to go today? I know you're in some pain with your feet."

"I don't know – maybe six miles to Whitley Gap shelter, perhaps camp somewhere after that. Why?"

"Well, I was thinking of going all the way to Low Gap shelter tonight."

Low Gap shelter is over ten miles away, and I know I won't get there in one night. But it's okay. We don't laugh at the same jokes, we don't hike at the same pace, and we just aren't kindred spirits – she doesn't know my soul – and we don't make the best hiking partners. At this point, I know I don't need someone to hike alongside me and hold my hand. "It's okay – I'm not sure I'll get there, but you go ahead and hike your hike. If I see you, I see you."

Some people at home had asked me, "Aren't you afraid to hike alone?"

Why would I be afraid to hike alone? I wonder. "No." I respond. "I'm not afraid to hike alone."

"Aren't you afraid of animals? Or crazy guys trying to hurt you?"

No, I'm not afraid. Maybe I'm naïve or stupid, but I grew up in a neighborhood where boys outnumbered girls 3-1. I've always considered myself equal to them. I've never been afraid of anyone hurting me. I use my gut instinct to tell me if I need to move on. At home, yes, I carried my keys between my fingers as I walked to my car in a parking lot at night. I always told a friend or my parents my plans or where I was. I always looked over my shoulder if I thought someone was following me, or I would cross the street if I were nervous. I use common sense. But out here in the woods? No, I'm not afraid, not one tiny bit.

Hiking in sock liners isn't the answer to my problem. There is no cushioning between my heel and boot, and my blisters are increasingly tender with every step. And because I'm walking so gingerly to avoid that pain, my knees and ankles are beginning to hurt. My pack is entirely too heavy, and my body is just not used to carrying all this weight. I'm a mess physically, but I enjoy myself out here strangely. I like the woods, the wide-open spaces, the animals running about, and the whisper of the wind as it flows through my hair. I like the people out here. There is no judgment, no comparison, just acceptance. My body tells me to quit, but my mind tells me to stay.

I arrive at the Blue Mountain Shelter and a bunch of people hand out Band-Aids, Advil, and anything else that might help me. Somebody hands me a quart of filtered water, telling me they have too much anyway. The guidebook says there is a beautiful view from the shelter, but it's cloudy and misty, and nobody can see more than 20 feet away. After dinner, as it's starting to get quiet, we hear a rustle of activity down the trail. A guy walks in carrying chili dogs, sodas, and cookies as a surprise for everyone. He introduces himself as Three Piece, a member of the Georgia Appalachian Trail Club. It's our first official experience of trail magic, unexpected treats, usually offered by locals trying to help out their fellow hikers. I've heard of trail magic, but this is much more amazing than the stories I've read. We have a great time sitting around, chatting, and laughing all night.

When I open my eyes in the morning, Three Piece offers to take me back to the Walasi-Yi Center. "If you want to make it to Maine, you will never be able to do it without proper fitting boots."

He knows a lot about hiking, so I accept his advice. We hike together until we reach his car and drive back to the center. He waits nearly three hours while I get properly fitted for new boots and spend $400 for them and new hiking poles. The new boots are a full two sizes larger than my previous boots. I can wear my cushiony socks with ample room, and my feet feel much better.

The hiking poles look like ski poles but have shock absorbers to help relieve some of the pressure from my knees, which enable me to hike a little better and a little further every day. I still have many bouts of pain, I take more Advil, and I do plenty of talking to my cousin, Greg, in heaven. I know there's a reason that I'm out here. I don't know what it is yet, so I just keep hiking north.

What makes hiking so different from the real world is that I need to make so few decisions. I get up in the morning, eat breakfast, pack my stuff, and hike north. I stop for lunch and grab something easy to eat from the food bag. Then I hike north again and then stop for the night. My fellow hikers on the trail are from all walks of life. But nobody talks about themselves in the real world. I've met a doctor, teachers, salespeople, and grocers. I've met unemployed people, wealthy people, poor people, and middle-class people. I've met people from Canada, America, England, and Australia. We don't even use our real names anymore.

Trail names are a thing out here. Usually, other hikers bestow a trail name on you, based on your habits, idiosyncrasies, or something funny you did. Ziplock received his name because every item in his pack is protected in a Ziplock bag. Kiwi was given his name because he's from New Zealand. Dana became Twin Bears because of two tiny stuffed bears on her backpack.

I introduce myself as April, but someone always says, "Yes, but what's your *trail name*? I am Trail Gimp. I have limped most of the trail, so people now know me as Trail Gimp. Nobody calls me April.

But how can I have a new name? I've been *April* for 25 years. I can't just suddenly start calling myself something new. Even back in French class back in high school, many students adopted a new French name. I couldn't. Because April is a month and had an actual French translation, my teacher simply called me *Avril,* French for April.

But a new *trail name*? It takes a little while, but now, I introduce myself as Trail Gimp. It's a little weird, but I'm getting used to it.

I'm enjoying myself out here. I'm meeting new people, I'm enjoying free time for the first time since I was 12, and I love seeing new places. However, I'm constantly hurting. I spend the next few days waffling between quitting or continuing to hike.

"Trail Gimp, you should get to the hospital to have someone look at your feet. You don't want to do permanent damage," Woody says to me.

"I'm fine," I say as I limp onward.

"Well, Sven and I are going to the hospital. I need my foot looked at, and Sven is going to have someone look at his ankle. You should come with us."

Fine. I reluctantly tag along.

As we walk through the small hospital, I see pictures on the walls, and I begin to get nervous. *Where the heck are we?*

A movie called *Deliverance* came out in 1972, about a group of friends from Atlanta who go to rural Georgia for a boy's weekend of canoeing and fun. They get a lot more than they bargained for, and it turns into a race for survival. The hospital scenes were filmed in the very same hospital I am in right now. There are pictures of actors and scenes from the film throughout the hallways. I've seen the movie, and it's interesting to see photos of the actual scenes. But it's weird and a little freaky at the same time.

I fork over $150 to hear the doctor tell me exactly what I already know. "You're carrying too much weight that your body isn't used to, and you're trying to heal from the blisters. It would do you well to take a couple of weeks off before you cause permanent damage to your feet."

A couple of weeks off? Well, that's not happening. Onward.

As I'm coming down the trail towards Deep Gap, I dread going up Standing Indian Mountain. It's the first mountain I'll hike over 5,000 feet above sea level. *How am I supposed to climb 5,000 feet?* I limp with every step and try to figure out a way to get to Franklin, NC, instead of going over Standing Indian Mountain. As I approach the gap, I see a pickup truck parked off the forest service road.

Who does that belong to? Can I ask that person to drive me to town?

No, you idiot, you can't ask a complete stranger to drive me 15 miles out of the way.

I continue walking and see an older gentleman kneeling and disappearing in the tall grass and reappearing a few minutes later. What the heck is he doing? He finally looks up and notices me as I get closer.

"Hi, I'm Paul. I'm here picking ramps."

Ramps?

"Ramps are a wild vegetable; they look a little like a green onion, and they have an onion-garlicky taste. They're pretty tasty. Where ya headed?"

"I'm hiking the Appalachian Trail, but since my feet hurt, I'm trying to get to Franklin to get a hotel room."

"Where is Franklin?" I realize this may not be a good sign from a local, if he doesn't know the local towns.

"Franklin is about five miles down this service road, and then when you reach Route 64, take a left and drive about ten miles, according to my guidebook, anyway."

"Well," he says with a thick Southern accent, "if you want to throw your pack in the back of that truck and get comfortable for a few minutes, I'd be happy to take you when I finish."

Paul is an older man with a pickup truck whom I just met in the woods. These are the beginnings of stories I read about in the newspapers. "*He seemed nice enough…*" but in the end, he kills her. I wrestle with the idea of being strangled, raped, beaten, or shot to death by this sweet-looking older man who reminds me of my grandfather or being driven to a nice little hotel with hot, running water and a restaurant with food. My gut instinct tells me he's just a sweet, local man offering a kind favor. I go with it and accept his offer.

I offer to help him pick his ramps, and he shows me how to find them, and how the leaf is different from that of garlic and green onion. We continue to chat once we're in the truck, and he gives me his name and address and asks me to send him a postcard occasionally to let him know I'm okay and if I make it to Maine.

He drops me off at Henry's Motel. I meet the proprietor, Lois, and she shows me to a cabin. There are about ten cabins on the property, and most are full of hikers. I end up sharing my room with The Accident Waiting to Happen, Drew, and Squirrel, hikers I've been around lately. I think they're a few years younger than me, but I'm not sure. Nobody talks about age out here because it doesn't matter. We spend Saturday doing errands – laundry, grocery shopping, and checking the post office for our mail drops. It's one of the things that make trail towns so unique.

People can mail things to a post office and write a thru-hikers name on it with "In care of general delivery, please save for Appalachian Trail hiker." The postmaster puts packages aside into a pile. When you arrive at the post office, you tell the postmaster your name, and they'll hunt out your package. The Post Office didn't have the box my parents told me they sent. The postmaster said, "Don't you worry, Sweetie. Come back around tomorrow, and we'll see if it's on the truck in the morning."

Puzzled, I said, "Tomorrow is Sunday; the post office isn't open on Sunday."

"Oh honey, the post office moves 24 hours a day. We don't mind giving thru-hikers packages since we're here anyway." I was astonished by her kindness.

The four of us decide to go to dinner, and we meet up with seven other hikers and take over the local Pizza Hut. After we stuff ourselves, I realize my foot hurts too much, and I refuse to walk back to the motel. I don't know why hiking a few miles in the woods is easy but walking a mile in town is so hard. Maybe it's because it doesn't count towards our 2,000 miles on the trail. The waitress overhears me and offers to drive us back to the motel if we wait for the end of her shift in about ten minutes. We gladly accept and give her a rather large tip. We put too many people into too small a car and laugh like crazy for the five-minute ride.

Here I am, in a small mountain town in North Carolina, and I'm doing things I would never do at home. Smart girls don't take rides with strangers. Smart girls don't share a motel room with three people she barely knows. But those types of girls wouldn't be out here anyway.

We accept some drinks from the other hikers. Some of them have instruments, and they play music, and I laugh the entire night with new friends. I'm learning the importance of being happy where you are and making the most of it.

Sunday morning arrives early, and Squirrel and The Accident Waiting to Happen decide to check out a local Baptist church. They aren't Baptist, but since they are in the South, they thought it would be interesting. For some odd reason, I also decide to go to church and select the Resurrection Lutheran Church. I put on my cleanest shorts and shirt, then throw my boots back on. I walk 15 minutes to church and sneak in without anyone seeing me. I'm not a regular church-going person. I attend for special occasions and holidays, but I usually work Sundays. I don't know much about religion, so I'm uncomfortable talking to pastors, ministers, or priests.

An older lady slides next to me in the pew as the church fills up. She is wearing her Sunday best. Her blonde-turning-gray hair is perfectly coiffed in contrast to my combed but un-styled straight hair. Her makeup accentuates her eyes and lips, and I feel almost naked without eyeliner and mascara. Her silk blouse, straight skirt and matching jacket make my quick-drying teal-colored shorts and light pink tank top look ridiculous and inappropriate. Her hands are smooth and pretty with manicured nails. My hands are scratched and perpetually dirty, and I've never had a manicure in my life. I look down and can't help comparing her pantyhose-covered legs and fancy high heels to my scraped and bug-bitten bare legs, my heavy wool socks, and my clunky, dirty hiking boots. I feel like an idiot. I am out of place, and I can't believe I came here voluntarily.

The pastor's sermon is about suffering and discovering our calling. I feel like he's talking directly to my soul. I don't come to church often, and when I do, he nails it? Come on! I can tell you about suffering – I've been doing that for quite a while. Now, if I could tell you my purpose or calling, that would be fabulous. But I can't. Can you tell me? Because I'm interested.

When the sermon ends, I learn why the church is so packed. A baby is being baptized today. Fabulous. Now I feel like I'm intruding on someone's privacy, and I look for ways to sneak out the door. Unfortunately, I'm sitting in the middle of a pew with no way of sneaking out past Ms. Fancy High Heels. Damn.

The service ends, and I bolt toward the door, hoping to get out without having to talk to anyone. The pastor is already at the door and reaches for my hand, thanking me for visiting his church. We make small talk, and I'm about to run down the stairs when Ms. Fancy High Heels loops her arm through mine.

In a thick Southern drawl, she asks, "You're not about to sneak out of church before going downstairs for coffee and cake, are you? You simply must come downstairs and join us to celebrate." She takes my arm and leads me downstairs.

This is great. I come to church by myself, hoping to go unnoticed, and here I am, watching someone get baptized, eating their cake and cookies, and drinking their punch and coffee. She introduces me to a few people who thank me for visiting and inquire about my hike. They are genuinely interested, and I feel my mood lightening. Greg and my aunts would be proud of me; I've always turned down their offers of attending church with them, using the excuse that I had to work. They would be thrilled that I came to church on my own, in a small town, and had a good time.

As the celebration dwindles, I thank everyone for their hospitality and head for the door. A few hundred yards down the road, one of the women I had been talking to drives by and offers to give me a ride. Once again, I hop into the car of someone I barely know. We chat for a few minutes in the car before she drops me off at my motel, wishing me well on my journey. It's been one of the strangest days of my life. When I get to the post office, *on a Sunday*, the postmaster gives me the box my parents sent me, full of freeze-dried gourmet dinners, beef jerky, homemade cookies and brownies, and various candy bars. I share my goodies with my new friends and smile when I see so many happy people.

The evening wears on. Squirrel, Drew, The Accident Waiting to Happen, and I stay up chatting, and it turns into something like a group therapy session. We discuss why we're on the trail and what led us to this point. The others talk of attempted suicide, an addiction to drugs and how they got clean, and the need for adventure. I listen, but I don't have much to say. At first, I think I don't have anything like that to share. When they push further, though, it all comes out. I talk about not being able to find a full-time job, how my college boyfriend and I broke up, which took me a long time to get over, and I talk about my cousin Greg, how he died in a house fire, and how it affected my family.

"How did it affect you, Trail Gimp?"

"What do you mean? It didn't really affect *me;* it affected his family but not me."

"But it *did* affect you, don't you see? You're out here, hiking and talking to him, so although you're still alive, his death did affect you. It's okay to miss him and talk about him."

These are things I know in my head, but I didn't know in my heart until that moment. We stay up until five o'clock in the morning discussing life.

∞o∞

Because I hike a little slower than everybody else, most of my friends have gone ahead. Every day I meet new people. When I get to a shelter, I sign into the register and look for notes from my friends ahead of me. It's always nice to see a note that says, "Hey, Trail Gimp, hope you're just behind us. Maybe we'll see you in town in a few days."

The trail is nice today. The sun is shining, and the temperature is perfect for hiking. I'm neither sweating nor freezing to death. However, my feet still hurt, and my ankles and knees ache. I'm hiking slowly. I know I won't make it to Wesser Bald Shelter, where most of my friends are heading tonight. That shelter is still six miles away, and I'm tired.

I happen across a small stream in the middle of a clearing and sit down to rest and filter water. And realizing I'm hungry, I decide to make dinner. While heating water, I notice a perfectly flat spot next to the stream. *That looks like the perfect spot to set up a tent.* And just like that, I unload the rest of my pack, set up my tent, and pull out my food. I make another meal of instant noodles and dehydrated vegetables, and some peanuts and dried fruit for dessert.

While I clean up dinner and gaze at the rising moon, I realize that for the first time in my entire life, not a single soul knows where I am right now. My fellow hikers know that plans can change, and nobody worries about others too much if they don't show up. They know that I'll catch up or I'll see them another time.

And I'm okay with this. I have my tent for shelter, my filter for fresh water, my stove, and food. I have everything I need to take care of myself. I go to bed smiling and genuinely proud of myself for the first time in a long time. I've never felt this empowered.

CHAPTER THREE

COED NAKED BRIDGE JUMPING

May 1996

The Scouts Motto is "Be Prepared." I am usually prepared with everything I need because I'm carrying it on my back. I am also learning that I am a bit dependent upon Mother Nature.

I'm spending a beautiful night by myself, admiring the full moon and the surrounding woods, and I open my eyes in the morning to see a blue sky with puffy, white clouds and the sun peeking through the trees. I examine my maps and decide to hike ten miles to the Nantahala Outdoor Center. I know The Accident Waiting to Happen will be there; hopefully, we can share a room. It's been about five days since we were in town, and as much as I love solitude, I also miss talking to people.

I hoist my pack and begin walking. I've only been out here a few weeks, and this "hiking thing" is already becoming a habit, though my feet still hurt. The trail is lovely, with gentle slopes and easy hiking. I arrive at Tellico Gap and rest for a few minutes. *I'm glad I didn't camp here last night*, I think as I look around. There's no place to set up a tent other than the road. I hear some voices, and I turn to see Malcolm and Mile-Back, a couple of hikers I met a while ago, coming down the trail. The three of us decide to climb Wesser Bald together. I can keep up with the guys, which makes me feel good because they aren't injured.

We climb the fire tower, and I sit quietly in awe while admiring the scenery. It's early May, and Spring has reached the Carolinas in the valleys, where the rhododendrons are blooming, and the trees are lush with new leaves. Spring flowers like bluets and trillium dot the landscape, but high in the mountains, the branches are still mostly bare, enabling views as far as the eye can see. We leave the fire tower and head for the Wesser Bald Shelter, where we decide to have lunch. I grab the shelter register to sign in, leave a note, and look through all the messages to see if any hikers have left notes for me.

The registers are better than an answering machine. I find posts from friends telling me their plans in case I catch up. I've been out here for about three weeks, and already, I feel like I have a network of friends. Some are far ahead of me, while some are just a mile or two ahead. Hikers get to know one another fast, and we develop friendships quickly. We learn that it's difficult to stick to a precise schedule, and that's okay. It's called "hiking your own hike." It means hiking when you want, where you want, and stopping when you want, on your own terms and conditions. So, we leave notes for each other, telling each other our plans and giving encouragement to others.

I throw on my pack and head out. The boys have left ahead of me, and I enjoy the quiet as much as I love the conversation. There is a freedom out here that I find satisfying. I'm free to go where I want, when I want, and with whom I want. My only "rule" is that I head north, toward Maine. Growing up, we're taught to go to school and get an education to get a job. Once we get that job, we get up every day and go to work like clockwork. I still wear my watch every day, but now, I use it more to clock my miles per hour than to know the actual time. Time doesn't matter too much out here. We wake up at dawn and sleep when it gets dark. It's easy to lose track of the days out here, so I try to remember what day of the week it is;

It's helpful so that my daily writing journal is correct and to know when to schedule stops in town to pick up mail drops.

After an hour or so, I reach for my water bottle and realize I am unprepared; it's the forbidden rule of scouting. I forgot to fill my water bottle at the shelter, and now, I have one pint of water to last about five miles. I immediately ration, and as I hike down the mountain, I scan the trail and mountainsides for any signs of a creek, spring, or anything resembling water. I'm finding out that an ounce of water at a time does nothing to curb thirst. Sweat is dripping down my face. My tongue has turned to sandpaper. I begin to trip over tree roots and small rocks. I slow down, control my breathing, and continue looking for water sources. The trail spirals down the mountain, and what usually would be a lovely spring hike with sunshine and blue skies has turned me into a grumpy, tired, and very thirsty person. I'm hiking down this endless mountain, dehydrated and angry. The guidebook says that water is usually abundant along most parts of the trail. Clearly, this section is not normal. Feeling stupid and sorry for myself again, my eyes begin to sting, but I'm so dehydrated that no tears will form.

I see the shelter down the mountain, and knowing there is a source of water nearby, I guzzle the last half ounce of water I have. It is warm from sitting in my water bottle for hours, but it's wet. A half-ounce certainly doesn't go very far. I pick up my pace to get to the shelter, only to realize in horror that the trail leads in a different direction, and whatever I saw was not the shelter after all. Where is the damn shelter? It HAS to be around here somewhere! *You idiot! Why didn't you fill up your water at the last shelter? How could you be so careless and dumb?* I imagine local newspaper headlines about a hiker found in the woods, shriveled to death from dehydration. But I hike on.

I hear something like a stream or moving water, and a quick glance at my watch tells me it's been an hour since that last water I drank. I continue scanning the woods while I hike, and I notice a small trickle of water coming down the mountain wall next to me. Without taking my pack off or grabbing my filter, I thrust my water bottle under the trickle of water, collecting water that I hope has been naturally filtered by rocks and moss along the mountain. I don't care. I pour a cup of water down my throat and repeat. Now that I have something to drink, I break out some snacks and gorge on snacks to refuel and get some energy. At home, I eat when it's meal-time, at specified times, as society dictates. Out here, I eat for energy. I eat when I need to, in the appropriate amounts, to achieve my goals. I drink another quart of water and now, fully rehydrated, head back on the trail.

I haven't seen a white blaze in quite some time. *Am I'm lost?* But it looks like I'm on the trail; the path is worn, well-traveled, and clear of extraneous debris. I MUST be on the trail. *Just keep going. Keep Walking.* Finally, I round a curve, and I hear running water that gets louder with every step I take. I pick up my pace, which isn't too difficult since I'm hiking about a mile per hour. Just as I see a stream, I see a tent, the light of a small campfire, and finally, an entire sea of tents. The shelter! I made it! I hobble as fast as I can, and Malcolm and Mile-Back greet me with "Trail Gimp! I can't believe you made it this far! We were certain you would quit back there; the trail was so hard."

I smile as big as I can, and my eyes fill with tears from gratitude and happiness. I throw my pack to the ground and grab my water filter, promptly filtering two quarts of water that I guzzle so fast that I spill it all over me. I chat with everyone for a few moments, and at 7:45 pm, I'm off again to hike the last mile to arrive at the Nantahala Outdoor Center, where The Accident Waiting to Happen will be waiting for me with a hotel room and a hot shower. I hope.

Within fifteen minutes, I hear the sound of the Nantahala River, but the river seems elusive. I stumble on, and at 8:45 pm, I cross the road and let out a cry of joy, partly in disbelief that I've just limped for 11 hours. Almost immediately, a car pulls up next to me, and an older gentleman says, "Hi, I'm Horace Holden. Are you going to stay with me like these two are?" Confused, I look in his car and see The Accident Waiting to Happen and our friend Derek in the back seat, looking like they're having the time of their lives.

"Are you serious?"

"Absolutely," he replies. "I have a couple of spare rooms with two twin beds and a double bed. Hop in."

Normally, if some random guy in his early sixties pulls up next to me in his car and asks if I'm going home with him, I would run in the other direction and call the police. What do I do on the Appalachian Trail? I eagerly jump in and begin a conversation.

Once at his house a few miles away, he offers to feed me since it's so late, but I decline because I'm actually too tired to eat. He shows us to our rooms, where The Accident Waiting to Happen and I bunk together in the twin beds while Derek takes the room with the double bed.

"Feel free to take a shower in the bathroom, and the phone is in the kitchen if you want to call your parents to tell them where you are." I hop in the shower to scrub off several days' worth of stink and dirt, and finally call my parents to let them know I'm alive and well. I finally thank Horace, and collapse into a soft mattress.

"Blat, blat…. blat, blat". I wake up to a sound I haven't heard since a visit to the county fair several years ago. I look out the window and see more than a dozen goats running around. I arrived so late last night that I didn't realize I was on a small homestead. Horace calls us for breakfast, and we sit around eating comfortably as if we were at our own table in our own home.

Since he tells us he has four adult children and that he looks a little older than my dad, I guess Horace to be in his mid-sixties. He has gray hair, cut short at the nape of his neck, with a side part and slightly longer at the top that he constantly pushes to the side. He's clean-shaven and has a nice smile, revealing straight white teeth. He doesn't mention a wife, and I don't ask if he ever had one. He used to be a guide on the river, and he's still physically in great shape.

Horace takes us back to the Nantahala Outdoor Center, also known as the NOC, where we spend the afternoon eating, shopping, lounging, and swimming in the river. "Trail Gimp, we're going to take off hiking today," The Accident Waiting to Happen says. "Why don't you spend some extra time resting, trying to let your feet heal? Or, maybe you can find a ride up to Hot Springs?"

I have heard that the hike out of NOC is incredibly tough. I am limping a lot and taking too much Advil, and I'm hiking a pathetically slow mile per hour. It doesn't take much convincing to get me to stay put. I do love this "town" thing, hanging around in trail towns and talking to people. At 3:00, they take off, and Horace stops by to take me back to his house. He shows me the washing machine and invites me to do laundry, make more phone calls, and relax. He invites me to stay another night, but I learned that his son is coming into town, and I don't want to intrude. "I'll just get a bunk at the NOC tonight, but thanks for the offer."

Horace says, "April, since my son is coming into town tonight, why don't you come along for dinner?" Dinner sounds great, although I really don't want to intrude.

"Oh, thanks, that's so kind, but I'm really okay. I appreciate the offer."

Horace smiles and, with a twinkle in his eye, says, "Okay, well, the offer stands, so let me know if you change your mind."

Around dinnertime, we leave for the NOC. Horace says, "I just need to drop by my son's house for a second."

As we pull into the driveway, I see an old cabin, which Horace tells me is 150 years old. His daughter-in-law walks over, hand-extended, and says, "Hi, it's nice to meet you. I know you told Dad that you weren't staying for dinner, but I absolutely insist. We have plenty to go 'round, and we love talking to hikers along the trail."

How can I resist?

I know I've just met these folks, but sitting around their family dining table makes me feel like I am home. Plates of homegrown vegetables and meats are passed around while people grab whatever they want; I feel like I'm celebrating Thanksgiving, and everyone treats me like family. It's easily one of the best meals I have had in a very long time.

No, we didn't know each other a few days ago. But people are people. We need food, water, shelter, and other people. Community is a big thing. We're taught, especially as women, not to talk to strangers, not to let our guard down, always be on the lookout for something "fishy" going on. There is little of that out here on the trail. Hikers need other people. Ironically, hiking by yourself teaches you how much you need your community.

After dinner, Horace gives me a tour of the area and then drops me at my bunkhouse. I learn that Horace is the co-founder of the NOC and, generally, this entire area. You would never know it by talking to him. He's honest, modest, and helpful.

Because we're right on the Nantahala River, many rafting guides travel frequently between here, the French Broad River in Hot Springs, North Carolina, and the Nolichucky River in Erwin, Tennessee. Earlier today, I decided to try to get to Hot Springs. Nobody from here is going directly to Hot Springs, about a two-hour mountainous drive north, but a guide named Woody is traveling up to Erwin, which is also a two-hour drive on the highways. Then another guide will be me back to Hot Springs, about an hour south through the mountains. It's a roundabout way of getting there, but it's the best I can do.

I call my parents once more to let them know of my plans. I chat briefly with my sister, who informs me that my parents are betting I'll be home in two weeks. Ha! I'll show them!

I meet Woody at 8 am at the camp store, hop in his NOC truck with some rafting gear in the back, and head north. I'm sad that I'm not hiking. I want to be in the woods, but to be honest, I'm also enjoying the spontaneity of going wherever the world wants me to go. I'm usually so scheduled and planned. I like the difference. After two hours of driving, he drops me off at the NOC outpost in Erwin. I make myself at home near the river, soaking up the sunshine and writing in my journal. The gnats drive me crazy and force me inside, sort of. The office has a covered porch with a screened door and six windowless frames, one of which has a screen. Nevertheless, it does lessen the number of bugs a little and prevents me from getting sunburned.

I spend the day snacking out of my food bag, re-reading my journal, and nearly memorizing my guidebook from reading it so much out of boredom. I would give anything to find an actual book. Ed shows up around dinnertime, I jump into his NOC truck, and we head south to Hot Springs. He tells me he's a former thru-hiker, and when he finished, he returned to this area to get a job at the NOC. He loves the area and frequently travels between the three towns. I realize that there is a kindred spirit that connects hikers, especially thru-hikers of the Appalachian Trail. We all have a connection to the trail and are ambassadors of it. We are responsible for caring for it and the hikers traveling along it. I've been hiking on this trail for 20 days. Already, I feel at home.

Around 9:00 pm, Ed drops me off at The Jesuit Hostel in town, as some other places seem full. Father Vincent comes out with open arms. "Welcome to our place."

"Father, she's a little banged up," Ed explains. "She's limping pretty badly."

"Don't you worry, young lady. We'll take good care of you."

I say thank you and goodbye to Ed and follow Father Vincent into the hostel. He shows me the women's bunkroom, the bathrooms, and the common area, where I eye the shelves full of books. "Sleep tight, and we'll see you in the morning."

The Appalachian Trail runs along Bridge Street in Hot Springs. There are white blazes on telephone poles and street signs, all leading down the main street to the other side of town. I like this town already. Bridge Street contains an Inn, post office, hardware store, restaurant, diner, laundromat, and motel for all the town's 500 or so residents. A set of railroad tracks and a creek divide the typical main street from "over yonder," which houses a campground, gas station, and the Hot Springs Resort, all next to the French Broad River. It's a lovely little town with all the necessities and none of the fluff. Everyone I meet is friendly, hardworking, and helpful.

I spend a few days in town, restocking supplies, getting my mail drops, reading books for hours on end, and running into hiking friends staying all over town. I move from one hostel, motel, or campground to another almost every day, depending on where my friends are. I'm having the time of my life with no schedules and no rules.

Today I'm at The Inn at Hot Springs, and I meet a bunch of new faces. We are on the porch, drinking beer and eating snacks when Tracie decides she's tired of her long hair. She says it's hot and sweaty, sticks to her face, and gets in the way. Doug offers to shave her head, and she agrees! I watch in horror and amazement as this beautiful woman shaves her head. And I learn a lesson. She is just as beautiful without her hair as with it. I'm jealous of her ability to be herself. My hair is part of who I am, and I know I could never shave it off. I realize I'm not as strong as I think. I am in total awe of her.

"Hey," someone yells. "We should take a walk down by the river!"

I'm game, but instead of walking down the main street, people head down the railroad tracks to jump in the river from the bridge. I remember watching the movie *Stand by Me* by Stephen King years ago, and I know that the kids almost get hit by the train, escaping death with mere seconds to spare. I follow along anyway, constantly watching for any sign of a train. We cross the bridge and find an open clearing, where our party continues.

Out of nowhere, we hear a giant crack of thunder, the skies turn gray, and it begins to rain. We are soaked to the bone within minutes. Randall shouts to no one in particular, "Since I'm soaking already, I'm going to jump off the bridge naked!" He peels off his wet shirt and shorts, throws everything into a pile, and walks to the bridge. He jumps in, lands in the river 20 feet below, swims to the edge, and crawls out. "That was great!" he yells.

"Let's all go naked bridge jumping!" I hear someone yell.

I stare in bewilderment as hikers drop their clothing here and there and start walking to the train trestle, completely naked. I'm too much of a chicken to get naked in front of strangers. As an excuse, I designate myself as the photographer, using the rationalization that my ankle is all bandaged and wrapped up for support. I snap some photos, and after everyone screams and jumps, they swim over and start coming out of the river.

"That was great!" I hear over and over. "Let's go again!"

There are 11 of us. I am the only one wearing clothes. Seriously, how do you look someone in the eye when they're standing in front of you, buck naked? I look down to avert my gaze, only to accidentally stare at everyone's private parts.

Sheesh, he's a hairy monster. That must be hot and uncomfortable.
That water must be really cold!
Who puts a tattoo there? That must have hurt!

I mentally slap my face and try to get back to reality. I'm uncomfortable. I look at the trees and the ground and divert my gaze anywhere so that I don't have to look at all these naked people. I'm so uncomfortable that I feel like I should rip my clothes off to be as naked as everyone else so I won't feel so out of place.

Luckily, I'm not in time, as everyone is already heading to the bridge for another jump. They jump in just as a train appears out of the woods and crosses the bridge. Saved by the bell. Or the train.

As everyone climbs out of the river, I notice that people scatter, but I can't figure out why.

"Howdy, ma'am. Can I see your ID, please?"

I look up and stare into the face of a police officer. *Where did he come from?* "Um, sure, but why?" handing him my license.

"How many of those drinks have you had?" pointing to the beer in my hand.

Two? Three? Five? Sheesh—I wasn't counting. I really don't know.

"Um, just this one. Why?"

"Well, we have a public intoxication law here in Hot Springs, and if I find you're intoxicated in public, I'll have to arrest you," he says slowly and matter-of-factly, in a thick, southern drawl.

I assume he's kidding, but I see no indication of humor. I look around, and it seems that most of the other hikers have scattered, hiding in the woods, and the few that haven't have ditched their drinks and are somehow managing to act completely sober.

I picture myself in a small jail cell in the middle of the North Carolina mountains. Who would I call for my one phone call? My parents? I can see that conversation going really well. *Hi Mom and Dad, please send bail money because I was caught intoxicated in public.* Maybe I should call my sister instead.

"Can you blow into this straw, please?" The police officer hands me a breathalyzer. *What?* I've never taken a breathalyzer in my life. *You've got to be joking.* I see that he's not, so I take the straw and blow into it so lightly that I wouldn't blow out a birthday candle. He accepts it, and it registers .02. Phew, I'm safe. And thank God I'm dressed!

"You're all set, ma'am. By the way, these railroad tracks here are the railroad company's property, so technically, you're trespassing. If I were you, I'd head back to town right away. And people have been hurt jumping off that bridge, so I'd suggest not doing anything stupid like that, you hear?"

I nod emphatically, saying, "Yes, sir." After he leaves, my hiker friends jump out of the trees, completely schnockered and laughing, and congratulate me on keeping my cool.

This will be a story to tell my kids someday.

I spend a few more days, including my birthday, hanging out with hiker friends as they come into town and saying goodbye to hikers as they leave. On my tenth day in town, I find myself on the lawn of the Duckett House Inn, camping out with others. We're spending a leisurely day lolling around the park-like yard and chatting about the trail and life in general. Garcia, a hiker I met this morning, pulls into the driveway with a van, announcing that he is taking some people up to Trail Days in Damascus.

Trail Days is a weekend hiking festival in Damascus, Virginia. Like Hot Springs, the trail runs directly through the small downtown, and it's known as one of the friendliest towns on the trail. There are supply vendors, food tents, reunions of past year hiking groups, a hiker's parade down Main Street, and talent shows, and it's supposed to be a lot of fun.

"I have room for a few more. Anyone want to go?" Garcia asks.

"I'll go!" I gather my supplies in minutes and throw my stuff in the van. We just watched *Forrest Gump* a few days ago, and I feel like Jenny, in the part of the movie where a stranger stops the car and asks, "Anyone want to go to San Francisco?" Without thinking, Jenny says, "I'll go." Now I know what that freedom feels like.

I've been hiking for about a month, spending about half of it in town. I'm doing things I never thought I'd do. I'm hiking alone. I'm sharing hotel rooms with people I just met. I'm accepting rides from strangers. I'm staying in strangers' homes. Yet, it doesn't feel wrong out here. This is the hiking life. We rely on others. And, though I may not know their real names, I know a lot about these people. I know where they're from, their likes and dislikes, whether they snore or not, how they get along with their family, and I know the most important thing: whether they are good people deep down inside.

CHAPTER FOUR

ADJUSTING

May-June 1996

Trail Days is a non-stop party. My family thinks I'm hiking alone in the woods. Things couldn't be further from the truth.

We arrive in Damascus, and local officials instruct us to set up our tents almost anywhere. There are scores of tents next to Laurel Creek, affectionately called Tent City, so I hunt for a few feet of open space between tents and set up camp for a few days. In a matter of minutes, I run into people I know, and the party begins. We get dinner at the local pub, where we end up partying all night long with more hikers as they come into town. Since I've been hiking slowly and skipping around towns here and there, I know a lot of different groups of hikers. It's like a reunion every time I turn around.

I spend the weekend with various groups at different times. The Coed Naked Bridge Jumping Crew is hanging out on an island in the creek, and I spend hours with them, while the bunch from Franklin is hanging out in

Tent City, where I spend hours with them. Almost everyone heads to Tent City late at night, and drum circles begin, with hikers banging on drums, water bottles, and anything else that makes a sound. Soon, they find a collective rhythmic beat, and the sound becomes almost hypnotic. People drum for hours while others dance around the circles, and eventually, singing ensues.

I never sing in public, fearing my voice is screechy and out of tune. This really isn't my scene. Drum circles? Making music by banging on water bottles? Nah, that's not for me. Yet, I find myself loosening up, enjoying the camaraderie. I start singing with others, dancing around the drum circles, letting my guard down, and enjoying the moment. There is no judgment, no mocking, just acceptance. It's a different world.

During the day, I meet the vendors selling their wares, offering advice on equipment, and repairing anything as necessary. The vendors of Gregory products offer to look at my backpack and adjust it perfectly to my body. Another company gives me a shirt to wear while hiking, asking me to test it out and report to them with comments and concerns. Local service clubs set up all-you-can-eat pancake breakfasts and spaghetti dinners. Hikers wander from tents to restaurants to convenience stores.

After five days of nearly non-stop socializing with almost everyone I've met on this trail, it's time to hit the trail again. I am still limping and wrap my ankle with first-aid tape for as much support as possible. Someone from the local hiking club offers me a ride back to Elk Park, North Carolina. I realize that if I go back to Hot Springs, I'll never make it to Maine before the winter weather. I hop in the car and get dropped off about a half mile from Apple House Shelter, about 110 miles north of Hot Springs. I vow to come back one day and hike the miles I missed. It's been nearly three weeks since I've hiked on the trail. It's getting late in the day, and I head to the shelter first to acclimate to the rigors of the trail again.

While unpacking, a hiker named Daisy walks into the shelter. She is from Maine and about my age. She is hiking a section of the trail and finishing tomorrow. She hopes to hike the entire trail someday in the future. She is friendly, and we chat while having dinner. Another female hiker comes in and sets up her tent a little bit away from the shelter. Daisy mentions that she hasn't seen many women out here; it seems like more men are hiking the trail. I point out that three women hikers are at this shelter, with no men. And I recall all the women I've met along the way, rattling off nearly a dozen names. It seems like many women are hiking until we start to remember the names of male hikers we met along the way. I came up with a list of at least two dozen guys without thinking, and Daisy came up with more. We are in the minority, though I never think about it.

I recall all the boys I grew up with in my neighborhood; I've always considered myself equal to them, and they always treated me like an equal. We all rode BMX bikes on the trails, walked in the woods and trails, and watched the same TV and movies. I grew up seeing men and women as equals, and I wonder why the public is afraid of women hiking the trail but not men. Do they think we can't take care of ourselves?

Daisy and I hike out together in the morning, and she makes her way to town since she has finished her section hike. I continue on the trail. I have a spring in my step for the first time in weeks, and I revel in the beauty of the mountains, fresh air, and wildflowers. I hike around large, round rocks and soon realize that the air isn't quite so fresh anymore. I realize I'm in the middle of a cow pasture, and those rocks are not rocks but dried cow plops. It's a good thing I hiked around them.

The spring in my step disappears within a mile as I realize I'm no longer in trail shape. I can't hike 100 yards without stopping and gasping for breath. My leg muscles are burning, and my pack is really heavy. After a few hours, I throw my pack to the ground and immediately lie down next to it and take a nap. A half-hour later, I grab a snack and begin again. It's hot. I'm sweaty and covered in dirt. *Why am I out here again? Why am I sweating my butt off in Tennessee? Is that where I am? Tennessee or Virginia? Tennessee, I think.* I've traveled around so much where North Carolina, Tennessee, and Virginia meet that it's difficult to remember where I am. It's no use feeling sorry for myself. Self-pity isn't getting me anywhere. *Hike on and deal with it.*

I am done for the day. I don't even know how far I've hiked today, but somewhere between 10 and 15 miles. I come across a small tent site located next to a babbling brook, partially hidden by small trees. It's the perfect spot to set up a tent. I am sweaty, and I feel gross. I look around to make sure there isn't anyone nearby, and I strip down to nothing to take a sponge bath in the brook and rinse out my clothes. So much for all that fresh and clean laundry I had yesterday.

At the next shelter, I stay with four male hikers I'm meeting for the first time. They are power hikers, easily hiking more than 20 miles per day. They make fun of anyone who got a ride to Trail Days, chastised anyone who skipped around from town to town, and in no uncertain terms, told me I should go home to rest my feet and come back next year "to have a real thru-hike." I can do without them, so I purposely sleep late in the morning, and thankfully, I wake up to an empty shelter. With any luck, I'll never see them again. Who needs that kind of negativity?

The next few days fly by as I slowly assimilate into hiker mode again. I spend beautiful time alone, pondering life in front of gorgeous waterfalls and rivers, and as hiker friends catch up to me, I spend time bonding with them. I hike my first ever night hike with the crew from Franklin and a few others, deciding at 11 pm that we should pack up and head towards town. I end up staying at a shelter with a section hiker named Randy, whom I met a few days ago. It's Saturday at 3 am, and I just spent four hours hiking in the middle of the night in the Tennessee mountains, oohing and aahing at the stars in the sky and the lights in the valley. I can't help but think that if I were home, I'd probably just be coming home from the bars. I also realize that I'm having a better time out here.

But my body doesn't like it. My ankles and feet hurt, and I can't walk anywhere without a limp. The first few miles every day seem to be okay, but then my limp becomes more pronounced, and I end up in agony. I'm not just walking on a flat path in a straight line; I'm hiking around rocks and over tree roots, on uneven paths with holes in the ground, sometimes filled with mud and piles of leaves, dirt, and twigs. I constantly shift my balance to maintain my equilibrium. It's difficult to do when my feet don't work properly.

I run into many people I know. Hikers leave me notes at shelters, and I see some in town. People I haven't seen ask others how I'm doing. I've developed friendships with a bunch of people out here, but I'm still hiking alone. I honestly don't know what I'm doing out here; I know that I want to do something different from what I was doing at home. That part is successful. I'm meeting new people, seeing new places, and doing things I would never do at home.

Getting rides from strangers on the Appalachian Trail is nothing new. Locals always watch out for hikers, offering to drive them from place to place. It's an entirely new experience to stand on the side of the road, put my thumb out, and hitchhike. Growing up, I learned that hitchhiking is equivalent to asking to be murdered. It's like waiting for Ted Bundy to come along and pick you up.

Here on the trail, however, hitchhiking is a part of thru-hiking. Hiking ten miles in the woods seems like nothing, but walking an extra two miles into town is simply not acceptable. The good thing is that people who live in nearby towns know hikers just by looking at them. They have huge backpacks, dirty boots, and hiking poles, and are generally unkempt. Most men stop shaving on day one, so they usually have good size beards within a month or two. Women typically have their hair in ponytails or braids or cut very short. Their clothes look dirty, and they can't see this from the car, but they know that they generally smell awful. And it's not just them; it's their gear. Sweat has seeped into their backpacks, and the stink never disappears. It seems easier for women to hitchhike near the trail than men. Maybe men have a scary persona about them, or they look like serial killers with their scraggly beards and dirty attire. Most people think women need some help, so if they smile nicely, they generally have an easier time getting a ride into town. In either case, hikers hitchhike, and locals pick them up.

I'm also getting used to the wildlife out here. I no longer freak out about seeing a mouse or snake and anxiously await seeing a bear. Black snakes can be more than six feet long and are scary looking but harmless. Thanks to my guidebook, I recognize and hike past aggressive female grouse protecting their offspring. Wild turkeys can be quite large, as I found when I rounded a curve in the trail. I'm not sure if I scared the turkey more or if she scared me more. But as I walked around that curve, I saw a giant turkey with wings outspread, seemingly six feet tall and wide, making noises I'd never heard before. She squawked and scared the dickens out of me, running around like the proverbial headless chicken, so I gave her a wide berth and crept through the trees to escape. I was several yards down the trail before she quieted down.

I recognize different trees, flowers, and shrubs. Trillium is a flower I don't see at home, and it's quickly becoming one of my favorites. Three flower petals meet in the middle, with the three leaves sticking out below and between the petals. They are about three inches wide and stand about a foot tall. I see bunches of them laid out like a carpet in colors of red, white, yellow, and pink. We hike through tunnels of tree-sized rhododendrons, walking on a lavender carpet when they drop their flowers.

I notice the big flurry of activity that animals take part in before a storm arrives. Chipmunks and squirrels run around like crazy, gathering whatever food they can find, and birds squawk to their family members to hurry up and find what they need. And then, just before the storm, the woods get quiet. Animals are tucked away in their nests, boroughs, or whatever they call home. Coupled with constantly watching the skies, this has enabled me to become quite the weather forecaster, predicting storms to get to safety in a shelter or town as necessary.

I continue hiking, primarily by myself, and occasionally meet up with others. The beauty can be astounding out here; it's nice to enjoy it myself or share it with others.

I'm heading toward the Mount Rogers Shelter in Virginia, finishing up an 18.6-mile day. A full moon rises next to the shelter. The large shelter looks like a tiny shack on a hilltop in the distance. The sun sets behind me, and the combination of the sun and moon lights the sky in a Picasso of different shades of blue. I gasp at the beauty and stop for a few minutes to admire the view.

The trail coming down from Mount Rogers in the morning is like a jigsaw puzzle. Rock outcrops are everywhere, and I hike over and around them, and for one 40-foot section, through. After the rocks, the trail leads to Grayson Highlands State Park, where wild horses roam free among the wide open, grassy plains. Looking backward, Mount Rogers stands tall in the background, and I feel small and insignificant in this most beautiful land.

One particular pony takes an interest in me, sniffing my pack, possibly smelling the snacks inside. Some people come here and feed the ponies apples and other food, though they aren't supposed to. To a thru-hiker, though, food is a precious commodity. I am not giving it up to a wild animal. Soon, other ponies join, and a small herd follows me on the Appalachian Trail. They neigh and snort, looking for their next meal. They are not huge animals, maybe four feet tall at the most. I grew up in a town where thoroughbred horse racing is the tourism draw in the summer, but these are anything but thoroughbreds.

The wild ponies are mixed breeds; some have larger feet, while others have larger heads. Their coats are longer than I've seen, and their manes are long and slightly unkempt, unlike the sleek and well-groomed racehorses I grew up watching. They are of many colors, with various shades of brown, white, tan, and black giving each pony a unique marking. The ponies are used to people, as they live in a heavily visited state park. I want to reach out and pet them, but I also know they are wild animals and can be unpredictable. I'm not taking any chances. They remind me of a litter of puppies chasing their mama, looking for milk, each trying to get in front of the other to sniff my pack. After following me for about 15 minutes, a mama horse comes along, whinnying and neighing, gently guiding them back to their herd.

But where did the ponies come from? Originally, the grassy balds came about because of extensive logging in the area, due in part to the blight of the American Chestnut tree, the predominant tree in these mountains. More open land served to graze cattle and some ponies. The soil composition changed, resulting in more open land for grazing.

In the 1960s, Bill Pugh, of Sugar Grove, Virginia, began breeding the Virginia Highlander, a small horse that was suited for the terrain, higher elevations, and colder weather of southwest Virginia.

In 1965, the area became The Grayson Highlands State Park, and cattle grazing ceased. Almost a decade later, the grasses became overgrown, and because of the elevation, Bill Pugh and another horse owner brought in 20 ponies to graze on the grasses and small shrubs to maintain the landscape. Shortly after Pugh retired in 1974, The Wilburn Ridge Pony Association was established to monitor the herd.

Though the ponies are technically wild, meaning they can wander almost anywhere, feed and shelter themselves, the association does keep an eye on them. The ponies get yearly exams, and receive salt and worming blocks as the weather dictates to keep them healthy. Additionally, the herd is kept to approximately 100 animals. Some members of the herd are gathered up and auctioned off every year to maintain a healthy herd.

I bid adieu to the horses and finally reach the new Little Wilson Stream shelter mid-day and stay for lunch. My feet are killing me from rock hopping all day, walking through countless streams, trying – and failing – to keep my boots dry. I also have a new problem.

I need to adjust my backpack again, probably from throwing or dropping it whenever necessary. A screw on my hip belt rubs my hip, forming a hole through my shorts and into my skin. Even after padding and taping my skin and the backpack, it still rubs and causes bleeding and intense irritation.

I hike anyway, miserable and in pain, and arrive at Old Orchard shelter at about 6:15 pm. I take my usual sponge bath in a stream, change into camp clothes, and set my hiking clothes out to dry. Hikers generally carry two sets of clothes – one set to hike in, and one set to camp in. There isn't much room for luxury out here.

I eat dinner and admire the sunset. This one beats the one over Mount Rogers. A spectrum of red, orange, and yellow colors fill the sky, and I sit reverently, knowing that only God can create a masterpiece like that.

I run into some of the Coed Naked Bridge Jumping Crew and hike with them for a few days. UberDave's friend, Keith, is visiting them, hiking with them, and slackpacking them for a few days. He takes their packs and shuttles them up the trail, while they hike without packs, walking easier and faster.

Keith offers to slackpack me as well, so I empty the contents of my backpack, only carrying what is necessary until tomorrow. Keith also supplies ample quantities of beer, of which we all freely partake. There is something about hiking all day in the warm sun and cooling off with an ice-cold beer afterward.

"Hey, why don't we do some trust falls?" Pump Jump suggests. I have no idea what that means.

"I'll go first, and you guys catch me." Pump Jump climbs up on the picnic table and turns her back to everyone below her. We form two lines close to each other and hold our arms out. Pump Jump falls into our arms when we're in place; luckily, we don't drop her.

"Your turn, Trail Gimp!" she says.

"Oh no, I couldn't."

"It's okay; we promise to catch you. You caught me, right? It's all about letting go of your fears and trusting us."

I can trust other hikers. Letting go of my fears? That's going to require more work. I nervously climb on top of the picnic table. It's only a few feet high, but it certainly feels higher than that now. My heart begins to race, and I want to get off. This is a dumb idea.

"Go ahead. Turn around, put your feet on the edge of the table, cross your arms over your chest, close your eyes, and fall back with your back straight, just like I did."

Um. Right. Okay. I can't do this. Can I? Yes, I can do this. I have done all sorts of things while hiking this trail. I'm going to trust them.

I slowly move my feet to the edge of the picnic table. I cross my arms and place them over my chest. I close my eyes. *Will they catch me? What if they don't? What if I don't fall straight? What if I land on the ground and break my back? What if I'm paralyzed? April, STOP! Relax, and fall back.*

I take a deep breath, lean back a little, and a little more, and eventually fall backward, keeping my back straight and having complete faith that they will catch me. And they do. I smile from ear to ear, and they put me down. I'm so glad I'm doing things out here that I never thought I'd do.

I retrieve my things the next day and hike on alone since they are getting off the trail for a few days to attend a wedding or to take care of injuries. There is something about Pump Jump that makes me feel jealous and small. She is fearless. I am in awe of her independence. I have difficulty talking to her, as I've put her on a pedestal, someone I aspire to be like someday.

I'm planning on hiking 12 miles into Atkins, Virginia, today. According to the guidebook, a Dairy Queen is located on the road where the trail passes. It's summertime, it's hot and sticky, and I'd like nothing better than a fresh ice cream cone or Blizzard. And possibly some greasy fast food as well.

As I walk north, anticipating my ice cream, I see a person walking toward me. *Who is hiking southbound?* It's Malachi! I haven't seen him since Hot Springs. We spent two days talking to each other almost all night long and playing games with other hikers.

We hug like we're old friends. "Do you know how difficult you are to track down?" he asks.

"What do you mean?"

"I've been hot on your tail for weeks trying to catch up to you. Every time I thought I was going to catch you, you got a ride somewhere, or hiked extra mileage, or hiked throughout the night or something, according to all the other hikers. I figured I'd get a ride up the trail and hike southbound until I bumped into you. Nice to see you!"

"Aww, I'm sorry, I didn't know. But it's so nice to see you." Malachi turns around and continues hiking with me to Atkins.

The trail begins to wind down the mountain, through fields and cow pastures, past an old, one-room schoolhouse that I eagerly run in to explore, and we stop to pick wild strawberries in the middle of the trail. I feel like I've found a kindred spirit.

We can see Interstate 81 and the town of Atkins in the distance, but it takes a few hours to get there. We hike together, talking about the trail, family, and life. And before we know it, we reach the Dairy Queen. We order a couple of greasy cheeseburgers, fries, and Blizzards. Then, we walk into town to grab some supplies for the coming days. On the way back to the trail, the heavens open.

There is nowhere to hide, so we miserably walk in the downpour. We are drenched from head to toe, so we decide to share the cost of a motel room where we can take hot showers and dry off. Even in the summer, I'm chilly after a long, cold rain.

We spend the next few days hiking together, discussing life, and realizing how differently we grew up. I grew up in middle-class suburbia, while he grew up poor in the South. I'm eating freeze-dried gourmet dinners like chicken and dumplings, a gift from Mom and Dad, while he forages around for wild salad greens. After camping by the side of a creek one evening, I pack up in the morning. Malachi is sitting alone, reading a book.

"I'm getting ready to go. Are you coming along?"

"Yeah, I'll pack up soon and follow. Don't worry about me."

"Okay, you sure?"

"Yeah," he says. "Don't worry; I'll catch up."

I hike on slowly, still nursing my injuries. I wonder why Malachi won't come along. We aren't exactly romantic, though we kissed and snuggled a few times in Hot Springs and again these past few days. I like his company, but not enough to be involved romantically long-term. Maybe we are just too different. Perhaps he senses that, too?

I tape my ankles every morning for support, but it seems the ligaments in my feet are injured, at least that's what someone suggested to me, and they are not healing. The only way to let them heal is to get off them. That means quitting the trail and going home, which I am unwilling to do.

I run into Twin Bears again, a woman I've met various times since I started. It's nice to hike alongside a woman again. Girl talk is most welcome out here among so many guys. She tries to convince me to take time off to heal, but I refuse. We also hear about two girls found viciously murdered just off the trail in the Shenandoah National Park. Details are sketchy, and we're unsure if they are thru-hiking the trail or just out for a short hike.

"Do you want to get off the trail for safety? They haven't caught the person responsible yet," Twin Bears says.

"Listen, the Shenandoahs are still a few hundred miles away, and I don't think we're going to run into some wacko on the trail this far south," I reply. "We don't know the details yet, so I don't see any reason to panic. Let's just hike on and take it day by day."

We meet up with many other hikers, and Malachi catches up after a few days, but he hikes alone. Perhaps he likes solitude. We all continue, and I do a lot of hiking with Twin Bears. We complain about going up steep ascents, throwing our packs to the ground in disgust when we reach the summit. We grumble about descents and how it hurts our knees, and I whine about my feet.

"Why are you out here, hiking in so much pain?" she asks.

"Girl, if I had an answer, I would tell you. I'm still trying to figure that out. But I feel like I *have* to. Like it's a *calling*. I can't explain it," I answer. "But I also want to find a teaching job in the fall. How can I find a teaching job if I'm not home to interview?"

"True," she replied. "But how many times are you going to be able to hike the Appalachian Trail?"

I love meeting new people. I love the scenery, and I love seeing new places. But do I want to hike over 2,000 miles? Do I really want to hike the Appalachian Trail? Or am I just using this as an excuse to escape my pathetic life at home?

We hike on. A few days later, Twin Bears announces, "Trail Gimp, I'm going to take a week or two off. I'm tired, and my body needs rest. I called my dad, and he's driving down from Massachusetts to pick me up. You're welcome to come along, and we'll bring you home if you want. He's picking me up in Pearisburg, so you have a few days to decide."

I spend the next few days tossing around the options. If I stay out here hiking, I may cause permanent injury. At the very least, even if I continue hiking, I'm so slow I probably won't make it to Mt. Katahdin before Baxter State Park closes on October 15th. Technically, I could still hike the mountain after that date with permission from the forest ranger, but the date isn't guaranteed. If I go home, perhaps I can find a job in September. And isn't that my lifelong goal – to find a teaching job?

I don't want to quit. I don't want to be known as a quitter or a failure.

But is it still quitting if you change your mind because your goals have changed?

I love the friends I've made out here, but I also miss my friends and family at home. I miss my pets. Perhaps, if I choose to go home, I can take what I've learned, and maybe my life won't seem so pathetic. I look to the heavens and ask Greg what I should do.

"You're not a failure, April," I hear him say. *"You're injured. Go home. Get rest. You'll recover and come back another time to do it all again."*

I visit the Catholic church in Pearisburg with Twin Bears and her dad. It's my first time at a Catholic Mass. I don't know the prayers, and I feel like an idiot not knowing what to say in response to what the priest is saying. I stand, sit, and stand again, following everyone else's lead. I'm completely clueless. But it's church, I'm here, and I feel like He will forgive me and accept me for who I am, even if I'm in a different house than usual.

I decide to listen to Greg. I don't want to cause permanent injury to myself, and I do want to find a full-time teaching position. Sad to leave but excited for the future, I hop in the car with Twin Bears and head home. My hike is over. For now, anyway.

CHAPTER FIVE

NORTH CAROLINA

July 1996

I wash my gear, put it in the garage, and look around my bedroom. I'm back home, and everything is the same as when I left. The last two months feel like a dream, except for my feet. I'm still limping.

I spent more time in towns than I anticipated, so I spent more money than expected, even though I was gone for less time than predicted. I need to find a job. It's summer, so there are no teaching jobs. Summer camps have already hired counselors. I usually waitress in the summer, but with this limp, I don't think I can carry full trays of food without dropping them.

Someone I know tells me she has a client looking for a housekeeper for the summer horse racing meet. She's looking for a few hours a day, five days a week. It pays well, and the hours can be slightly flexible. The last thing I want to do is clean someone's apartment every day, but with a lack of options and limited mobility, I accept.

For the first time in my life, I have only one job in the summer. I enjoy it, and I love the client. I have free time to go out and enjoy all that my town has to offer. I also send out resumés to countless school districts in my area.

There are few teaching jobs available. I heard that the schools receive so many resumés that they can't even read every one. They randomly pull a few to read and interview, then choose a candidate. How is it even possible to get a job interview when there are 800 applicants per job?

September comes without a permanent job. My car is ten years old, and it's beginning to need more expensive repairs. Before my hike, I quit my mall retail job, and I don't want to return. I'm back to daily substitute teaching. A few weeks pass and I realize I need a second job. I find one at a mall jewelry store.

The days come and go. I'm teaching during the days and working at the mall nights and weekends. It dawns on me that hiking part of the Appalachian Trail has not changed my life one iota, except for the awareness that life does, in fact, exist outside New York State. I'm stuck in the same routine, day after day. My weekends are the same. I meet the same friends on Friday and Saturday nights, visit the same bars and clubs, drink the same drinks, and dance to the same music. I feel like Bill Murray in the movie *Groundhog Day*. Is there a way to stop this thing?

New Year's Day arrives, and I'm working in the jewelry store. It's now 1997. *Will I ever have a job where I don't have to work a holiday?*

The phone rings, and I hear, "Hey, April, it's your mom on the phone."

"Hi, mom, what's up?"

"April, (sniffle) you need to come home (sniffle) right away." I can picture the tears in her eyes as she speaks between sniffles.

"Why? What's wrong?"

"I'll tell you when you get home, but you should come home now."

My boss lets me leave early. When I arrive home, Mom tells me that my Nana passed away sometime last night or early this morning. She recently retired and moved to Saratoga to be with her family. She is the first to pass away since Greg died, which throws the family into a general depression again. We get together for her funeral and spend time reminiscing. *I'll miss you, Nana.*

I love my family, but I need to do something different. I just don't know what that is. My sister tells me that Laura, one of her high school friends, recently moved to Charlotte, North Carolina. The local school district is looking for teachers, and it turns out that Laura needs a roommate. I know Laura a little; she was a fellow bridesmaid in my sister's wedding.

I'm 27 years old. I have little savings and an old car. I'm still living with my parents, and I don't have a boyfriend yet. I graduated six years ago, and I still don't have a permanent teaching job. Something needs to change. Something drastic.

I'm going to need to talk to Laura.

"Okay, Laura, tell me about Charlotte."

"It's beautiful down here! The weather is nicer, it doesn't get as cold, and the city is bigger than Saratoga. There are a lot of opportunities down here."

"But you're not a teacher. How do you know about the schools?"

"Well, you know my boyfriend, JT. His brother went to school with a girl named Leah, and she moved down here last year with her best friend, Kathy, who teaches here. She always talks about how they don't have enough teachers. They are looking to hire teachers from up north because New York State has such good schools."

It takes all of two minutes to decide that if I want to change my life, I need to *change* my life.

"Okay, I'm sold. I need a few weeks to get organized and make sure I have enough money." Looking at the calendar and doing some quick figuring, I add, "I'll be down in three weeks. I'll come down on Martin Luther King Jr Day. Just give me an address."

I spend the next three weeks working as much as possible, giving my notice at schools and the store, and beginning to pack and organize. For years, I've collected pots and pans, blenders, and anything else I might need for an apartment when I saw a good sale. It's time to hunt them out of storage and organize them.

I run to Mrs. Tobey's house to say goodbye. She is one of my mom's best friends, and I've grown up with her family. She's like a second mom to me, and we have a special bond. I wore her prom gown to my prom in high school 25 years later. As I'm talking to her, her son overhears me. I've always loved Pat; he's like an older brother I don't see very often.

"So, you're just picking up and moving to Charlotte, just like that? And you don't have a job lined up yet?" he asks. "That takes balls," nodding his approval.

That's the biggest compliment I've ever received, and I beam with pride.

Martin Luther King Jr Day arrives. I spent the previous day packing my car and getting ready for this moment. My dad looks over my car and eyes the tires.

"Be careful driving. And try to avoid the potholes," he says.

"Call us when you get there," Mom adds.

After 12 hours in the car, I look around at the city of Charlotte as I drive through it. *So, this is where I live now.* I feel like I'm heading off to college again. I meet Laura at our new apartment and unload my car in short order. Now, it's time to find a job.

It's already January, and I'm assuming that I won't be able to find a permanent position until the next school year. I drive to the school district headquarters Tuesday morning to bring my resumé and teaching certificate to sign up for substitute teaching. I also peruse the malls and restaurants in the area to look for a part-time waitressing position. I give Laura money for rent, and after groceries, I'm embarrassed about how little cash I have. I still have a few large paychecks coming to me from various schools for substitute teaching, so I'm not panicking. Yet.

I spend a few days with Laura getting our apartment set up, buying second-hand furniture, and learning about my new city. I buy a roadmap from the gas station and sit down to memorize the larger roads and the easiest way to get from one place to the next and drive around getting acquainted with the area.

A week later, the phone rings. It's the principal of a local junior high school, wondering if I could interview the next day. My certification is in Elementary School, but because I've been a substitute teacher in a junior high and foreign language for so long, he thinks I'll be a fit for the full-time, permanent position.

Thursday morning comes along, and I head to inner city Charlotte for a job interview.

"So, April, what brings you to Charlotte?" he asks.

"Well, sir, I'm from upstate New York, but I hiked part of the Appalachian Trail last spring, and I loved the North Carolina area. A friend of mine lives here and told me that the local schools were looking for good teachers, and since there aren't many jobs available at home, I thought I'd come down to see how I can help down here."

"Wow, the Appalachian Trail! How many miles did you hike?"

"I hiked about 400 miles but was injured, so I had to go home early."

After a few cursory questions about my family and teaching experience, our conversation inevitably turns to the Appalachian Trail. I answer question after question about my pack weight, how many miles I hiked per day, what happened to my feet, and how I happened to move south.

"Well, April, you must be one tough girl to handle all that pain and adversity."

"I suppose so, sir; I'm not one to give up easily."

"Well then, we need tough people like you at this school. We need people who won't give up on these kids. We need people to show them how it's done and to lead them. I'd love for you to take this teaching position and start Monday. How does that work for you?"

Monday? Today is Thursday. That's in four days! How am I going to set up a classroom in four days?

"I'd like that very much, sir. Thank you for the opportunity," I answer, smiling.

He leads me on a tour of the school and shows me my classroom while introducing me to teachers here and there.

While the principal is chatting with someone, one teacher leans over and whispers, "You don't want to work here; this is a tough school. The environment is awful."

Yes, I do. I'm a good teacher, and I'm up for the challenge. Most importantly, I need a job. If it doesn't work out, I can try to transfer to another elementary school later if necessary. This will be fine.

Teaching school is going to be more complicated than I expected. The position I am in is newly created, and they were looking for the right person. I must develop a new curriculum, focusing on teaching reading and math to those students falling through the cracks. These kids are not special education students; they barely pass but don't qualify for any other special programs. The principal assumes this will be a perfect spot for me with my extensive substitute teaching in junior high, mostly in foreign languages and special education. He hands me the standardized test scores of all the kids in the school and their current grades and tells me to pick out students for my five classes.

How am I supposed to know which kids to take? And how many kids? The special education classes at home have less than ten kids per classroom, but this isn't special education. It's not a regular class either, so I can't have 25. Maybe 15 kids per class? The principal tries to convince me to take 20 kids per class, but I talk him down to 15 - 20, depending on the course. I will need to spend individual time with every student; 20 kids is too many and won't allow me to give them the necessary time they need.

Once I select my students based solely on test scores and grades, I need to create a letter to them and their parents explaining the new remedial program. Because the second semester of school has already started, I need to take them out of their elective class to put them in my remedial class.

What genius thought of this idea? I need to take kids out of their electives to put them in a remedial class? Sure, that will go over well. And the kids are going to just love me for this. Nevertheless, I write the letters.

I spend the first week of school choosing the students, sending the letters, and developing an idea of a curriculum. I head to the main office to see what books are available.

"Oh, Miss Peterson, this is a new program, so we don't have any books yet." *You're developing a new program and don't have books for it?*

"If you want to order some, let us know what to order, but remember, we don't have much money for supplies." My mind races back to my teaching supplies, remembering all the classes I took about teaching reading and math, and I try to remember what I have in my arsenal that might help me.

The receptionist hands me two reams of paper.

"What are these for?" I ask.

"That's your allotment of paper for the month."

"My *paper for the month*?"

"Yes, you're allowed to use 1,000 sheets of paper each month. When you need to make copies, just put your paper in the holder and copy what you need."

She leads me on tour through the copy room, where I see one older model of a copy machine and a ditto machine. *A ditto machine? Do people still use those?* As an affirmation of that thought, someone comes into the room, puts their paper on the designated holder, and starts cranking the handle in circles to create copies in bluish-purple ink. I haven't seen a ditto machine in 20 years.

I have no idea what kind of books to look for or where to look for them. I have materials from college, so I simply decide to make up material as I need it. This way, it's customized for the students. But 1,000 pages per month? That's roughly 50 pages per day, divided by five classes a day. I'm going to need to buy some extra paper.

Classes start on Monday, and as predicted, nobody is happy to give up an elective like music to be in my remedial math and reading classes. The students don't listen and could care less that I am here. The majority of my students are Black, Hispanic, or Asian, and none of them have blonde hair. They are only interested in my naturally light blonde, straight hair. A few even ask if they can touch my hair, and I oblige, thinking it will give me a personal edge to get them to listen to me.

It's early February and today is cold, and all hell breaks loose when a few snowflakes fall. My classroom is a science room with heavy stone desktops and floor-to-ceiling windows facing the courtyard. Coming from the north, the idea of snow makes me cringe. These kids don't see snow very often, so trying to get them calmed down is like herding cats. Some even manage to escape into the courtyard to try to catch snowflakes. I finally get them inside and use this as a writing exercise. "Tell me about the snowflakes. How do they make you feel? What do you think about the shapes? What memories do they bring up? What do you hope for when you see them?"

Teaching in this grade and location is challenging. I love the teaching aspect. I don't love that I'm not receiving any help. These students lead complicated lives. I don't know anybody whose parents have been to prison, yet some of these kids have one or both parents in jail. For some, one or both parents are dead, and many students live with someone other than a parent. It's a new reality for me, and I try to give these kids a reason to be on the straight and narrow and believe that crime doesn't pay.

During my breaks, I try to get outside. I walk around the neighborhood and notice bars on the windows, multiple door locks, and heavy iron gates in the doorways. In the lunchroom, I tell a fellow teacher about my walks, and she scolds me. "Never, ever, walk around this neighborhood by yourself. You drive your car with the windows up, park in the faculty parking lot, come right inside, and get right into your car when you leave and go home. You got that?"

How can I help my students if I don't know what they are going through?

I finally start to make some strides. Many of the students are musically inclined. They love the beat; they love drumming their hands on the desks. Asking them to stop becomes futile. Finally, I decide to use that skill. We practice our multiplication tables to the beat of their drumming hands. *Nine times nine is eighty-one* is easier to remember if they sound like song lyrics. Before long, every student repeats the multiplication tables in unison, like song lyrics to the beat they are drumming on their desks. I'm creating magic, and I smile.

The principal of the school doesn't like this idea. It's loud. It's disruptive. It's not traditional.

"But, sir, we're the only classroom in this hallway. It shouldn't be disruptive to any other students. And they're learning! They're almost 15 years old and finally learning their multiplication tables! Shouldn't this be something we can celebrate?"

"I can hear you in my office, and I can barely hear myself think. You get these kids to be quiet! You need to give them an environment where they can learn," he scolds and walks away.

How does he not see that these kids clearly can't learn the "traditional" way? They've muscled their way through life, learning only what they need to survive.

I like my job, but it's tough. I'm always trying to come up with new material to teach, which is difficult without a syllabus, a mentor, books, or the help and support of my administration. To decompress, I look forward to the end of the week.

When I moved down, my roommate introduced me to her group of friends. Each friend convinced another friend from home or college to move down. I developed a crush on Luke the moment I met him. He moved down here a few weeks after I did. He's a tad quiet and doesn't always say what he's thinking. We have a few things in common since his hometown is only about 30 minutes away from mine. It's nice to chat about places we both know about. The problem is that it's clear he has no interest in me. I'll try to work on that, but it's hard without being too pushy or obnoxious. And sometimes, I think I come across that way.

Occasionally, I escape to the mountains to hike my beloved Appalachian Trail. In three to four hours, I can get lost in the woods and forget about school, kids, and responsibility. I hike for myself, remembering the quiet and solitude of my hike only a year ago. But as sure as the sun rises and sets, Monday comes right on schedule.

The end of the school year arrives, and it's difficult to gauge if the students actually learned anything. There are no standardized tests to take, only a passing score on a test I created. The principal suggests it was all subjective, that I couldn't prove any actual gains. The fact that my students read an actual book and know some of their multiplication tables is positive to me. I'm not trying to get them into Harvard yet. I'm trying to instill a love of learning, to get them to understand that education can help them reach a goal, whatever that goal may be. Additionally, I only had them for a few months, and it took half of that time just to get them to stop hating me for taking them out of their elective classes.

My principal disagrees with me and doesn't ask me to come back for the next school year.

I run to the mountains for solace.

Trees don't judge, they are just *there* for us. The trees are all different, yet they all live together in harmony. The trees understand. I'm reminded of the book *The Giving Tree* by Shel Silverstein. Oh, how that tree loved her boy so much, she gave everything to him – her shade, her apples, and eventually, her whole self. The book always made me a little sad, and I hope he learned what a gift she was to him.

I love the trees out here. I wonder what secrets they hold, whispering as the wind whips through the mountains and rustles their leaves. The trees with the two-by-six-inch painted white rectangles are my favorite. I wrap my arms around them, hugging them, silently thanking them for the gift they are to me. They allow me to move forward. They are my strength.

CHAPTER SIX

THE DREAM JOB

Summer 1997

My best friend, Kathy, tells me her school is hiring a fourth-grade teacher for the year. Fourth grade is my favorite grade to teach. I love the age level of the students, and I like the curriculum for that age. I apply for the job the very next day. School starts on August 11th for teachers, and it's already nearing the end of July. Where are all these teaching jobs that people say are so badly need to be filled?

The phone rings, and I answer with optimism and hope.

"Hello?"

"Is April Peterson there, please?"

"This is April."

"Great. This is Mr. Mancini, Principal of Great Meadow Elementary School. I have a fourth-grade position open this year and was wondering if you'd be available for an interview this week."

I can't believe my luck. I jump for joy in my living room, covering the phone's mouthpiece lest he hears my excitement. We schedule an interview in a few days. He reminds me that the school is under construction, so he'll be in the trailer up front, temporarily set up as the main office.

I jump up and down and call Kathy to tell her the good news. I look in my closet to plan the perfect interview outfit. Finding nothing appropriate for an interview during a hot summer day in the south, I take to the malls and go shopping. I settle on a yellow and white, cotton, casual suit. It's summery, professional but not corporate-looking, and has just enough whimsy to reveal my personality.

I arrive at school a few minutes early, park my car, and walk eagerly to the trailer in front of the school. I am interviewing for my dream job and want to ensure everything is perfect. Weather: perfect. Hair: perfect. Makeup: perfect. Outfit: perfect. Shoes, handbag, dossier: perfect.

I enter the trailer and gasp. The inside looks like a hoarder's paradise. Every piece of paper, book, and folder in or near the main office has been crammed onto tables and in temporary cubicles, piled onto the floor in giant stacks. These are leaning against other stacks, threatening to push them down in a domino effect. I locate a person behind a tall stack of binders and introduce myself, adding that I am here for an interview with Mr. Mancini.

"Mr. Mancini, your interview is here!" she exclaims as loudly as possible, trying to carry her voice over the sound of the construction behind the trailer.

A man comes out of an office a few minutes later, clearly annoyed at the noise and chaos in the building. "Hi, I'm Mr. Mancini. Nice to meet you. Clearly, we can't talk here, so follow me, and we'll find someplace quiet where we can chat," as he hands me a well-used, once-white hard hat.

"We'll be walking through the construction zone, so you'll have to wear that," he adds, putting on his hard hat.

I follow him, and my hard hat bobbles on my head with every step I take. It's entirely too big, but the only way to tighten it is to remove it and pull the belt on the inside, and I know I don't have time for that. It's only temporary. I'll be fine.

I follow Mr. Mancini into a classroom, where he says, "Good. At least it's quiet in here, and we can talk." I sit down in the seat in front of him and take off my bobble hat.

"Oh, sorry, you can't take that off. We are still in an active construction zone."

Perfect outfit, perfect makeup, perfect hair, and now I need to wear this god awful dirty, disgusting hard hat that doesn't fit and shakes every time I move my head? I lie and say, "It's no problem at all," in my sweetest voice, as I put the dreaded thing back on.

"So, April," he states, looking at his paperwork. "It says here that you were a substitute teacher for six years in New York state, moved down here and got a job right away at Hathaway Junior High, and that they didn't ask you back at the end of the year. This tells me that you can't get a job. Why is that?"

Umm. Wow.

I finally understand what it means when people say they want the earth to open and swallow them. I'm speechless. Or rather, my mouth is quiet, but my brain is abuzz with exclamation points.

What?! Are you kidding me?! That's your first question?! How dare you accuse me of being unable to get and keep a job! You don't know anything about me, you pompous ass! Kathy didn't tell me her principal was such an asshole! How the hell am I supposed to answer that question?

An eternity passes, though the tick-tick-ticking wall clock assures me it's only been a few seconds. I calm my brain, take a deep breath, and steady my voice.

"Well, Mr. Mancini, I graduated from SUNY Geneseo in New York in 1991, along with about a million other teachers. We joined the workforce that year and learned that there were so few jobs available because all the teachers in New York hadn't retired yet, as predicted just five years earlier. You see, every single teacher I had from kindergarten through twelfth grade was still teaching in the fall of 1991 and still is to this day. I started to substitute teach, but there were so many substitute teachers that I even had to sub in the middle, junior, and senior high schools if I wanted to be in a classroom. I'm not sure if you know anything about the schools of the capital district of New York, but if you did, you would know that they are some of the best public schools in New York and indeed, the entire country. Because of that, many people want to teach there, and the competition is just outrageous. I decided to move down here because I heard the Charlotte schools were looking for good teachers…

"Regarding my placement at Hathaway, I'll remind you that I was neither trained nor certified in junior high grades. I had to remove students from their elective classes and put them into remedial math and reading classes. The principal felt I could handle the assignment because he thought I was tough and could take it. Respectfully, I wasn't given any guidance, curriculum, books, or a mentor, yet I was expected to change the lives and grades of those students within a few months. It was an impossible situation to begin with. No, I was not asked back, nor would I have gone back even if I was."

I want to stand up and accept my Oscar for Best Performance. Instead, I sit there, stoic, and wait for more.

The interview continues in the same tone. Mr. Mancini is accusatory, and I'm defensive, offering explanations and ideas whenever possible. It is easily the worst interview in history.

He releases me from torture and says, "April, it was nice to meet you. Thanks for coming in."

LIAR!! You big fat lying asshole!

I refrain from saying my thoughts and somehow stammer, "It was nice to meet you, too. Thanks for your time. I hope you have a nice day."

I fight back the tears as I racewalk to my car. As soon as I reach my apartment, I grab the phone and call Kathy. Tears sting my eyes as I recount the awful interview and tell her I never want to see that evil man again.

School starts in less than two weeks, and I'm pretty sure I won't get a teaching job this school year.

I need to clear my head; I need the mountains. It's finally time for me to get back to Franklin, NC, to hike over Standing Indian Mountain, which I was so afraid to climb last year. After my stay in Franklin last year, the shuttle driver drove us to the trailhead, and I skipped about 24 miles of the trail. It's time to hike them.

I'm up and out early for the four-hour drive. I park at Deep Gap and grab my backpack. It's August 1 in North Carolina. It's 80 degrees. But I plan to camp on top of Standing Indian Mountain at 5,499 feet in elevation. Should I bring my summer sleeping bag or my winter bag? I opt for my summer fleece bag because it weighs less, and I begin climbing. The hiking is easier than expected, fueled by lingering anger over my disastrous interview.

In no time at all, I'm in trail mode. I forget about work and teaching and everything related to my life in Charlotte. I concentrate on breathing and enjoying the trees, wildlife, and fresh air. I arrive at the summit around dinner time and find a small spot to set up my tent. Northbound thru-hikers are long gone, and the southbounders, those starting in Maine, won't arrive in this area for a few more months. A few people are hiking for a night or a weekend, and I chat with various people and their kids. They ask if I'm afraid to hike alone, and for the thousandth time, I explain that I have no reason to be any more fearful out here than I do in town. Hikers are usually pleasant people, conscious of the environment and aware of their actions. I generally find more kindred spirits in the woods than in the real world.

After dinner is cleaned up and conversations wane, many people retreat to their tents for the evening. I do the same, write in my journal, and check out the trail guide for the next day. I plan to hike to Big Spring Shelter the next day, 15 miles away.

I settle into sleep, but I realize I am a little chilly. I remove some extra clothing from my stuff sack, which serves as my pillow, and wear them to keep warm. I can sleep without a pillow, I guess. I fall asleep, only to wake up really cold a few hours later. My fleece sleeping bag was a poor choice, and I should have brought the heavier winter bag. I chastise myself because the winter bag was only one additional pound.

I try to go back to sleep, but my teeth chatter, and I'm shivering.

Should I hike back to the car to get my sleeping bag?

In the middle of the night? You are an idiot!

I've hiked in the middle of the night before. I have my headlamp. Maybe I'll just sleep in the car and head out in the morning.

If you sleep in the car, people up here will panic when they find an empty tent in the morning.

I could leave a note.

And then you'd have 20 miles to hike tomorrow. There must be a better idea.

Suddenly, I remember my emergency blanket. Stuffed into the crevices of my backpack is my emergency space blanket. It's made from mylar, and it reflects body heat rather than having it escape.

In the middle of the night, I unpack my foil space blanket. It's about the size of an apple and unfolds to the size of a twin bed.

It's not quiet.

It's worse than someone trying to quietly open and eat a bag of potato chips at the movies.

I probably wake everyone in the local towns until I finally place the blanket over me and try to sleep.

I'm not exactly comfortable, and every move makes me feel like I'm trying to sleep in that foil bag of chips. The good thing is that I don't die from hypothermia.

I eat breakfast in the morning and say hello to everyone I bothered last night, apologizing if I kept them awake. I consider returning to my car in the daytime to swap bags, but the next shelter is at a lower elevation, so it should be warmer, and I will be all set. I'm back on my beloved trail and couldn't be happier. I'm enjoying the fresh air and being out in the middle of nowhere. The lack of cars and people and bosses and classrooms makes me smile.

I climb the Albert Mountain fire tower and admire the endless views. The mountains are like waves of an ocean, one coming right after another, as far as the eye can see. The sun gets lower in the sky, casting long shadows across the mountains. It's time to get to Big Springs Shelter.

A half dozen people are camping here, and someone sets up a campfire. I introduce myself as April, and that I hiked part of the Appalachian Trail last year. One guy is working in the mountains of North Carolina for the summer and wants to thru-hike the trail next year. I share some thru-hiking stories, and we have a good time chatting. We started as strangers, but after a few hours of talking, I feel like I know many of them well.

I retreat to the shelter and use my tent as an additional blanket to keep me warm. It's not enough. Before I begin shivering, I unfold the dreaded emergency blanket, laying it over and tucking it under me. I toss and turn again, trying to stay warm but failing miserably.

Luckily, I don't freeze to death, but I'm somewhat tired and cranky from two semi-sleepless nights. Everyone begins to stir, and I start to pack up, folding my space blanket to the amusement of everyone around me.

"Hey, April, did you get any sleep at all? I think I heard you every time you flipped over last night," Steve, the guy working in the woods, asks with a giggle.

"Well, I left my heavier sleeping bag in the car, thinking that we are in the middle of summer, and it would be warm enough for this fleece bag. I was wrong. I'll never make that mistake again."

"Where's your car?"

"I left it at Deep Gap. I'm hiking to Winding Stair Gap today, and I'm hoping that once I make it to the main road, I can find a ride back to pick up my car."

"Well, I can drive you back if you want. My car is at Winding Stair Gap."

"That would be great. Thanks so much."

He's not a serial killer. He's a graduate student obtaining a botany degree and working in the mountains doing something with trees. He did tell me what he's doing, but it's botany. Seriously. I have no idea what he's doing with the trees.

After breakfast, we finish packing and begin our eight-mile hike for the day. It's a perfect hiking day – low sixties in the morning, zero rain, clear skies. It's fun to talk to someone new, someone who loves the woods and the trail as much as I do. He has a thick, Southern accent, and I giggle at some of the words he says.

He's smart, though. He asks about my hike last year, and I tell him more stories. He tells me about his classes and how he's working on his Ph.D. He teaches me a little about the plants we pass, which ones are edible or poisonous, and their uses. We're fast friends after a few hours when we get to Winding Stair Gap.

After loading our stuff in his car, we begin the drive on the main road, heading toward the forest service road. I'm sorry that I will get to my car so quickly. I really like talking to this guy.

"April, I'm a little hungry. How about we get some lunch in Franklin before heading to your car?"

"I'm starved too! I bet B&D's is still open. That's a great diner; I ate there a few times while I was in Franklin."

"Okay, perfect. B&D's it is."

We talk all through lunch, including the must-have peach cobbler for dessert. He talks about his plans to take classes from September through December and to begin hiking the Appalachian Trail in early March of 1998. I talk about how I don't expect to get a job this school year after that disastrous interview, and I'm not sure what I will do. I talk about my failed teaching attempts, but I love living in Charlotte.

We babble until we reach my car and chat for a few minutes longer. We exchange phone numbers and addresses, just in case.

Sheesh, I finally meet a guy I think I like, but he's working in the mountains, and I need to go home. Something isn't fair.

I hop in my car to drive home with stars in my eyes.

At home the next day, I organize my apartment, try to figure out what I will do about school, and head out for some errands. When I return, the answering machine is beeping. I push the button.

"Hi, this message is for April. This is Mr. Mancini from Great Meadow Elementary School. I'd like to discuss the teaching position we spoke about last week. Could you call me at the following number to discuss the details? Thanks so much."

I stare at the answering machine. Did he dial the wrong number? Was I the only one in that room? Does he not think that was the worst interview in the history of interviews?

I consider throwing away the number, but curiosity gets the best of me, and I call him back.

"April, thanks for returning my call. We'd love for you to join us next week as part of our staff at Great Meadow Elementary School."

I'm still confused. Is he actually offering me the job? Did he interview two Aprils? Does he have the right person?

"August 11 is the first day of school for teachers; you'll have a week for set up, and the students arrive on August 18. Will that work for you?"

Well, it works for my wallet. The rest of me will have to deal with it.

"Absolutely. Thank you for the opportunity. I'll be there," I say, and hang up the phone in utter disbelief.

CHAPTER SEVEN

A NEW DREAM

August 1997

My first day is full of meetings and motivational speeches, boxes of Krispy Kreme doughnuts, and the excitement of setting up my own classroom. It also comes with a warning from some other teachers.

They glance at my class roster. "Ohhh, you have Mandy. Good luck with her – she's a handful." They also give me hints and clues about other kids in the class.

The fourth-grade teachers teach in teams and divide the students into four groups, and we each lead a level. I will teach Social Studies to two classes, the highest-level math group, and the lowest-level English.

Social Studies is a problem right away. I'm excited about the first part of the year, when I get to talk about the different geographical areas of North Carolina. I know a lot about the mountains. I can share information with pictures! But towards the end of the year, I see something in the textbook called "The War of Northern Aggression." I read further and wonder, do they mean The Civil War? After reading more, it's clear that the textbook discusses the American Civil War. I take the book down to the principal. "Mr. Mancini, I have some issues with this textbook. How can I teach "The War of Northern Aggression" when it's clearly The Civil War we are discussing?"

"April, it's semantics. Teach it the way it says."

"It's NOT semantics. There was a significant difference of opinion about slavery. The Northern states weren't more 'at fault' than the Southern states. When President Lincoln was elected, opposing slavery's expansion into the west, the Southern states seceded from the United States, forming the Confederacy. The rest is history, but not THIS history!"

"I've got nothing more to add. That's our textbook, and that's what you will teach."

This is going to be another challenging year.

∞o∞

I send Steve a letter, thanking him for driving me back to my car, and I am surprised when he calls me. We talk about his work in the mountains and my work in the classroom, and we decide to have a hiking date. Last year, I skipped a section of the North Carolina mountains, so we decide to hike the Stecoah range until Fontana Dam. My friends make fun of me, laughing and saying, "Only you could walk into the North Carolina mountains and come out with a date."

Steve and I meet up at The Nantahala Outdoor Center, one of my favorite places on the trail last year. We greet each other like old friends.

"That is the most coordinated hiking outfit I've ever seen," he says with a smile.

"Thanks." I'm happy to see that he recognized my efforts. I was not about to admit that I spent an entire day shopping for new matching hiking clothes so I wouldn't look like a schlep with my dirty, stained clothes from last year.

We fill our water bottles, ensure we have what we need, and follow the trail into the mountains. The Stecoahs are steep, and I let Steve lead the way.

Man, he has some good-looking legs! I follow along, thoroughly enjoying the wilderness and not thinking about my classroom. It's challenging to keep up a conversation when you're huffing and puffing, trying to catch your breath, so he does most of the talking, and I answer occasionally with a few short words and grunts.

After seven very steep and challenging miles, we stop for the day, set up our tents, and begin to make dinner. I pull out Lipton noodles, and he pulls out some gourmet concoction, adding wild ramps and greens. He makes this fantastic nutritional powerhouse dinner, and I have, well, noodles. He admits he made enough for two, so we share our dinners. He's a good cook. Maybe there is something to botany after all.

After dinner, we take turns at the creek, taking sponge baths and changing into camp clothing. He creates a small fire, makes hot chocolate for us, and we sit around sipping and talking for hours until sleepiness sets in and we retreat to our tents. I love this wilderness date.

The next day is nine miles of rugged hiking, but the amazing views of the Smoky Mountains and rugged North Carolina mountains from the summit of Cheoah bald make all the effort worthwhile. It's endless mountains as far as the eye can see. The company and conversation are great as well. That is, when we can talk between gasping for air. We have several more ups and downs before finally resting at Brown Fork Gap Shelter.

He makes hot chocolate again, and after dinner, he excuses himself and heads for the creek. He returns with a no-bake cheesecake that he secretly made while I was cleaning up. We sip and snack until exhaustion ensues. This is the most effort I have ever put in for a date, but I'm impressed at the amount of effort he's also putting in.

Eleven slightly easier miles the next day brings us to Fontana Dam, where the Great Smoky Mountains begin. The dam is impressive; Fontana Lake is full of clear blue water, and the Little Tennessee River forms at the base of the dam. It's an engineering marvel. After sightseeing for a little while, we get a shuttle back to the Nantahala Outdoor Center.

We grab an early dinner at the on-site grille and chat about our favorite parts of the weekend. I have a three-and-a-half-hour drive home, yet I don't want to go. I will miss Steve. His summer is almost over, and he'll be headed back to graduate school out of state. After delaying the inevitable, we finally part ways and head home. We promise to stay in touch.

∞o∞

School starts early. Students arrive by 7:20 am, and teachers are expected to arrive by 7:00 am every day. I'm not a morning person, and I squeak into the building right on time. My students shuffle into class, and I have butterflies in my stomach. I'm excited to meet them, and nervous about having my own classroom. *Can I actually teach them something? Am I as good a teacher as I think I am?*

The other teachers weren't kidding about Mandy and the other students. I notice the talkers, the quiet ones, and the ones that need to be the center of attention. They are about ten years old. They have distinct personalities, likes and dislikes, and their own will, but they are still young enough to be teachable.

Good teaching involves explaining something, reteaching it for those who don't get it, and repeating it another way until every student finally understands. The first day of school involves getting to know each other, passing out books, and explaining how the schedule works. We are on our way to a productive year within a few days.

Everything I teach needs to involve literacy, which is the primary goal of the school district. I must note in my lesson plans where they match the North Carolina State syllabus.

"Joe, will you please read your answer to number four, please?" I call out.

"Um, (pause), sorry, Miss Peterson, but I can't read what I wrote."

"You can't read the answer to the question you just answered about five minutes ago?" I reach for his paper, and I understand. I have been in classrooms for years, and I can decipher almost any writing at all. But Joe was right; it was difficult to read his handwriting. I glance at a few other papers; their handwriting is also illegible. It's nearly impossible to teach reading if the kids don't know how to write their letters. I scrap the lesson and begin to talk about how to form cursive letters. Seriously, the school should have taught this for the past two years.

"Miss Peterson, can I see you for a moment?" I look up to see Mr. Mancini standing outside my classroom door. I instruct the students to write their names in cursive several times while I sneak out of the room for a moment.

"Hi, Mr. Mancini, what's up?"

"Are you teaching *handwriting* in class?"

"It didn't start as a handwriting lesson, but it's turning into that. Why?"

"Miss Peterson, the North Carolina State Syllabus doesn't allow the teaching of handwriting. Everything we teach MUST deal directly with literacy."

"I see your point, Mr. Mancini, but handwriting directly correlates with literacy. The students in that class can't read *their own* writing to me. If they can't read handwriting, they can't read. I'm not sure how North Carolina doesn't see how that relates to literacy."

"It doesn't matter what you see. It's not in the syllabus, so you can't teach it. If I see you teaching it again, I will fire you instantly. Do you understand?"

"Yes, I understand."

No, I don't understand! But I can't say that. If you can't read and write letters, how are you supposed to be able to *read*? As instructed, I turned around and walked back into my classroom to end the handwriting lesson.

It's September 10, and I'm excited to receive my first teaching paycheck today. Teachers get paid once a month in this district. I've already borrowed money from my roommate to pay the rent for September. Today, I'll be able to pay her back. I arrive at the library for our faculty meeting and spend a few minutes chatting with Kathy and the other teachers. Before we are all seated, I see Mr. Mancini making a beeline straight to me.

"Miss Peterson, I need to see you before the meeting." I rack my brain to figure out what I did wrong this time. "Miss Peterson, I wanted to inform you that you won't receive a paycheck today." I stare at him, trying to understand if I heard him correctly.

"You see, Miss Peterson, since you are technically a substitute teacher for the year, you will be paid on a substitute schedule, and their paychecks are a month behind. You'll receive your first check on October 10th."

"Mr. Mancini," I said, trying and failing miserably to control my anger, "Are you telling me that I just worked in a professional capacity for an entire month, yet I won't be receiving a paycheck for another 30 days?"

"Well, yes."

"Well, that's not acceptable. I haven't had a paycheck in over a month. I have 76 dollars in my account. I still need to pay rent and insurance, buy food, and put gas in my car to get to school. How do you suppose I do that? And if I was on this alternative payment schedule, you should have told me that from day one because I would never have been able to afford to accept this job. Do you know why the school district has trouble getting substitute teachers? Because nobody can afford to work here!" I am yelling now, and I storm out of the library. My eyes are burning, and I need to get away from this man before I say or do something I regret.

I walk a few laps around the school, trying to calm down. After about 30 minutes, I quietly enter the school and sneak into the back of the library, where the faculty meeting is underway.

The school district calls me to the main office. They can issue me a partial paycheck. It's not ideal, but at least I can eat. I'll receive the second half of the check on October 10th, so I'm still a month behind. It's frustrating to know I'm putting all this effort into my dream job and still have no money. Even with an entire paycheck, money is scarce because the pay scale is so low. Like many teachers, I realize I need to get a second job.

There is a small movie theater only a few hundred yards from my apartment. They are looking for people who can work in the evening and they hire me. The theater runs second-run movies, so it's not very busy during the weeknights. Additionally, the management allows me to take the leftover popcorn to school, where I can share it with the students who don't bring a daily snack.

I usually find a few minutes to chat with Steve once or twice a week. He discusses his plans for beginning his thru-hike in March of next year. I am entirely jealous.

"Why don't you come with me?" he suggests.

"What? I can't go hiking with you. I'm teaching. The school year doesn't end until May."

"You could quit. You don't like it anyway."

He's right. But I can't go there.

"No, I can't go. I've been waiting all my life for this. It's just hard as a first-time teacher."

"Okay, but the offer stands. I need to begin my hike on March 7th to finish in August for another round of classes."

I dismiss the idea as ridiculous.

The next day, Tommy raises his hand during a social studies lesson. "Yes, Tommy, what is it?"

"Miss Peterson, I feel like I'm going to throw up." Oh, dear. How does one handle this in the middle of teaching?

"Oh, okay. Why don't you run down to the main office, and they can call your parents to come to pick you up?" He gets up and runs downstairs. A minute later, the office calls me over the classroom intercom.

"Miss Peterson, did you just send Tommy to the office?"

"Yes, I did. He's not feeling well."

"Well, did you call his parents?"

What? "No, I didn't have a chance. I'm in the middle of teaching a social studies lesson."

"Well, did you take his temperature? You know we don't have a full-time nurse."

"No, I didn't take his temperature. As I said, I'm in the middle of teaching a social studies lesson. I don't have time to run down the hall to call his parents from the lounge, and I don't have time to take his temperature.

Since we don't have a full-time nurse, I thought perhaps, you could call his parents for me."

"Okay, we'll do it this one time."

Sheesh.

As expected, Mr. Mancini approaches me at the end of the day to discuss this. Apparently, I'm supposed to verify a student is ill by taking their temperature, then call a student's parents to have them pick up their child from school.

"Mr. Mancini, the room with the phone is at the other end of the hall. We are not supposed to have our classrooms unsupervised, and the teacher next door was out of her room with her kids in specials. How do you propose I find supervision for my room while I leave to make a phone call down the hall?"

"That's not my job, Miss Peterson. That's yours."

This job is not going well.

I arrive at school every morning and wait in my car, watching the clock until it's precisely 7:00 am when I must get to my classroom. Life shouldn't be like this. I should be excited about school. I've been waiting for this my entire life, and I'm not happy with it once I get it. What's wrong with me? I could understand suffering through this misery for a while if I were making more money. But I'm not doing that; I need a second job simply to survive. I'm 27 years old. Can I see myself doing this for the next 40 years?

I think of the financials. Most teachers have a state retirement plan. Financially, at what age are you *stuck* teaching because you need to keep your retirement funds? Doing a little figuring in my head, I figure that if I am ever going to leave the field of teaching, the time is now. I can't wait five or ten years. Financially, it's now or never.

I don't fit in with this principal or this school district. I don't agree with district politics, and I am not one to teach things the traditional way all the time. Traditionally, fractions are complex for students to learn. I've learned that the best way to teach the addition and multiplication of fractions is to use recipes for baking things. Using two half-teaspoons of water, doubled in a recipe, is one teaspoon of water. Nobody wants to practice boring fractions on a worksheet but doubling or tripling a recipe is much more fun. Or take a chocolate chip recipe and make 50 recipes instead. It gives the students real-world examples of why the lesson is essential and how they can use it in everyday life. Teaching this with water in a classroom can be fun and practical but also messy. The principal doesn't like this.

A few days before Thanksgiving break, I receive a message through the intercom.

"Miss Peterson, please come to my office after school," Mr. Mancini calls out.

"Sure. I'll be down in a few minutes." I enter his office and sit down as he instructs me.

"Miss Peterson, I think it's time we evaluate the job you've been doing here at this school."

I could only think of that horrible interview before the school year started, and I knew what I had to do. "Don't you worry about it, Mr. Mancini. I've decided to tender my resignation. I'll write something formally and put it on your desk tomorrow."

"Oh, may I ask when you plan on leaving?"

"I thought Christmas break would be appropriate."

"Well, if you're going to quit, why wait until then?" he pushes.

Gathering every ounce of strength and civility in my body, I continue. "Well, I think staying until the holidays is only fair to the students, don't you agree? The district has a hard enough time finding substitute teachers, so I thought giving a month's notice is only fair so they have enough time to find a suitable replacement. Additionally, the students will have a two-week break to get used to the idea of a new teacher, and it will be toward the end of the marking quarter."

"Well, when you say it like that, I agree, that makes the most sense."

"Great, you'll have an official letter tomorrow," and I walk out the door.

Feeling simultaneously proud for standing up for myself and shameful for not being able to teach well, I stop by Kathy's classroom to break the news to her. She understands my predicament. She knows I am not a rule follower, even if I don't realize that whole truth myself. I stop by the grocery store to pick up some beer to drown my sorrows, and as I walk through the grocery store, I buy some flowers instead. The flowers are beautiful, make me think of the trail, and make me smile.

What if I did hike next year? Do I want to hike with Steve? No, I don't want to hike with him. As much as I like him, I know we're not a couple, and it's tough to have a partner on the trail if you're not a couple. And he needs to start so early. I don't know if I can save enough money by early March. No, I need to hike my own hike if I'm going to do this.

My lease will end at the end of March, I don't have a car payment, and I can have Kathy mail out my insurance and credit card payments. The rest of my stuff can go into storage.

Creating a plan without intending to do so, I only have to work up the courage to tell my parents. I wait on this as long as possible. They fully paid for my college education to get that teaching degree. How could I possibly tell them thanks but no thanks? Eventually, I break the news.

"Hi, Mom; yes, things are going fine. Um, I wanted to tell you and Dad something. You know I don't get along with my principal at school, right? Well, I decided that I'm going to quit teaching, I'll get a temp job after Christmas, and I'm going to rehike The Appalachian Trail next year, beginning in March." And before they can utter a word, I add quickly, "and I can tell you really don't want to talk about this right now, so I'll talk to you about it a little later. I gotta run. Bye!" and I hang up the phone as quickly as I can.

That was the hard part. Now, I have to plan.

Financials are the most difficult part of the plan. *Can I afford to hike? How can I save up enough money to hike if I don't have any money saved to begin with?*

In a stroke of luck in a roundabout way, being on a substitute pay schedule allows me to collect paychecks well into February. So if I find a temp position from now until March, and continue working at the movie theater, I could feasibly work enough to pay my bills and save some, and put those teaching checks into a savings account just for hiking.

What about my current situation? My apartment lease ends on March 31. That will give my roommate enough time to find another roommate. Car? My car has been paid off for years. It's a good thing I didn't buy that new car when I got that first teaching job! Insurance? I can have Kathy send out pre-written checks to pay for the insurance, and she also offered to keep my car at her apartment to keep an eye on it. Luke offers to drive it occasionally to keep fluids running and keep it in working order. Lease, check. Car, check. Money, check. What else?

When to begin? Steve invited me to at least start the trail with him, and I consider it. There are two issues. One, he begins hiking in early March, and according to my calculations, I'll need to save more money than that time frame would allow me. No, I need to work until the end of March. It's the only way I can make it work. Hiking with Steve would bring up another problem. We aren't a couple. It's difficult to hike with someone when you're not a couple. No, if I'm going to hike the Appalachian Trail, I need to do it by myself on my own timeframe. I need to hike my own hike.

Equipment? What do I keep? What do I get new?

Sleeping bag. It's too heavy. Luke and Kathy come with me to a local outfitter store so I can look at new sleeping bags. Looking at weight, I select a 20-degree synthetic bag and put it on the floor, get in, and roll around a few times to see if it's comfortable and big enough. I think they are embarrassed about me doing this. Luke is looking away, pretending not to know me, and would probably leave the store if he didn't drive us there. I really like the softness of down, but I'm concerned about it getting wet. When down gets wet, it loses its insulating properties. The bonus with this bag is that it comes with an additional down liner to make it a zero-degree bag when necessary. Sold. I sell my other sleeping bag in the newspaper to help pay for it.

Cooking stove, pot, fuel canister: everything stays the same. My pot is bigger than necessary – but knowing how much pasta I'll be eating, I need to boil noodles and not just let them simmer. Food preference. I'll keep what I have.

Backpack: I definitely need a new one. I like the Gregory brand, but exterior frame packs are bulkier, and they don't sit as close to the body as I'd like. I'm drawn to the Gregory Wind River. It's a huge internal frame pack, but it has a horseshoe-shaped zipper in the front, enabling me to pack from the top, or pack from the front. It has a lot of bells and whistles. I don't pay any attention to the almost seven pounds that the bag actually weighs.

Water Filter: a filter is necessary to remove contaminants and bacteria from water sources. I have the Pur Hiker, which weighs 11 ounces and filters water quickly. I've never had a problem with it. Keep.

Boots: I LOVE the Scarpa brand boots that I bought at the Walasi-Yi Center last year. But with all the hiking I've done, they already have about 600 miles on them, if not more. I don't think they will last the entire trail. So, I buy another pair of Scarpa boots and break them in. My old pair will serve as my back up boots in an emergency.

Tent: I have a Eureka Rising Sun. It's a small tent, and one or two people can fit in it. It's a free-standing tent, and if I don't carry the tent stakes, it weighs less than four pounds, plus the additional plastic footprint. I'll keep this.

Clothing and socks: I buy some updated shorts and thermal pants, keep my raingear, and grab a few new pairs of Smartwool Expedition weight socks. I like the cushiness they provide.

Hiking Poles: keep.

With all my gear set, I think about getting back into shape. I work a lot. I have a full-time temp job and a night job at the movie theater. I usually get Sundays off, and I realize that the only way to get in shape for hiking is to go hiking. Crowders Mountain is a small mountain about 30 minutes away from Charlotte. It's easy to get there. Every weekend, I grab my backpack and fill it with all my gear, plus additional canned goods from the kitchen to make it heavier. I head out to Crowders and hike to the summit, and back down to my car. I do this until it's easy. Then, once it's too easy, I do it *again*. People I pass while going down the mountain look at me funny when

I head back up the mountain, and they are coming down. "Practicing," I explain.

When I am walking around my apartment complex, I walk barefoot. I step on stones and pebbles, and I rub my feet with alcohol. I am told that this toughens up my feet, and I will have fewer blisters. I will do *anything* to have fewer blisters.

I work, I save money, I practice hiking. This is my life for three months after teaching.

Luke and Kathy offer to drive me to Dahlonega, Georgia, to begin my hike.

It's March 28, 1998.

CHAPTER EIGHT

THE SECOND ATTEMPT

March 1998

Kathy and Luke take me to Dahlonega, Georgia, where we find a hotel room for the night. I begin my journey tomorrow. I have a mixture of emotions. I remember being in this hotel two years ago with Melissa and her father. I've had an abrupt change in my life in two years, yet I'm here in the same spot.

I will miss my friends. I moved down here knowing one person, and I quickly found a group of friends that kept growing. Kathy has turned into my best friend, and my crush on Luke has only gotten stronger, even while having that temporary crush on Steve. How will I live without seeing them both?

After breakfast, we drive to the entrance of Amicalola Falls State Park and weigh my pack, a traditional "pre-hike" custom. 50 pounds, fully loaded with two quarts of water, a bit high but much better than my pack two years ago. I change into my hiking boots, use the ladies' room for the last time for about a week, and they drive me up the road a little to the trail, missing the climb up the waterfall like two years ago. I hug them goodbye and hoist my pack.

I am not alone.

Kathy doesn't want to see me go. Luke chases her up the hill to force her to allow me to leave. I hug her again and say, "I'll be back in six months!"

Then Luke reaches out to hug me. I hold on tight and tell myself that if he doesn't let go, I'm not hiking, and I'll go home with them. He whispers into my ear, "Stay safe, you hear? Give us a call every once in a while and let us know how you're doing."

He lets go, and I begin to hike. I glance back after a few minutes to find them still watching me. I wave once more, and they are soon out of sight.

I'm on my own. I'm excited and terrified. I gave up my career, and I better not fail this time. Based on my last hike, I know I have the willpower to finish; I only hope I have the health to do it this time.

I have six miles left on the approach trail, then only four. The hiking is much easier than last time. I'm not gasping for air every few steps, nor do my muscles or feet hurt.

I am more prepared this year. All that hiking and practicing on Crowders Mountain has paid off. At one point, I was carrying nearly 70 pounds. This 50-pound pack is light in comparison!

I arrive at the summit of Springer Mountain hours earlier than expected. Several people are at the top, and I look around, wondering who is thru-hiking and which of those hikers will make it to Maine.

A woman says, "Hi, I'm Susan."

Instinctively, I answer, "Hi, I'm Trail Gimp." Somehow, I am no longer April. With all the hiking and preparation for the past two years, I am Trail Gimp. And that's good because I like her more than I like April. April is quiet. Mostly, she's afraid of what people think of her a lot of the time. Trail Gimp is nothing like that. Trail Gimp is fearless. She doesn't care one iota what people think of her. She's brave and isn't afraid of anything.

"Oh! I've heard of you!" she exclaims. "Weren't you in a book that came out last year?"

"Yes, I gave my journal to Lynn Setzer, who was writing about the 1996 thru-hikers in a book called *A Season On The Appalachian Trail*. I'm glad you read it. I wanted to let people know that not everyone makes it to Maine, and some of the circumstances around people leaving the trail."

We discuss the book for a while, talking about some people in it and why I returned to the trail.

"Well, good luck this year! I know you'll make it this time," she says as she takes off down the mountain with her friends.

I walk towards Springer Mountain Shelter to claim my spot before it gets too crowded. I am now a professional at hanging my food bag under the tuna fish can and hanging my backpack. I find the shelter register, sign in as Trail Gimp, and read the entries of other thru-hikers as they begin their journey. I continue reading back to March 7, where I see Steve's entry and a note he left for me: "Catch up, Trail Gimp!" He's a full three weeks ahead of me. There is no possible way for me to catch up with him. And although we get along incredibly well, this is my hike. I am out here to complete something on my terms. I am out here for a reason. I just don't fully understand what that reason is.

I make an early dinner, grab my journal, and head back to the summit to watch the sunset while recording my thoughts.

Everything about this hike is different from my last hike. Last time, I didn't know what to expect. I was out for an adventure and to do something different with my life. This time, I'm here to finish what I started. I'm looking for a new beginning that will guide me for the rest of my life. I know what the trail brings. I understand the hiking, the willpower needed to continue moving when you're tired or cold or hot or hungry. And I know the discipline required to continue to hike through pain and adversity. I know what it's like to walk alone, get lost, and listen to the heavens and let them guide your way. And for the first time, I feel like I am finally in the right place at the right time. I hear my cousin Greg's voice say, *"You are."*

That's enough confirmation for me.

I develop a massive blister on my foot within two days, but it's not nearly as bad as before, and I hardly notice if I tape my foot well. I'm not writing in my journal as much as I did two years ago; I'm much more social, talking to more people more often. This is prime time for hikers to begin, so I see 30 or more people every day. All hikers are generally friendly toward others. We are all stewards of the land and the trail and do our part to keep it clean.

With so many people on the trail, the thru-hikers tend to stick together, wondering who will make it or who our trail family will be. Even hiking by oneself, you develop a trail family – a group of kindred spirits you often see while hiking and hang out with. I'm hiking alone, but I look around at everyone and wonder who my trail family will be.

At Gooch Gap shelter, after three days of hiking, I am lucky enough to find a spot within the shelter because it's raining, just like it was two years ago. Some people here were at Hawk Mountain Shelter from last night, including Gail and Brent, Walk-A-Week, Rick, and Shane. Rick and Shane are best friends from a town near Atlanta, hiking between college semesters. Growing up near the Appalachian Trail, they have always wanted to thru-hike, so they took this semester off, hoping to complete a thru-hike before next semester starts. They are only 20 years old, and they crack me up with their jokes and impersonations. Shane talks a lot in his sleep, and Rick is a sugar fanatic, constantly nibbling on some candy, so they've been dubbed with new trail names: Nightgrumbler and Sugarfoot.

I arrive at Blood Mountain after hiking over 12 miles, more than I expected in the first week. It's a beautiful day, and although the shelter at the summit is old, decrepit, and looks like it is probably haunted, the views from the top are amazing. As the sun sets, Sugarfoot and Nightgrumbler point out the teeny tiny tips of buildings in Atlanta, so far away. I grab my journal, intending to write my deep, profound thoughts, but I end up watching a small grey junco jump around the ground, trying to find food and curious about who I was and why I was there. Finding enjoyment in the habits of birds and woodland creatures is a nice by-product of hiking.

After a lovely night and a hike down Blood Mountain, a bunch of us reach Neels Gap for a break. I find my maildrop and open a box I mailed to myself, containing Snickers bars, beef jerky, Lipton Noodles, and some other food. Gail, Brent, and others chose to get a cabin in the next town since the hostel I stayed in two years ago is closed. I don't want to waste the day and decide to continue after restocking and eating. Sugarfoot and Nightgrumbler are staying at Whitley Gap shelter. It's over a mile off the trail, and I don't want to walk that far, but they want to stay there because they camped there once as young Boy Scouts. I'm sure I'll see them soon.

I hike until I reach Hogpen Gap, where I see Walk-A-Week, Frank and School Bus, Katie-did, and six other hikers I can't remember if I've met yet. We set up our tents in a circle around a fire. Conversations revolve around who we are and why we are hiking. Quitting a career and hiking to figure out your life is a fairly common theme. I'm glad I'm not alone.

It's a beautiful night, so I sleep without the rain fly on my tent, enabling me to sleep like a baby with the mesh fabric and cool mountain air. It's hard to believe I'm in the north Georgia mountains and I'm sleeping in a tent without a rain fly, and I'm enjoying myself with mostly strangers. At home, I would never do this. I'm beginning to like this Trail Gimp person, wherever she came from. She takes chances and has fun. I like her.

I wake at the ungodly hour of 6:15 am, but it's not that early for some hikers who are already up and eating. Just as I finish getting dressed, I hear a few sprinkles of rain hit the tents. And then I hear zip-zip-zip, and before the rains come, everyone is frantically packing their tents and stashing things in packs. I am second out of camp at 7:15 – a record for me.

Low Gap Shelter is only four miles up the trail, so a bunch of us head there and plan to make breakfast undercover in the shelter. We hike rather quickly, arriving in less than 90 minutes. I can't believe my luck when I hear, "Hey, Trail Gimp, would you like some hot pancakes?"

"I'd love some pancakes. Thanks!" I drop my pack and fumble around for my plate and spoon. Growler arrived at the shelter first, so he had taken out his stove and pancake mix and decided to make breakfast for all the hikers coming in after him. We are all wet and cold, but we're huddled together in the shelter eating and laughing. Sugarfoot and Nightgrumbler show up for a quick break but then continue on their way. Just before noon, I decided to don my rain gear and head to the next shelter. After all, the saying goes, "You can't get to Maine if you don't walk in the rain."

For safety, I purchased red rain pants, just in case I am ever lying in a ditch and rescuers are looking for me. I figured red would stand out better and be more obvious in the woods. My coat is red for the same reason. I'm beginning to regret that decision. After getting dressed in all my rain gear, including my knee-high black gators, and hoisting my pack with a dark-colored rain cover, I looked a little like Santa walking up the trail. I walk away, hearing giggles and laughter coming from my fellow hikers. I hear someone call me "Santa Pants," and I really hope that trail name doesn't stick.

The constant rain has turned the trail into a muddy river, causing me to slip, slide, and use my hiking poles for balance. Mileage is slow until I finally get to Blue Mountain Shelter. This is the shelter where Three-Piece walked in two years ago with trail magic and took back to Neels Gap, nearly forcing me to buy new hiking boots. I pray for him to come today, but that's not how trail magic works. I catch up with Nightgrumbler and Sugarfoot; their jokes and antics make me laugh until my cheeks hurt.

It's no longer raining, but everything is white. The air is white with a light fog, and the view, which is supposed to be miles of gorgeous mountains, looks like a white curtain. I couldn't tell you if there were trees or an ocean 15 feet away from the shelter. Another hiker, Spot, listens to his weather radio. "Careful, everyone," he says. "The weather service has issued a tornado watch for our area until ten tonight."

Fabulous. Everyone hightails it into the shelter, deciding to get some early sleep. It's 7:37 on a Friday night. Trail Gimp is in on the Appalachian Trail during a tornado watch, trying to go to bed. At home, April would just be getting home from work, making plans to go dancing with friends. This is a crazy, mixed-up world.

I'm the last one out of the shelter the next morning. It's not raining, and thankfully we didn't have a tornado last night, but it's still kind of misty out. I'm cold, lazy, and unmotivated. I hike slowly.

A few miles later, exhausted and needing energy, I stop at a forest service road at Indian Grave Gap and eat a bagel. Tray Mountain is next; if I remember correctly, it is a nightmare of a steep climb. I see a few cars drive by on the service road. One car stops, and a woman pokes her head out of the window. "Hey, are you headed to Tray Mountain Shelter?" she asks.

"Yes, I am. Why?"

"No reason, but just don't fill up on bagels!" she hollers as the car drives off.

I hike three miles to the shelter, arriving at nearly the same time as a few people in the cars that had passed me. One by one, I watch as they unload their packs and bags, set up a table, and then load it up with hot dogs, potato salad, coleslaw, baked beans, wine, and key lime pie! They create a huge bonfire and set up tarps as a wind block. They explain that they are the Kennesaw Outdoor Activities Club and like to hike in with trail magic a few times a year. Some other campers with three dogs filter in to see what's happening, and suddenly, we have a party. It's a different world out here. Nightgrumbler, Sugarfoot, a hiker named Second Chances, and I settle down for the night, warm and toasty, stuffed with food.

In the morning, we wake up to juice and fresh coffee. The club members had forgotten to bring cream, but they have a can of Reddi-wip, which is sufficient. I'm still not a big coffee drinker, but when it's cold outside, and someone offers fresh, hot coffee, I've learned to take it and love it. I've decided to take a short hiking day today and rest a bit at Deep Gap Shelter, only seven miles away. I could hike the extra three miles to Dicks Creek Gap and get a ride into Hiawassee, but I'm already rationing my funds, and I'm not sure if I can afford two nights in town.

I'm still in Georgia, and I still have 2,000 miles to hike. I've got a few thousand dollars in my account. I spent more than I expected two years ago because I spent so much time in towns. Town = money. Towns mean resupplying and comfort. How much resupplying, where you resupply, and where you rest dictate the amount of money we spend. I could spend $10 for a night at a hostel, or $50 a night in a motel. The motel is worth the cost if enough people share the room, but that's not always possible.

Likewise, I can get dinner at a diner, or find a steakhouse somewhere. Most hikers juggle the comfort versus money issue in town, every town we get to, all the way to Maine.

Additionally, we only have a limited amount of time to make it to Maine before cold weather comes in. It's nice to take a day off, also known as a zero-mile day. A day off enables our bodies to rest and recuperate a little. Hiking up and down mountains all day long wearing 40 or more pounds on our backs is no easy feat, and our bodies take a beating. A day off is welcome respite. But how many days can we take off and still make it to Maine?

I arrive at Deep Gap Shelter to find Sugarfoot and Nightgrumbler, who have already set up camp and are sitting around reading. It's warm and sunny, so I join them, and we set up a clothesline to dry out our clothing, which is still damp from yesterday. Nightgrumbler has a travel chess set and offers to teach me how to play. As the dinner hour draws close, many hikers filter in and find a place in the two-level shelter.

I recognize almost everyone, but there is one guy that I don't know. Nobody seems to know who he is. He's not dressed like a thru-hiker. His pack is like something you'd find in an army-navy store. He doesn't talk much, but I hear him tell another hiker that he bought his boots from Sears for 50 bucks. He has regular household pots and pans; his pack cover is a black Hefty trash bag. There is something about him that I just can't shake.

Hikers have been talking about Eric Rudolph, the man accused of planting the bomb that went off in Centennial Park in Atlanta during the Olympics two years ago that killed two and injured more than a hundred people. He's also accused of setting off some other bombs down south, killing more people. Rumors say he is possibly hiding out along The Appalachian Trail, posing as a thru-hiker. I heard he is probably in the North Carolina Mountains, but we are only a few miles away from the North Carolina border. Is this close enough? Is this Eric Rudolph staying with us?

My peaceful and quiet night is interrupted with thoughts of this possible psycho-murderer camped with us. It's not like I can just ask the guy. He makes his way to the top floor of the shelter to sleep, and I opt to stay on the bottom floor, directly at the shelter's entrance. I try to sleep but keep waking up to ensure everyone is safe. And alive. I have this horrible vision of hearing this guy start slaughtering the hikers upstairs before working his way downstairs. By that time, I can put on my boots, which I've kept right next to me for this reason, and run down the hill as fast as I can until I reach the highway, where I can flag down a car or police officer to alert them of the carnage.

The sun rises, and thankfully, hikers emerge from their sleeping bags. Nightgrumbler, who slept next to me, looks at me and asks, "Did you sleep alright? You look a little tired."

"I'm fine. I just didn't sleep well last night."

I'm relieved to see possible bomber hiker guy leave the shelter and head up the trail. I leave with Nightgrumbler and Sugarfoot, nearly skipping down the trail, knowing we're planning on going to the Blueberry Patch hostel. I missed it the first time I hiked around here, and the other hikers raved so much that I will not miss the opportunity again.

We find a ride right away and arrive at the Blueberry Patch, an organic farm and hostel, just before ten in the morning. Gary is a former thru-hiker, and he and his wife Lennie own the place. They remind me a little of hippies. Lennie is thin, has long brown hair, and doesn't wear makeup; she is pretty without it. Gary is thin and muscular, assuming the muscles come from farming. There is a blueberry patch on the property, and this place is known for the yummy blueberry pancakes they serve every morning.

The bunk room has eight wooden hand-made bunks, and there are several tent sites outside. There is room to spread out and relax in the large yard, lounge in the hammock, or enjoy the mountain views, listen to the water flowing, and soak your feet in the creek at the back of the property. After a shower, I hang around the backyard in my raingear with Scrabble, Katie-did, Minnie Pearl, and Tigger, soaking our feet in the ice-cold creek while Lennie washes our clothes – a huge benefit of staying here.

In a few hours, all clean with fresh-smelling clothes, Nightgrumbler, Sugarfoot, Second Chances, and I hitch a ride to town to eat and shop. As soon as we stick out our thumbs, a commercial flatbed vehicle slows down and offers us a ride into Hiawassee, about ten minutes away. We jump into the back and hold onto the very short sides of the flatbed for dear life as he navigates the twisty mountain roads at top speed. We pray we won't fly out the back, as there is no tailgate on the truck. We laugh hysterically, although I think this is the most dangerous ride I've ever had in my life. Finally, he slows down and stops at Hardee's, allowing us to get a much-needed, calorie-laden meal.

We run to the grocery store to resupply, and since it's Nightgrumbler's 21st birthday tomorrow, Sugarfoot and I want to surprise him with a birthday cake. But how do we buy it without him knowing? I spy Weatherwoman and Growler on the other side of the store, so we give them money and ask them to buy the cake. They are also staying at The Blueberry Patch, so they can easily sneak it into the kitchen and have Lennie hide it.

We find a safer ride back to The Blueberry Patch, and Nightgrumbler and I sit by the creek for over two hours until dinner. We soak our feet in the icy water, share a newspaper, and I get butterflies in the pit of my stomach when our feet accidentally touch in the creek or our hands touch while exchanging or sharing parts of the paper.

Lennie brings out homemade pizza for dinner and the surprise cake for dessert. And now, it's a waiting game for the phone, with each person taking turns calling friends and family. Very few people have cell phones; they are too big and heavy, and there aren't many cell towers along this rural path. I know some people already sent their phones home from the Walasi-Yi center because they were mostly useless.

I'm finally able to chat with my parents to let them know I'm in Hiawassee, Georgia. I'm alive and well and enjoying myself. I leave out the part about the possible Eric Rudolph hiker and the death-defying hitchhike into town.

Nightgrumbler and I hike together a lot. We have the same hiking pace. Sugarfoot is either slower or faster than us, depending on his mood. But the three of us stick together in the evenings. We arrive at the border of Georgia and North Carolina and take an obligatory picture of the infamous gnarled oak tree. I hope I hike with these guys for a while. I feel like they could be my trail family.

We set up camp tonight at Muskrat Creek Shelter, and Nightgrumbler and I take off to explore the area. Our guidebook describes the amazing views from the Raven Cliffs and mentions the remains of an old plane crash. We quickly find the 25-year-old remnants of the Cessna, and instinctively, we know that nobody could have survived this crash. The tail section, fuselage, and cockpit are scattered over a large area. We are quiet with the knowledge that someone died right here.

We head over to the Raven Cliffs, which are pretty steep. Nightgrumbler offers a hand to help me with a steep climb, a large rock, or a difficult step. At the edge of the mountain, we find a small boulder upon which to sit and admire the view. It's a large rock for one person, a snug rock for two. The butterflies in my stomach return as we sit next to each other. The breeze coming up from the valley makes my hair fly, and Nightgrumbler spends a few minutes removing stray hairs from my arms and removing leaves from my hair. Why is he always finding an excuse to touch me?

We hear the voices of other hikers and scramble from our rock. We chat with White Glove and Duster, a couple we've been hiking around for a few weeks.

Nightgrumbler and I tackle those steep spots on the trail as we head back. I slip on a rock, and he turns around quickly enough to grab my arm and prevent me from falling. Usually, he is a few inches taller than I am, but since I am standing on a rock, we are face to face, mere inches away. *Lord, he has the biggest blue eyes I've ever seen.*

It's awkward, like an awkward first kiss moment, but without the kiss. Flustered and not knowing what else to do, I mumble "thanks" and step off my rock—moment over.

In the morning, we begin the hike over Standing Indian Mountain. Sugarfoot and I are in happy-go-lucky moods, but something is up with Nightgrumbler. He's quiet and moody. The three of us usually hike within eyesight of each other, but today, Nightgrumbler is off on his own, and when I round a bend in the trail, I see him throw his pack on the ground and throw himself down next to it, sulking. I stop next to him, asking if everything is okay, and he simply grunts, "I'm fine."

I continue hiking, and he arrives at the summit shortly after me. Once again, he throws his pack to the ground, finds a snack, and sits down to admire the views and watch the birds. Thirty minutes later, he stands up, smiles, and simply says, "Animals are therapeutic."

We leave the summit together and chat until we reach Big Spring Shelter, where I initially met Steve. Sugarfoot discusses Easter plans and suggests that we hike 12 miles per day to make it to the Nantahala Outdoor Center for Easter dinner in three days. It would be a great way to talk to family on the holiday.

"Trail Gimp, are you coming with us?"

"Absolutely," I reply. "It sounds like a great plan."

"All right, you're coming to Maine with us!" Sugarfoot shouts.

I'm grinning from ear to ear. I found my trail family. We laugh, cry, hike, and cook dinner, and are still friends after a long, crazy day.

It's cold tonight, and nine hikers are sleeping in the shelter meant for about five or six. Everyone is squished together, and when I open my eyes in the morning, I am nose to nose with Nightgrumbler, and his giant blue eyes are staring directly into mine. I recoil from the shock of waking up literally face to face, but I feel those butterflies in my stomach again.

We arrive at the Nantahala Outdoor Center on Easter, as planned. I race for the payphone to call my mom, and since my extended family members are there for dinner, I talk to sisters, aunts and uncles, mom and dad, and my grandma.

"Well, April, what are you eating for Easter dinner?" my grandma asks.

"Well, Grandma, I'm only at a cafe, so I'm eating a cheeseburger for dinner."

Appalled, she screams, "A cheeseburger?" That's not a proper meal for Easter!"

"It's okay, Grandma, at least I'm eating dinner on Easter."

I also call Kathy, and she passes the phone around so I can chat with everyone. When Leah passes the phone back to Kathy, I hear her tell everyone, "Oh, she sounds so *happy!*"

I am so happy. Finally.

──── CHAPTER NINE ────

NIGHTGRUMBLER

April-May 1998

Two days later, Sugarfoot gets ahead of us on the trail. Nightgrumbler and I catch up to him at Stecoah Gap. His pack is on the ground, semi-unpacked, with the tent and some cooking gear lying next to it.

"Hey, Sugarfoot! How long have you been waiting for us?" I call when I finally see him. And then, looking around, Nightgrumbler adds, "What's going on?"

"Shane, you know I love you like a brother, and Gimp, I love you too. But I miss my girlfriend. I miss her a lot. I'm going to go home and ask her to marry me."

Nightgrumbler and I look at each other, then look at Sugarfoot. We know that look; We will not deter him. Shane speaks first. "All right, man, I wish you luck. But how are you getting home?"

"This road leads to Robbinsville, so I'll try to hitch a ride and then grab a bus from there."

I speak up next. At this point, he's no longer Sugarfoot. He's Rick. Trail names are like that. For most of the trail, your trail name is your name. But sometimes, in times of real friendship and closeness, when things get personal, real names comes out.

"Rick, I'm really happy for you. Just be sure you're going home for the right reasons. Missing someone and proposing to someone is not the same thing."

"I know," he assures me. "I love her."

Nightgrumbler grabs the rest of the gear and repacks his pack.

Is Nightgrumbler going to follow? Is he going to hike? Our group is gone; where does that leave me?

As if reading my mind, Nightgrumbler says, "Don't worry, Gimp, I'm not going anywhere yet. My goal is to make it to Damascus, at least."

I feel a little better.

It's different hiking without Sugarfoot. There isn't any banter in the shelter. A few weeks ago, since we signed into the registers at all the shelters, the boys "created" a hiker. The Passion Piston is a hairy Italian guy who thinks he is God's gift to women and the trail, and he hikes without a shirt. Other hikers would ask if we met The Passion Piston because they kept missing him. They wanted to see what a jerk he was in real life. It seemed that Nightgrumbler, Sugarfoot, and I were the only ones who had ever met him. The Passion Piston's register notes are hysterical, and everyone would comment on them. Sadly, after Sugarfoot leaves the trail, The Passion Piston also says his goodbyes.

But without his friend, Nightgrumbler becomes more daring.

We're at Cable Gap Shelter, and I go to bed early because I am exhausted. We're only five miles from Fontana Dam and the beginning of the Smoky Mountains. I wake up at one in the morning with the full moon shining directly into my face. It's so bright that I sit up to admire the beauty before me. After a few minutes, I feel a hand on my back. Nightgrumbler reaches out to rub my back and stroke my hair. He sits up and whispers, "You're beautiful," and gives me a soft kiss, careful not to wake anyone else in the shelter. He wraps his arms around my shoulders, and we watch the landscape without saying a word.

Only the moonlight could make a dirty, smelly hiker appear beautiful.

We get chilly from the cold mountain air and retreat to our sleeping bags. Nightgrumbler kisses me once more, and we fall asleep with his hands holding my face.

I'm content.

We stop for the night in Fontana Dam, then begin hiking through the Smokies. The Appalachian Trail traverses the Great Smoky Mountains National Park for about 70 miles along the North Carolina and Tennessee border. Hikers need to obtain permits before entering, a way to keep track of the number of hikers passing through. The shelters are old, made of stone and wood, and they have chain-link fences across the front of them, keeping the bears out. It's kind of a zoo, in reverse. The amount of people visiting the smokies in recent years have caused an increase in bear activity. Bears are looking for easy access to food, so staying in shelters behind chain-linked fences is helpful.

We quickly learn how the Smokies got their name. There is a lot of fog in the mountains, and it gives the mountains a smoky look. In addition to that, the fog often takes a bluish effect from the escaping water vapor scattering blue light from the sky. It's beautiful and serene, and I can see why artists paint these mountain scenes.

It's also very rainy. We walk through mud and slosh our way along the trail. We play chess at the shelters in the evenings or talk about books. It's refreshing to chat with a guy who knows about books. I've learned that we need to take turns having a bad day. We can't be in a rotten mood simultaneously – it doesn't work well. When I'm having a lousy day, slipping down the muddy trail, or not having enough energy because I didn't eat enough the night before, Nightgrumbler offers me water or a snack or sits there for support without saying a word. When he has a bad day, it's the opposite. I offer to cook dinner, filter water, or whatever he might need.

We hitchhike into Gatlinburg to dry off after several days of rain. The first stop we make is the laundromat. I wear nothing but my raingear as everything goes into the washer. Days of dirt and mud disappear after 45 minutes, and then into the dryer everything goes, including the tent.

Nightgrumbler and I transform from cold and miserable to warm and happy in less than two hours. The simplicity of clean and dry clothing cannot be overstated. It's a simple luxury that can have some of the biggest effects on a thru-hikers state of mind. This is one reason that rain for an extended period of time is so hard. When you are wet and live outside, it takes a lot of willpower to keep going, not knowing when you will dry off or warm up again.

We get some food and walk quickly through the village. Once we get a hotel room for the night, he drops his bombshell.

"Gimp, I'm leaving the trail in Hot Springs."

Mentally calculating, that's less than 100 miles – not quite a week of hiking. I'm speechless, and my eyes well up with tears.

Don't cry, April! Don't cry! You didn't come out here to hike with a guy. You came by yourself to learn some lessons.

"I understand, Shane. You came out with your best friend, and now he's gone."

"April, I've been thinking about this for a few days. My friends are home, my family is home, and my school is home. You're the only reason keeping me out here." I smile that at least I'm some consideration.

But I'm not enough.

I make the best of the situation and try to enjoy myself. I try to see the humor in situations, like when we stay at Mountain Mama's Kuntry Bunkhouse and are assigned The Honeymoon Shack. We have a great time hiking, laughing, singing along Rocky Top Mountain, and singing in the rain. I'll take his company while I can.

After leaving the Groundhog Creek Shelter, we run into the RAT Patrol. Randy is a former thru-hiker and comes out to offer trail magic and feed thru-hikers occasionally. He's a member of a few trail-maintaining clubs and does anything he can to help the trail community. His crew gives us breakfast and then immediately follows with lunch. After gorging ourselves, Randy asks, "Hey, do you two want to slackpack? If you slackpack into town today, which is another 23 miles, we can hang onto your packs and bring them into Hot Springs tomorrow."

Nightgrumbler has never slackpacked before and is intrigued at the thought. He's also never hiked at night. We chat quickly, grab whatever we need from our packs for the day and give Randy our things. We run up the mountain at 2:30 in the afternoon, determined to make Hot Springs tonight.

We climb Max Patch, another bald mountain, and admire the endless, 360-degree views. Shane says, "Other than you, Gimp, this is my favorite part of my hike so far."

We run into lots of hikers and chat for a while, hiking through dusk until I trip over a tree root, forcing us to turn our headlamps on. Our pace slows a little in the dark, and we get frightened for a moment when we see yellow eyes staring at us from a bush not far in front of us. Shane stops abruptly, and I bump right into him. The eyes eventually disappear, and we can only guess if it is an owl or a bird. Still, we proceed with caution, not knowing what kinds of animals might be around us.

We finally arrive in town at 11:10 pm. It's a sleepy town, and there isn't much going on. I want to continue to the motel in the middle of Main Street, but Nightgrumbler is complaining of aching feet, so we stop at the Jesuit Hostel instead, knowing that bunks will be available. Without supplies, we use a towel for a blanket and retreat to our separate bunkrooms. Hikers can sleep just about anywhere, anytime.

Sugarfoot is expected to arrive today to pick up Nightgrumbler, and Kathy, Leah, and Luke are supposed to show up today to visit me. We shower and put on the same clothes, and head into town. Hot Springs is celebrating Earl Shaffer and his 50th anniversary hike this year with a festival this weekend. I buy Earl Shaffer's book *Walking With Spring* and David Brill's book *As Far As The Eye Can See* at the local outfitter's store. I'm excited and a little awestruck to meet these trail legends and have them sign my books.

Sugarfoot, his new fiancée Sue, and another friend from home, John, arrive midafternoon, and Sue shows off a beautiful diamond engagement ring. Sugarfoot is glowing, and I'm glad he made the right choice for himself. They take off to meet the RAT patrol to retrieve our backpacks, and I reserve a room at the motel. Once in the room, I take another shower, and Kathy, Leah, and Luke show up minutes later.

It's the first time I notice how young Sugarfoot and Nightgrumbler are. They are 21 years old, while my friends and I are about 27. The maturity level is noticeable off the trail. My Charlotte friends talk of work and apartments and responsibilities. My trail friends discuss college, tell immature jokes and laugh at things like teenagers would. I love them all, but they are different.

The eight of us go to dinner, and my friends listen in awe at the stories we tell and the sights we've seen. They are more shocked at the *amount* of food we eat. At this point on the trail, we burn 4000 or more calories every day, and it's impossible to eat that much while hiking. So when we're in town, we have to eat rich, calorie-laden meals with huge serving portions. It's not uncommon for hikers to eat an entire pound of pasta in one sitting or have multiple plates of pancakes at breakfast.

After dinner, we head back to the motel, and it's time for the boys to head home. Nightgrumbler gives me many of the things he received in his mail drop today since he doesn't need them anymore. He hugs me and holds me for a minute. Then he looks me in the eye and says, "You have a lot of reasons to finish. I'll write to you, and maybe we can meet you over the summer to hike for a week or something." I hold back my tears and nod.

I wave goodbye to Sugarfoot, Nightgrumbler, and their friends and let out a few tears as they drive away. Then, I stand up straight, turn around, and walk into my room full of friends from home.

We stay up talking and laughing until almost two in the morning. Kathy and Leah are roommates, so they share one bed. That means I have to share the second bed with Luke, something I have dreamed about since I met him. And I realize I don't want it anymore. I miss my trail boys. I miss laughing until my stomach hurts, the conversations about books, learning how to play chess, and the camaraderie that living on the trail brings.

Kathy, Leah, and Luke leave in the morning, and I'm happy to say that my crush on Luke is officially gone. I guess I've been away from him for a month, and I've grown up a bit.

There are still a lot of hikers in town today since the festival with Earl Shaffer was yesterday. I meet a hiker named Baltimore Jack, who is not from Baltimore, and I'm not even sure if his name is Jack, but he doesn't tell me how he got his trail name. It doesn't really matter anyway. He has hiked the trail a few times. He likes to live on the trail, and in the colder months, he finds odd jobs like caretaking or something to sustain him until he can start hiking again. One of his knees has an ace bandage wrapped around it, but it looks like it has been there for ages. And I think I glimpsed a small bottle of whiskey tucked neatly into the bandage. I've never met anyone like him, and I find him fascinating.

After dinner, I call my parents to update them on my progress, and my mom asks about some of the people I've met.

'Well, Sugarfoot and Nightgrumbler left the trail, so I'm alone again, but there are a lot of girls in town that I might be hiking with when I leave tomorrow. I met one guy today named Baltimore Jack." I explained that he hikes the trail every year and how much he loves it.

"Nah, there's something wrong with him," she replies. "Everybody wants a house. Everybody wants the stability of a job and a place to live." I've lived with my mom long enough to know there is no arguing about a situation like this because I can't change her mind. But she's wrong.

If my mom is wrong about everyone wanting a house, what else is she wrong about? What if I finish the trail in Maine and want to keep hiking? What will I do for money? I shake my head as I finally realize that my mom's life, though perfect for her, is not ideal for everyone else. What if everything she taught me is not perfect for me at all? For the first time, I know it's okay to think differently than my parents.

CHAPTER TEN

THE HAVEN FARM

May 1998

After four days in Hot Springs, I finally drag myself away with a heavy pack, carrying extra supplies, including Nightgrumbler's and my own food drop. Someone told me that if you buy a pint of Ben and Jerry's ice cream, the unofficial ice cream of the Appalachian Trail, and stuff it into the middle of your sleeping bag, it will stay insulated enough so it won't melt for several hours. With that in mind, I hope to have ice cream at the shelter tonight for dessert.

I can't get accustomed to hiking without Nightgrumbler. I keep imagining walking around a bend in the trail to find him waiting for me as he did so often. I'm hiking with Tigger and Weatherwoman because we left town together. The trail isn't as steep as the guide makes it out to be, but it's still climbing up a mountain. With extra supplies, we are all complaining about our knees and feet. We finally arrive at the shelter. There are about a dozen hikers here, including some in tents. I'm delighted with my dessert, which luckily did not melt into my sleeping bag. I will remember to hike out of town with ice cream more often!

We begin hiking downhill, and almost simultaneously, everyone complains of sore knees. Weatherwoman has short, semi-curly hair sticking out from under a baseball cap and has a fun and lets-do-this attitude. She is about my age and since knee surgery several years ago, claims to predict bad weather when her knees start acting up and getting sore, thus being given the name Weatherwoman. She has a brace on one knee, and other hikers have braces on their ankles or knees. Carrying a heavy load up and down mountains is beginning to take a physical toll. We take a break at Allen Gap, where everyone starts discussing their maladies. Free Spirit catches up to us, only to mention that she felt sick last night; Minnie Pearl's ankle is swollen and painful, Weatherwoman has sore feet. My knees hurt, and Tigger says that we should all take time off. Someone suggests getting a ride back to Hot Springs, but I have a problem going back and getting sucked into the black hole of that town. A lovely couple stops and asks if we want a ride, and they offer to take us up to Erwin, Tennessee.

We jump into the back of their truck, and they drop us off at the hostel on the river. The wife is a nurse and insists on giving me ice and a couple of Ace bandages for my knees. I'm all wrapped up, looking eerily similar to Baltimore Jack, without the requisite bottle of Jim Beam. Since we skipped about 40 miles of trail, we finally meet up with some of the people we'd been reading about in the shelter registers. We talk to Pilgrim, Wisconsin Dave, Free-at-last, Seinfield, Guided by Voices, and more. I ask if anyone knows who Moby Dick is. He's a hiker ahead of me that draws cartoons, usually relevant to the trail conditions for that day. He's a fantastic artist, and I look forward to seeing his drawings every day. I've never met him.

"He's a nice guy, but very quiet," someone tells me. "He doesn't look like a typical thru-hiker. He uses an army rucksack and a trash bag for a pack cover and wears cheap boots he bought at Sears," someone tells me.

I think back to the hiker that camped with us before Hiawassee, Georgia. Was that Moby Dick, and not the serial bomber Eric Rudolph, as I feared?

As though reading my thoughts, someone says, "Trail Gimp, have you seen the FBI agents? For people trying to be discreet, they stuck out like a sore thumb."

"What FBI agents? I never noticed them." I respond. "What made them so obvious?"

"They were clean! Their gear was brand new, they were clean-shaven, their clothing smelled like fabric softener, and they didn't know how to use their equipment properly. They're out on the trail posing as thru-hikers, trying to find information on Eric Rudolph, who may be hiding out along the trail."

How I could be so wrapped up in my own hike to not notice FBI agents?

We talk for a few more hours, and my thoughts turn to Moby Dick. I'm sorry I judged him based on his gear. Lesson learned: Never judge a book by its cover, and never judge a person based on their gear.

It's April 29th, and I have been hiking the trail for precisely one month. Everyone here is nursing injuries, and many hikers want to go to The Haven Farm, where hikers can stay for a few days. A guy named Bob lives there, so when he finishes work today in Erwin, he's bringing all of us over to The Farm, about ten miles away. We eat lunch, snack for hours, and watch movies; I call my mom to tell her where I am, and she gives me some bad news. My Grandma is in the hospital with some kidney issues. She's doing better, but she suggests I call her back for updates before getting back on the trail.

Weatherwoman, Tigger, Minnie Pearl, Second Chances, and I pile into Bob's truck with our gear. He invites us to stay until Saturday, which means we can relax all day tomorrow. As soon as we arrive, I feel like I'm in another world – it reminds me of a throwback, hippie style of living. June is a social worker and owns the main house, while several people live in separate cabins or campers scattered throughout the farm. A barn, community organic garden, and greenhouse sit near the front of the property, near the main house, which everyone uses for the bathroom, kitchen, living and TV room, and music room. A large flat area where thru-hikers are allowed to set up tents is behind the garden. Mookie is a former thru-hiker, and after his hike, he found his way back to the farm. John is a section hiker and stopped here on his way from Damascus to the Smokies. It's been several weeks, and he hasn't left yet. He's living in a camper somewhere on the property. Adam and Patty are a couple who live in a cabin, and they really tend to the garden. Patty has straight, dark brown hair that falls to the middle of her back. She is dressed in a casual, bohemian-style dress and sandals. Adam wears clothes that look like he just came out of the fields – clean – but with a few embedded dirt stains and small tears in the fabric. His boots look perpetually dirty. Friends drop into the farm at any hour of the day. They seem to be one big happy family here. It's a fascinating environment, and everybody accepts everyone for who they are.

I wake up late in the morning and find that Tigger is gone. She packed in a hurry and went back to Erwin. I'm not sure why. The farm residents have apparently been "sizing us up" before tomorrow's event: a wedding! But it's not a typical wedding with a bride and a groom; there are two grooms. Technically, gay marriages are not legal here in Tennessee in 1998, but who am I to judge? We are invited to the wedding.

I decide to make myself useful and help in the kitchen, baking cinnamon bread, brownies, and strawberry shortcake for the wedding tomorrow. After all the baking is complete, I call Mom to chat with her, and I call my grandma in the hospital. She is doing much better, and she tells me how proud of me she is. I'm doing something amazing and learning "life lessons", as she called them. She made me feel good about my hike.

On the morning of the wedding, I make my family's recipe for Norwegian waffles for brunch. Since I don't have a gift, I can at least make myself useful by feeding everyone.

The grooms finish getting dressed in their tuxedos. Men and women wear suits and dresses. Hikers dress in our cleanest hiking clothes. And it doesn't matter. All that matters is that two people who love each other are getting married. Love and acceptance are in the air, and everyone is happy.

I sneak away from the festivities for a few minutes to call my grandmother again tonight, and she tells me everything is fine and she is going home tomorrow. I call Mom to double-check, and she gives me the green light to begin hiking again. I collapse from exhaustion at ten o'clock and plan my hike for tomorrow.

∞

Weatherwoman, Minnie Pearl, and I are returning to the trail today. We've had a few days of rest, and our knees, ankles, and feet are healing. Bob brings us back to Devil's Fork Gap. This means I've missed 20 miles of trail. I vow to come back and hike them someday.

The sun is shining when we begin hiking, but clouds form quickly, and soon, rain and hail are upon us. We're at the edge of the weather front; half of the sky is gray and rainy, and the other half is blue and sunny with pretty, white clouds. We get to the shelter before the thunder and lightning come, so we make dinner and chat with everyone there. I like to read the shelter registers, and now that we know so many people, it's fun to read their entries. I look back for any notes from Steve, now called Grunts-n-Groans. The shelter registers are the best way of communicating with fellow thru-hikers.

In the morning, Weatherwoman, Minnie Pearl, and I head out, each hiking at a different pace. I arrive at Sam's Gap to find Minnie Pearl waiting for us, and I join her as we wait for Weatherwoman. Just as she arrives, another hiker who passed us a few minutes ago returns. "Are any of you April?" he asks.

"Yes, I'm April," I answered.

"Well, there is a message for you at the greenhouse just up the road. Something about your grandmother."

Oh, God. This can't be good.

The girls and I walk over to the greenhouse, a large roadside store selling flowers, plants, and vegetables. The woman inside invites me to use her phone to call home. I call Mom. No answer. I call my aunts. No answer.

I call my two sisters. No answer anywhere. Finally, the woman says gently, "April, I'm so sorry you can't reach your family. I guess I should tell you that your grandmother has passed on."

I knew it. Dammit. I'm so glad I spoke to her on Easter and the other day. Now, what do I do?

Minnie Pearl hugs me and continues hiking, but Weatherwoman's knees still bother her, so she says, "I guess I'm going back to Erwin with you."

We hitch a ride to Erwin again, and Bob takes us back to The Farm. Apparently, my mom called The Farm a few hours after I left to tell me of my grandma's death, but I had already left. June and Bob knew where I was staying that night and that I'd be passing the greenhouse the following morning. It's incredible how communication works along the trail.

Instead of hiking The Appalachian Trail as planned, I'm figuring out how to get home immediately. Luke offers to drive to Tennessee to pick me up and take me back to Charlotte so that I can fly home, but that's too much driving. June offers to drive me to the Tri-City airport tomorrow on her way to work, and Jeff, whom I met at the wedding, offers to pick me up from the airport next week when I return.

Within 24 hours, I'm home in Saratoga, and I learn more about Grandma's death. She was getting ready in the morning to come home when she just fell on the floor and died instantly. Perhaps a pulmonary embolism caused that? I feel a little guilty about not being here when my grandmother died, but I remind myself that I can't live down the road from her forever. My family understands and doesn't blame me for wanting to move away.

I answer a million questions about the trail, but I'm itching to get back. I miss my friends and call Nightgrumbler and Sugarfoot to update them on my whereabouts and catch up. They are getting on with their lives; it seems the trail was a brief disruption, and they are ready to move on. They still say they will surprise me for a week in the summer and hike with me, but I have a sinking feeling that it will never happen. Sugarfoot is engaged, and Nightgrumbler is figuring out his classes. I'm not sure if I'll ever see them again.

It's May 12, and I'm finally on a plane heading back to Tennessee. It's been a whirlwind of a few weeks, and I can't wait to get back to the trail. Jeff picks me up at the airport as promised, but since it's so late in the day, he offers to let me crash at his house for the night, where we stay up late talking about the wedding, The Farm, the people that live there, and our backgrounds. He's about my age, and he's taking some college classes now. He was in the military for a few years, but he's still figuring out what he wants to do. He's hiked on the Appalachian Trail, but not extensively.

Jeff has taken a liking to me, but I'm not as interested in him as he is in me. I don't get butterflies in my stomach when I talk to him. I can't break his heart, though, because time will take care of that. I am returning to the trail tomorrow, so I'll probably never see him again anyway. But I feel bad, nonetheless.

I wake up on my 28th birthday, and I'm excited to start hiking again! I'm not worried about celebrating, because we celebrated at home with friends and family, and plenty of birthday cake. But Jeff insists on taking me out to lunch for my birthday, then drives me to the farm because I left my fuel bottle there; I wasn't allowed to take it on the plane. We don't arrive until 3:30. Once we arrive at the farm, they say, "You can't start hiking now! It's your birthday! We need to celebrate!" So, we celebrate some more with dinner, drinks, and more cake.

I had hoped to hike into Damascus, Virginia for Trail Days, but today is Wednesday and Trail Days is this weekend, and more than 100 miles away. In order to make up some quick miles, Bob offers to drop me off at Sam's Gap so I can slackpack into Erwin, stay at the farm one more night, and then head to Damascus for Trail Days. I accept his offer and use one of his small bags to carry water and snacks for the day, hiking 24 miles in one day. At this point, the members of The Farm are so comfortable with me that they invite me to sleep on the couch in the house, an honor not usually bestowed upon passing thru-hikers.

I'm beginning to get comfortable here, too. Although it's different from anything I've ever known, or perhaps because of it, I'm starting to feel like

I'm part of the extended family. I know I need to get back to the trail. I just keep getting sucked back in.

Jeff picks me up Friday morning, and we drive to Damascus for the Trail Days celebration. It's an eventful two days, similar to 1996. There are all-you-can-eat pancake breakfasts, vendor tents, a hiker parade, and a talent show, and since it's a reunion as well, I see a bunch of people from 1996 in addition to hikers this year. It's a little different being here with Jeff, though. It's hard to be footloose and fancy-free because I'm always worried about leaving him alone, or bored; it's also difficult to balance being nice and friendly with his attempts at romance. Do I hold his hand or not? It's already snug enough in the tent; technically, it's a two-person tent, but I think the people they tested it on are two small children. How do I tell him to stay on his side when there isn't much of a *side?*

On Sunday, Jeff takes me back to Erwin, and I start hiking the trail again. I'm alone this time. Weatherwoman has gone home to heal. Minnie Pearl is ahead of me, and I have no idea where Tigger is. I see Second Chances at the first shelter and run into her frequently on the trail. All this time off has allowed my knees to heal, so I'm no longer limping. I spend the week finding my trail legs again and discovering my hiking groove. Once again, I'm comfortable by myself, sleeping in shelters, eating whatever food is in my bag, and hiking 12-15 miles every day. I'm learning how important it is to be flexible. Schedules change, weather changes, hikers leave the trail, fall behind, or hike ahead. I can only rely on myself right now.

I've come far in two years. Since I hiked in 1996, I've moved to another state, quit my career, and made new friends. Yet here I am, camped at the very same spot I camped precisely two years ago to the date. I don't know whether to laugh or cry at the irony. Have I learned anything? Yes. I've learned that men and women can sleep platonically in the same hotel room, and it's pretty normal to do that when you're hiking. I've learned not to judge people based on appearances. I've learned to listen to my intuition – if it feels wrong, it is. I've learned to love adventure and live in the moment, embracing what life throws at you. I've learned to trust myself and believe in other people. I think I'm a better person than I was two years ago.

I see a hand-written sign for the Kincorra hostel on a trailpost, and I'm looking forward to getting there later today. I haven't showered in five days. Taking sponge baths in cold streams doesn't do justice to the dirtiness in which hikers live. Sweat and dirt are ground into my skin; it takes some serious scrubbing and soap to get clean. And washing my hair in icy water just gives me brain freeze, so I try not to do that very often. I also don't like to use too much soap around natural water sources.

At Kincorra, Pat and Bob Peoples welcome me and give me a tour. There is a notice on the wall that states: "$4. More if you can, less if you can't. It all works out."

Selkie, a hiker I met a few days ago, tells me that some guy had called looking for me. *Who knows where I am, and why would they call me?* Jeff called and wants to spend the day with me tomorrow.

I spend the weekend with him, slackpacking during the days and camping in the evenings near Laurel Falls and Laurel Fork Gorge. Laurel Falls is one of my favorite spots along the Appalachian Trail, and I even came here a few times on my weekend escapes from Charlotte. A flood had come through a few weeks ago that knocked out some bridges, so hiking through re-routes and skipping some parts becomes necessary. Later in the evening, we go to the drive-in theater to see the movie *Titanic*.

Working at the movie theater in Charlotte allowed me to see *Titanic* about a million times. I am numb to the sadness of the sinking ship, and as someone who grew up with a pool, I know it sometimes takes a few attempts to get onto a raft properly. So, I find myself annoyed at Jack and Rose that he only tried to get on the door with her once. While I'm sitting in the truck silently scolding them, imagining the perfect way for both to fit on the floating door, I glance over at Jeff, silently wiping away the tears falling down his cheeks. I get it. It's a sad movie. But it's not like the sinking of Titanic is a secret. I keep my mouth shut with Jeff and stare straight ahead at the movie.

On Monday morning, I say goodbye to Jeff. He's clearly upset that this is the last time he'll see me, and he tries to hide the tears beginning to form in his eyes. He's such a nice guy, and I wish I could like him more than I do. Love is like that. You can't explain it, and you can't force it.

I give him a long hug. "Thanks for taking such good care of me these past few weeks. I really appreciate everything you've done for me."

"You're welcome. I'll write to you along the trail. Keep me posted on your whereabouts."

I put my pack on, grab my hiking poles, and say, "See you later, Jeff."

He wipes a tear from his cheek and says, "Please forgive me if I don't watch you walk away. I don't know if I can bear that."

My heart breaks a little for him. But the trail calls, and I must go.

I begin the long hike up to Vendeventer Shelter, overlooking Watauga Lake, 30 miles shy of Virginia. I don't feel well this morning, and I hike slowly. I barely eat lunch at the shelter because I'm tired, and my stomach is in knots. Maybe it's because I'm on the trail again after being in town so much. Perhaps it's a lack of salt causing my muscles to be tired. Could it be that I miss Jeff more than I think? Or maybe I miss the luxuries of town. Whatever the reason, I stop at Route 91 to debate my options. Someone drives by and offers me a ride into Damascus. That would mean skipping about 20 miles of trail, but since I hiked them in 1996, I feel it's okay. So, I'm off to Damascus.

I head to the laundromat and run into Desperado and Little Bus, a couple of hikers I met earlier this week. They plan to go to the local bar for dinner and drinks tonight and invite me along. When I arrive at Dots, I join them, and about eight of us hang out for the night. It turns out that Little Bus graduated from the same college as me, three years later. Seven years ago, we were on the same small college campus. Imagine that.

He lives in New York State, so we compare notes of all the mountains we've hiked in the Adirondack Mountains. Who knows, maybe I've met him before, and I just don't remember. Hiking is like that – you meet so many people, but usually, it's for a brief period, and you move on.

The more we talk, the more I blush, and the more I want to be closer to him and talk more. By the time I collapse in my bunk at bedtime, it occurs to me that I have the biggest crush on Little Bus.

It doesn't matter, though. Little Bus leaves town early today, and I'm still doing chores. I'm resupplying with food, fuel, and restaurant food. I won't catch up to him. As I'm sitting around at The Place, a hostel in town, someone offers to drive me up to the new Partnership shelter at the Mount Rogers National Recreation Headquarters. It would mean skipping another 60 miles, but I remind myself that I've already hiked them two years prior. I'm still a little depressed; I miss my trail family –Nightgrumbler and Sugarfoot. I miss their banter and the way they make me laugh. I miss my family from The Farm. And here I am, alone again. *You dummy, you came out here alone.* But I'm still sad.

I accept the ride without understanding why and get dropped off at the brand-new shelter. There are several people here, but nobody I've met before. I'm tired and cranky. Reading through the register only reminds me that all the friends I've made along the way have left the trail or are nowhere near me.

One of the hikers here makes me a little uncomfortable, and I don't know why. Her name is GI Jane. She recently shaved her head, and she's a badass woman. She portrays an image that she does what she wants when she wants. Maybe I'm jealous of her. I wish I could be like that. Trail Gimp is like that; she's confident and happy, but April is shy and apprehensive. Lately, I haven't seen much of Trail Gimp. I miss my alter-ego. I sulk in my sleeping bag until I fall asleep.

CHAPTER ELEVEN

CHASING LITTLE BUS

June 1998

The hiking is easier in Virginia than in the past few weeks. The mountains aren't as steep, so, like everyone else, I'm trying to increase my mileage. The only problem is, it's hot. It's summertime in southern Virginia. And because the trail traverses so many mountaintop ridges, the sun beats down all day. I don't think I ever drank this much water before. I drink four to six quarts throughout the day and guzzle another quart of water before bed to rehydrate my body while I sleep. The other hikers are amazed that I'm not getting up in the middle of the night to go to the bathroom all the time.

I'm hiking by myself, but with many friends. I'm still in awe of GI Jane, and I seem to clam up whenever I'm around her. She knows what she wants and is going for it. I'm hoping to find what I want by following the white blazes. I suppose we're doing the same thing, but I feel so *inadequate* around her.

I've been trying to hike more miles lately and have been nursing some shin splints. I remember from high school that tight shins mean you need to stretch your calf muscles, so I've been doing that a few times a day. It doesn't seem to be helping.

My cousin Greg has been on my mind a lot lately. Memories of us growing up together keep popping up in my head, making me giggle. He was such a goofball sometimes, but always a good kid, always trying to do the right thing, always a gentleman. Sometimes I can hear his laughter, and sometimes I hear him say, *"Just keep going, April."* When I get to town to check and with family, I realize it's his birthday today. I miss him.

On my first thru-hike attempt in 1996, I didn't stop at Woodshole hostel, just outside of Pearisburg, Virginia, because I was leaving the trail in Pearisburg. Everyone said missing Woodshole was one of the biggest mistakes on the trail. This time, I'm going.

There is no fee to stay in the bunkhouse at Woodshole, but the owner, Tillie, asks that hikers bring a rock from the road area to the rock wall that hikers have been building for her for years. After I gather and place my stones, I tell Tillie how much I love the creek running by her house. "Oh honey, so do I. But, that creek hasn't always been there, you know."

"I did notice that the creek runs along the other side of the road until it gets to your house," I answer.

"When my husband, Roy, and I first moved here, I told him that I wish I could hear the creek from the house. Do you know what he did? Since he worked for the forestry department, he asked his boss or someone in upper management if he could relocate the stream from across the road and closer to our house. At the end of our property, he would relocate it under the road and back into its original creek bed. So, one year, as a gift, he gave me a creek. I love listening to the running water outside my bedroom window. I fall asleep to that sound all the time. It's my favorite sound in the world."

I've heard of moving mountains before, but *literally* moving a creek? That is the sweetest gift I've ever heard. I don't think I'll ever forget their love story.

The main house is an 1880's log cabin, complete with chinking between the logs. It has a large front porch and a few rocking chairs on which to sit and relax. An old barn has been converted to a bunkhouse, complete with bunk beds or mattresses on the floor in the loft. A dozen of us relax for the night, putting puzzles together, chatting on the porch, and getting to know one another. I'm no longer afraid of GI Jane. She's a nice person, and I'm able to talk to her just like any other hiker.

I drag myself away from Woodshole and realize I should start hiking longer days. But I'm limping again. I've got something wrong with my feet. It's possibly tendinitis or pulled muscles; my feet hurt, and they are swollen every night. I've been slathering Ben Gay all over them and taking ibuprofen for the burning and swelling, but it's not really working.

I limp into Laurel Creek Shelter shortly after noon and stop to rest my feet. I'm eating lunch, and plenty of hikers are coming and going, but I'm here alone. Although it's June, I'm down in a valley, and it's cold and windy. I make a little fire to sit by and warm up, but it's been hours, and I'm still chilly and miserable. I hear some hikers coming around dinner time, and Desperado, Jingle, Kevin, and Little Bus show up. GI Jane, Frenchy, and four other hikers show up next.

I'm on Cloud Nine, talking to Little Bus all night around a bonfire. After everyone is in camp trying to sleep, Little Bus and I stay up another half hour whispering since our sleeping bags are next to each other. I just love everything about him. He's smart, and tall, maybe six feet two. His light brown hair is almost shaved, and it's apparent he shaves in town, as his beard has only a few days growth, not the typical bushy-unkempt beards that so many male hikers adopt. His roundish glasses give him a scholarly look. He's single, adventurous, and likes his family.

In the morning, I rise early with Little Bus and his gang. They are planning to hike 22 miles today. I desperately want to get that far, but I'm not sure I can make it there with my bum foot. So I'm off, hiking rather slowly, counting the miles, and hoping I get to 22. It takes me almost 12 hours, but I drag myself into the Pickle Branch Shelter just as everyone seems to be getting ready for bed.

"Trail Gimp! You made it! We're so glad you got here," Jingle says.

Since everyone has already eaten dinner and is getting ready for sleep, I grab my cookware and move over to the picnic table to make dinner, giving them some peace and quiet. Little Bus comes over to keep me company while I eat and then clean my dishes, and when I finally set up my sleeping gear next to him, we stay up for another half hour talking about life, the trail, and a little about Geneseo, where we went to school. He's a nice guy, but he clearly doesn't have any romantic notions for me, so I'm trying to hide my feelings for him. I wonder if I can somehow change his mind before we reach Katahdin. Is this why God has me hiking the trail? So I can meet Little Bus?

My feet throb because of the rocky 22 miles today. My ankles were bending in all sorts of directions that nature never intended. I'm popping ibuprofen tablets like they're M&M's lately.

Little Bus's group tends to hike fast and long. I'm not sure I'll be able to keep up. They are out of the shelter just as I am waking up. "Goodbye, guys! I hope you have a good day. Maybe I'll catch up with you later." It breaks my heart, but I don't think I will. Troutville is the next trail town, and most hikers stop there to resupply, so perhaps I'll see them in town. Until then, I will try to enjoy myself with the hikers I'm around. At least, that's what I tell myself.

I've been hiking around Fireball lately, and we get along well. She's thru-hiking too, but she has some injuries and is hiking until her body gives out. She's short and bubbly and has a smile that makes you want to be her friend. I bond with her instantly. I giggle when she tells me how she received her trail name. She didn't practice using her stove before she started hiking, and she nearly set fire to the picnic table her first night, creating a giant fireball that rose from her stove.

We plan to get up before dawn to see the sun rise over McAfee Knob, but at 4:30 am, it's raining and thundering, so we go back to sleep. We arrive at the summit around ten in the morning, just as the rainy mist is clearing off. McAfee Knob is one of the most iconic photo ops of the trail. The flat, rocky summit provides 180-degree views of the valley and surrounding mountains. But the iconic part is the giant, flat outcropping that juts out from the summit, enabling me to sit on the edge and dangle my feet a thousand or more feet above the valley floor.

Fireball takes a picture of me doing a cartwheel on the summit. It's more difficult to do a cartwheel wearing heavy hiking boots than one would think.

We hike along the edge of the cliffs all day long, with beautiful vistas, but hearing the highway off in the distance is disheartening. Our day will end at that highway in Troutville, yet it seems elusive. Finally, nearly 12 hours after we begin hiking, we arrive in town. Our first order of business is to find a motel room to drop our gear and take a shower, and as we're walking by the Best Western, I hear, "Trail Gimp! We're over here!"

I look up and see Jingle, Desperado, Kevin, and Little Bus.

"Hey, guys! I didn't know you would be here. I thought you would have left town today."

"Oh, we got in earlier today and spent the day resupplying. We are thinking of taking tomorrow off as well." Jingle said.

"Why don't you stay with us?" Desperado added.

"You already have four people, though."

"Oh, don't be silly," Desperado said. "One of us can easily sleep on the floor."

"Well, if you don't mind, I would love the floor," I answered.

I drop my pack, hunting for my camp clothes, the cleanest ones I have, and take a quick shower. Since these guys have already eaten, I hurry to meet Fireball, Moose, Papa Smurf, Hawkeye, and Wandering Bear at Western Sizzler for dinner.

I easily eat enough food to feed an average person for days. With all the hikers coming in and out of this restaurant, I'm not sure how they can afford to stay in business, considering how much we eat at the buffet. All-You-Can-Eat (AYCE) buffets are a huge draw for hikers and are generally listed in our guidebook. Hikers generally can't pass up AYCE anything.

Back at the motel, the five of us talk for hours before everyone heads to bed. It feels like we've known each other for years, even though I've only seen them occasionally for the last two weeks. Desperado jumps up from his bed and says, "Trail Gimp, I'll take the floor. You sleep on the bed next to Little Bus."

I'm not sure if this is a hint or a gentlemanly gesture. Despite my protest, Desperado is already on the floor with a pillow, getting ready to sleep. I crawl into bed, apologizing to Little Bus, and he says, "Don't worry about it. You're much better looking than that ole guy over there anyway!"

I do appreciate a man with a sense of humor. I wake up frequently, paranoid that I will accidentally wrap my arms around Little Bus in my sleep, scaring him off forever. As much as I want to snuggle up to him, I remain on my side of the bed.

I spend the first part of the day with the group, but they leave halfway through the day to get to the next shelter. I'm not ready to go; I need to rest my foot and repack after resupplying. I think Little Bus is my dream man, but I'm afraid I'll never see him again. I simply can't hike that fast every day. *April, you're out here by yourself. You can't hike someone else's hike; you need to hike your own. God has a plan for you. You just need to have faith.*

Why am I enduring all this misery out here, especially when my favorite people either left the trail or hike too fast? Having faith is difficult when you're not getting any answers.

I spend the next week hiking alone, though there are several other hikers I see every day. I finally run into Pilgrim again at Punchbowl Shelter. I hadn't seen him in almost six weeks since I learned my grandmother had died. We've been flip-flopping around each other; some days, I'd be ahead of him when he took a day or two off, or when I took some time off, he'd get ahead of me.

About a dozen of us are squeezed into Punchbowl Shelter, and just as the sun sets, a bullfrog begins his evening serenade, trying to find a mate. It's like he has a megaphone, and the sound amplifies and echoes over the pond into our shelter. The evening is quiet, the air is still, hikers are dozing, and then CROAK. Silence. CROAK. Silence. I try my best to sleep but that frog could wake the dead.

Sometime in the middle of the night, with our bullfrog still croaking, one hiker screams, "Shut the fuck up!" and everyone erupts into hysterical fits of laughter. Nobody was asleep anyway, and it takes a good 20 minutes for the giggles to subside. The moon is shining directly into my face again, so I sit up to admire the pond and the scenery, and Pilgrim sits up to chat. We talk until nearly four in the morning when I finally sleep from exhaustion.

I enjoy hiking, meeting new people, and experiencing new things on the trail every day. I pick wild strawberries and blueberries, meet trail angels, and see small towns along the way. I'm still trying to figure out why I'm on this trail, and since I met Little Bus, I wonder if he might be the reason. Was I supposed to meet him on this trail? If I'm supposed to meet him, then why aren't I hiking with him? What am I supposed to learn out here?

When I arrive at a shelter, I grab the shelter register, sign in, and read through past posts to look for messages. Grunts-n-Groans is more than a month ahead of me, so I look for his entries, but he doesn't leave me many notes anymore. He is hiking his own hike.

I also look for Moby Dick's entries because I love to see his drawings. But what I really search for are notes from Little Bus. By reading his entries, I can gauge how far ahead of me he is.

I set my current sights on Waynesboro, Virginia. Waynesboro is a must-stop for most hikers, as there is a large lawn behind the YMCA where hikers can camp and shower. Since it's one of the larger towns on the AT, there are many things to do, places to resupply or fix things, and take a well-deserved break. If I can increase my pace a little, I might be able to see Little Bus for a day.

I don't know exactly when I did it, but I injured the quadricep muscle in my right leg, and now it's increasingly painful to hike. But I pick up my pace anyway, hiking longer days with more miles for the remote chance of seeing Little Bus.

Kathy is coming to Waynesboro to meet me for a day or two. I haven't seen her since Hot Springs, and I can't wait to catch up with her. She is on summer vacation, so she offered to meet me to bring my summer fleece bag and take home my winter gear, saving me a few pounds.

I am camping near the Tye River with about a dozen other hikers, and it's fun hanging out with everyone, but that leaves me 27 miles to hike to get to Waynesboro tomorrow. This is a stupid idea, considering I am limping with sore feet and a possible pulled muscle. But I must move on. I must see Kathy and hopefully Little Bus.

It's 3:30 in the afternoon, and I've hiked 20 miles so far today, starting at 6:15 in the morning. I have seven miles to go. At the Blue Ridge Parkway, I stop to eat a snack and talk to the hikers I've been running into all day. One of them is a day hiker, and since his car is here at the parking lot, he offers a ride into Waynesboro. I resist at first, until about a dozen hikers convince me that 20 miles by 3:30 is enough mileage for a day. I'm not sure I'm happy about it, but I pile into the car with several others. He takes me to the Post Office to pick up mail drops and then leaves me at the YMCA. More miles skipped that once again, I vow to return and hike.

Tents litter the lawn, and with so many hikers here, it's almost like a mini trail days festival. We catch up with one another, asking if we've seen someone or updating each other on trail gossip. I hear Little Bus and Jingle were in town this morning but left today. Someone else tells me that he saw Desperado hanging out on the lawn near Rockfish Gap. Perhaps they are staying there for the night?

I sit in my tent and look through my mail. Aunt June sent me a card with some money, Nightgrumbler sent me a letter, and Mom and Dad sent me some money and the upcoming maps for the trail. There are dozens of maps detailing the Appalachian Trail. Some people don't carry them because they are fairly heavy, and the trail is well-marked with white blazes. For safety reasons, I think it's important to carry them in case I somehow get lost. Besides, it's helpful to look at the profile map to see what kind of hell we will be hiking each day. When Kathy gets here, I will give her the maps I've finished with. Having extra money in town is helpful because we can eat real food and a lot of it.

I had given Kathy directions to the YMCA, so she pulls into the parking lot around lunchtime. It's so good to see her! We grab some lunch in town, where we see Got Milk, who gives me the best news ever!

"Hey Trail Gimp, Little Bus has been asking around for you, wondering where you are. He's spending the night at Rusty's with Jingle and Desperado, just in case you want to know."

Little Bus was asking about me!

Rusty's Hard Time Hollow is a thru-hiker institution. I've heard all the stories, and I wasn't planning on going, partly because it's a few miles out of town. According to legend, Rusty has a wood-fired hot tub, no electricity, and it used to be a non-stop party, though he's trying to curb the party scene a little.

Kathy agrees that it sounds interesting, so we decide to head over. Kathy is not thru-hiking, and Rusty only allows thru-hikers to spend the night, so we pack up my things, intending to get a hotel room a little later. I'm so excited about seeing Little Bus that I can hardly sit still.

We reach the entrance to Rusty's, but the gate is closed. Signs read "no swearing" and "no violence". Another sign makes us rethink our decision: "*Private Property*". We park the car outside the gate and continue to walk in. We relax a little as the signs get more comical, "*Grownups allowed if accompanied by children*". The driveway is made of dirt and aluminum, or rather, squashed aluminum cans. Thousands or millions of crushed soda and beer cans litter the driveway, flattened by feet and vehicles driving to and fro for years.

We see the main cabin and several other buildings, supposedly spring houses and bunk houses. We walk toward the main door, and Desperado immediately sees us and hugs me. I introduce him to Kathy, and he leaves without a word but returns momentarily with Little Bus and Jingle.

Rusty is an agreeable fellow, with a long white beard and a wide smile, round glasses, and usually wearing a bucket hat. He takes a photo of every hiker that comes through the door, so he takes a Polaroid of me, prints my real name, Trail name, and date, and pins it to the wall alongside the thousands of thru-hikers that came before me. I feel a sense of pride having my photo there, and I look for any 1996 hikers I might recognize.

Rusty took my photo because it's clear that I'm a thru-hiker. I wear heavy, worn hiking boots and trail clothing that look dirty, no matter how many times they've been washed. I have numerous scrapes and cuts on my legs, arms, and hands, mosquito bites everywhere, and a perpetual dirty appearance.

Kathy, on the other hand, is clearly not a hiker. She's dressed in regular clothing. She's wearing makeup. Rusty tries to take Kathy's photo for the wall, but she refuses, insisting it's an honor for thru-hikers only.

Rusty asks, "So Trail Gimp, are you staying here tonight?"

"Well, I'd love to, but Kathy is visiting me, and I know non-hikers are not supposed to spend the night here. We're probably going to get a hotel room down the road," I answer.

Rusty looks over at Kathy. He eyes her up and down, then looks back to me, over to Little Bus, and then back to Kathy. "Well, now, this young lady looks like she won't cause any trouble. If you want to spend the night, you're both welcome to a bunk in the bunkhouse. Make yourself at home. Drinks are in the springhouse, the hot tub is down in the yard, and you're welcome to anything in the kitchen."

I can't believe it. Rusty doesn't charge a fee for staying at his place, but he does rely on donations to keep everything running. Since Kathy brought my summer bag, we both have a sleeping bag to use. We get set up in the bunkhouse and walk to the springhouse to get a soda. Hikers always filter water from streams and springs; I've even had to filter water out of a mud puddle once in the Smokies, so when someone offers a fresh, cold soda or other beverage, it's a treat.

The springhouse is old-fashioned, and I find it interesting. Ice cold spring water comes from the ground and forms a stream, and small, shallow pools were created long ago, where Rusty stores food and beverages that need to be kept cold. In addition to beer and soda, there is milk, butter, and other items for the kitchen. The soda I grab is ice cold, and I wonder at the simplicity and the lack of electricity and think about how things were about a hundred years ago when the cabin was built.

We look around and see an expansive lawn with a wood-fired hot tub, a solar shower, an outhouse, and a few areas where hikers are encouraged to pee, like the target where guys are supposed to "aim", trying to hit the bulls-eye.

Anything goes here at Rusty's, as long as you are respectful.

Kathy, Little Bus, Desperado, Jingle, and I hop in the car and head to town for a nice dinner. I just love Little Bus, and I can't stop looking at him.

After dinner, we head back to Rusty's. Kathy is holding her own with the other hikers, so Little Bus and I go out to the back lawn to watch the stars. Sitting on the grass, side by side, I'm loving my life right now. I'm hiking the Appalachian Trail; I'm talking about the stars and life with this guy that seems to have zero faults. Like me, Little Bus had gone to Geneseo in New York, but he is also living in North Carolina, recently obtaining his master's degree. I can easily see myself with him in North Carolina forever.

"Hey, Gimp, how about we sleep under the stars tonight?"

"I'm up for that. It's a beautiful night; it shouldn't rain."

We traipse back to the bunkhouse, gather our sleeping gear, invite Kathy and Jingle to join us, and lie in the grass, warm and cozy in our bags. We chat about life and the trail, and I fall asleep next to Little Bus with a giant smile on my face.

I wake up without a smile. I'm not sure how we can be so smart yet so stupid at the same time. Our sleeping bags are cold and wet because the morning dew settled right on us. We run back to the bunkhouse to put on warm clothing.

I walk into the kitchen where Little Bus has already prepared a cup of coffee for me, and Rusty is making pancakes to feed an army.

"Here ya go, Trail Gimp," Rusty offers. "Hot pancakes! Maple syrup and butter are over there if you need them." I grew up on regular pancake syrup, which, if you read the label, is primarily corn syrup. Rusty has the real stuff – 100% real maple syrup from trees.

Life can't get much better at this point.

It's time to go, so Kathy, Little Bus, Jingle, Desperado, and myself, pile into Kathy's car with our gear. We drive to the trail, hug each other a thousand times, and the three of them take off up the trail. It's good that Kathy is here to prevent me from crying and chasing after Little Bus.

Since we have a car, we pick up some hikers and drive them around to do errands, and finally, Kathy and I wind up at a cheesy motel, soaking in the air conditioning. It's mid-June in Virginia, and sitting outside for five minutes causes you to sweat until you're drenched. I've never been so happy to have air conditioning.

After a good night of sleep, I take off hiking just before noon. I miss Little Bus already. I guess I'm just going to have to catch up to him.

CHAPTER TWELVE

STILL CHASING LITTLE BUS

June 1998

My leg and feet still throb, but a few days of rest has helped. I still take my Advil every four hours, hoping to prevent more severe aches from returning. Hiking 20 and more miles per day doesn't help, though.

I've entered the Shenandoah National Park, and I'm acutely aware that I'm getting closer to the point where those girls were murdered in 1996. As of today, they have not caught any suspect. But there are about a dozen hikers near me at any time, so I keep my eyes open and listen to my gut instinct.

Hiking through one of the most heavily visited national parks in America ensures people are always around. We emerge from the woods to follow Skyline Drive for a while. It is the only public road in the park, and it traverses 105 miles along the crest of the mountains throughout the park. Tourists can enter the park from four separate places along Skyline Drive, and they look at us with curiosity and humor as we carry our homes on our backs, wearing heavy hiking boots, preferring to walk on the softer grass over the paved paths and roads.

A bunch of us are sleeping in a shelter, and a weird noise wakes me up in the middle of the night. It sounds like someone is sucking on a popsicle that is melting faster than it can be eaten. Sluuurp. Suck. Lick. Lick. Sluuurp. I look around, but it's pitch black, and I can't see a thing. This slurping sound is awfully close to my head! I fumble for my flashlight, turn over to look outside with the light, and I see a deer only a foot or two away from me, sucking on the webbing straps of my backpack, presumably to get the salt from sweating so much.

Oh gross! My straps are covered in gobs and gobs of deer saliva. If my backpack could talk, I'm sure it would say, "He slimed me." I shoo the deer off and head back to bed. In the morning, we see that I was the lucky one. I can easily wash off my pack straps. Other hikers find socks, shorts, and tee shirts slimy, mangled, or missing altogether. Even the shirts that are just slimy or so gross, the owners say, "Yeah, I'm never wearing that again!"

One of the great things about hiking through the park, other than the wildlife and fantastic scenery, is the abundance of camp stores and restaurants. Thru-hikers have been known to roam from restaurant to restaurant, not using their stoves for days. I eat more than my fair share of ice cream from camp stores and have lunch and dinner with other hikers for several days. I'm meeting more hikers, but I spend lots of time in shelters reading the registers and looking for notes from Little Bus. I finally find a message from him that says he and Jingle are taking a few days off the trail to visit a friend in Baltimore. I know I won't catch up to him, and I'll probably never see him again. The thought makes me want to cry. *Remember, April, you didn't come out here to meet a man. I have no idea why you're out here, but you'll figure it out soon enough. Move on.*

There is nothing to do but move forward—one agonizing step at a time. So, I hike. At least it gives me a direction: north.

A hundred miles later, I arrive in the town of Front Royal, and I'm ready for a break from the trail. I need food and comfort. I'm sad, not knowing what my future holds, and anxious about what I might do when I finish the trail.

While I sit outside a convenience store, trying to decide whether to accept Lobo's offer to share a motel room, I hear some guy mention the town of Berryville. Berryville is a tiny town about 30 miles north of here, and even people who live near Berryville don't know the town's name. But I know it!

"Excuse me, did you just say Berryville?"

"Yes, I live there. You've heard of it?"

"Of course! My mom's longest best friend lives in Berryville, and her daughter and I have long been best friends since we were two years old! I used to visit them during college vacations. I was going to call them and see if I can stay with them for a day once I get up to Route 7."

"Well, I have a few errands to do, but I'm heading home in about half-hour if you want a ride up there. I'd be happy to take you along."

I'm excited to see long-time family friends since I haven't seen them in three years, but I caught them at a bad time, and they only agreed to let me visit because I wouldn't take no for an answer. It's an awkward stay, and I feel bad for interrupting them. They take me back to Front Royal in the morning, and I feel worse for my stay.

I'm at a busy part of the trail – there are various roadside convenience stores and towns near the trail, and I happen to have relatives in this area. I'll be up near Route 7 tonight, and I'll call my mom's cousins, Diane and Trent. It's cold, rainy, and gloomy outside, so I stop at a convenience store to get a cup of coffee to warm me up. I call Diane from the pay phone to plan a visit.

"Hi, April! I can't wait to see you! When are you coming?"

"Hi, Diane; I was hoping to see you later today. I have about 12 miles left to hike today."

"Oh! I can come to pick you up right now if you want. I can't wait to see you!"

I consider this, but I really need to stop skipping north to come back down to hike again. No, I need to walk there. "Thanks, Diane, but I need to get these miles in. How's this? I'll get to Route 7 by 7:30 pm, and there is a restaurant called the Horseshoe Curve Restaurant close to the trail crossing. I can call you from there, and you can meet me there. Does that work?"

"Okay, that works. We'll plan to go out to dinner. See you later, honey!"

And with that, I drink the rest of my coffee and hit the trail, hobbling through the "rollercoaster" section of small hills with constant ups and downs. They are small enough that they don't appear on the profile maps, and I'm annoyed. I had planned a leisurely walk on a flat trail; It's not happening, I'm limping, and I'm pissed off.

Finally, I reach Route 7 and turn left until I get to the curvy road that leads to the restaurant. My excitement comes to a screeching halt when I realize the restaurant is closed. I look around for another restaurant or a pay phone, and I don't see anything. How am I supposed to call Diane? I wander back to Route 7 and face a decision. Do I hike south on the trail to return to the Bears Den Hostel, which I passed about an hour ago? It has a phone, but the guidebook says it's strictly for their guests' use. Or do I hitchhike into a town and call them from a payphone?

I stick my thumb out and walk down Route 7, closer to the town where Diane and Trent live. A few minutes later, a car stops.

"Hi, young lady. Are you looking for a ride?"

"Hi, yes. I'm supposed to call my aunt, but the restaurant around here is apparently closed. Can you give me a ride to the closest payphone?"

"I surely can, but just beware, we're less than an hour away from a major city; you shouldn't be hitchhiking in these here parts. You never know who might stop. You're lucky I stopped before anyone else."

"Well, thank you. I appreciate it. I'm just looking to go down the road to the nearest convenience store, or anywhere they have a pay phone. My aunt's been expecting me for a while now. I don't want her to worry."

I put my pack in the backseat and climb into the front. George tells me he's lived in this area his entire life, which appears to be about 70 years, and he loves it here. As we drive down the road, George takes a right.

"I live just down this road. You're welcome to use my phone. It'll be faster than driving to a pay phone."

I look over at George to determine if I just got picked up by a serial killer. Trying to remember what I learned from documentaries about Ted Bundy, I glance at my door to ensure it has a handle if I need to escape in an emergency. Door handle, check—the door lock, usable. I'm not trapped; I can relax—sort of.

We arrive at George's house, and he invites me to use the phone. I quickly head for the kitchen and grab my guidebook, where I have all my phone numbers and addresses listed.

"Hi, Diane, it's April. I was supposed to call you from the restaurant, but the darn thing was closed. This guy named George drove me to his house so I could call you," and I gave her his address.

"Oh, that's only a few minutes from here. I'll be there shortly."

I hang up the phone to find George looking my way. "April, here's my address. Do me a favor. Can you send me a few postcards along your trip? I like to keep up with some of the hikers I meet. Can we stay in touch?"

Stay in touch? I'm not looking for a pen pal! Oh boy. How do I get out of this situation? I'm beginning to get the creeps, and all my radar is going off. He keeps looking at me like I'm his new best friend. He's probably harmless and just lonely, but I bet that's what all of Ted Bundy's victims said.

"Sure, George, I'd be happy to send you some postcards," I lied. He hands me an envelope with his address written down. "You know, my aunt is going to be here any minute, so I think I'm just going to wait outside for her. It's getting dark, and I don't want her to miss your house."

"Oh, you don't have to wait outside. You can just sit down and make yourself comfortable until she gets here. It's been miserable weather all day today."

"Oh, I know, and thank you for your hospitality, but I should be heading outside to wait for her. Thank you again for allowing me to use your phone." I grab my pack, glance around to ensure I didn't leave anything behind and quickly head out the door.

I feel a sense of relief when I'm standing by myself at the end of the driveway. Diane is taking longer than expected to get here. I hope she didn't get lost. I glance back at the house, and George is gazing out the window at me. I pretend to smile and offer a fake wave. *Oh please, Diane, hurry.*

Ten minutes feels like an eternity when Diane shows up. She jumps out of the car to hug me.

"Thank you for saving me, Diane! Now let's go before this crazy guy follows me."

It's nearly 10:00 pm when we arrive at her house, and I apologize to her and Trent that it took so long for me to get there. I recount my experience with George and promise I'll never hitchhike again. At least, not within an hour of a major city. We sit around the table, eating dinner and talking until one in the morning. I'm so sleepy I can barely keep my eyes open. They show me to the spare room where I'll be sleeping.

I'm used to sharing a shelter with a dozen or more people. This room has a king-sized bed and my own bathroom. The bed could easily fit three hikers, four if it's raining, plus another dozen hikers sleeping on the floor, and more, if you put them in the bathroom. It's a big space for just myself.

Two days later, I walk into Harpers Ferry, West Virginia, the unofficial halfway point of the trail and where the Appalachian Trail Conference has its headquarters. I'm happy to reach another state. I've spent over a month in Virginia. There are more trail miles in Virginia than in any other state. From here, I'll spend anywhere from a few days to two weeks in most states, so the milestones will come quickly.

I stop into the building that runs and manages the Appalachian Trail to say hi and have my photo taken for their records. Lobo is another hiker I've hiked with for a few days, and we get some lunch and then return to the ATC headquarters to hang out. My dad's aunt lives not far from here, and they told me that I MUST call them and stay with them when I get to this point on the trail. The problem is that I've been calling them for hours, and they aren't answering the phone. I've left messages but can't get in touch with them.

Not knowing what to do, Lobo and I decide to go to the local campground. We sit outside the campground office door on a bench with other hikers, debating what to do. It starts to rain again, so we are considering getting a room at a nearby Inn. Sheesh, I'm spending so much money lately! The weather begins to clear, so we decide to set up our tents in the "thru-hiker" section to save a few dollars. Just as we stand up, a car pulls up and stops about two feet in front of my face. I look up to see Little Bus, Desperado, Jingle, and their friend from Baltimore piling out of the car.

Lobo and I cook dinner, buy some beer, Little Bus' group buys some more beer, and we have a party around the campfire. It's funny how I can go from being discouraged and pessimistic to cheerful and jubilant within a few minutes.

After the beer is gone, we walk to the Inn to visit the bar, and Little Bus and I spend lots of quarters and giggle while playing Galaga in the game room. I haven't played that arcade game in a decade, and I revel in the simple joy.

I'm so in love, and I have no idea how he feels about me. He laughs and giggles with me but never tries to kiss me.

Our group closes the bar, and the others head back to the campground while Little Bus and I head to the 7-Eleven for a snack. We wander the streets for a while and wind up on the local high school football field. I try unsuccessfully to climb the goalpost, and as I slide back down, Little Bus grabs my arm to ensure I don't fall.

It's now or never, Trail Gimp. Just do it.

I finally kiss him, just for a moment. But he stops. And reality hits. I probably stink. Or he just doesn't like me at all. Whatever the reason, I try to hide my disappointment.

We walk back to the campground, crawl into our tents and crash. We don't mention the kiss.

I wake up early with a slight hangover, drink water, and fall back to sleep. When I finally crawl out of my tent, I see Desperado and Jingle have left. "Where did everyone go?"

Little Bus answers, "Desperado and Jingle left this morning. I figured I'd wait for you, and we could hike together. Whenever you're ready."

Honey, I've been ready for you my whole life. Let's go!

CHAPTER THIRTEEN

KEEPING UP

July 1998

I run to shower in the campground facilities and head out of town with Little Bus around noon. We pass a group of schoolchildren hiking south, and I hear one boy exclaim in exasperation, "Where does this trail end?"

"Georgia," I answered.

"Uuuuggghhhhh!"

The weather is perfect for hiking. The sun is shining, the temperature is warm but not hot, and the trail is nearly flat as it follows the C & O Canal towpath for a few miles out of town. I feel like I'm walking in a park instead of hiking to Maine. Little Bus hikes faster than I do. I hike two miles per hour, sometimes a bit faster. Little Bus is easily a three-mile-per-hour hiker, if not more. He often gets ahead of me but waits for me to catch up in certain spots. It reminds me a little of hiking with Nightgrumbler – walking with someone but not attached at the hip. It's nice.

We hike 17 miles to the Dahlgren backpacking area, where we set up tents and take hot showers. In the morning, Little Bus says, "What do you think about hiking into Pen Mar tonight?"

My guidebook says it's 23 miles to Pen Mar. That's an average hiking distance for Little Bus, but that's a lot of mileage for me. *But to be with Little Bus?*

"Sure, that sounds fun. We can plan to get dinner somewhere in town."

We begin hiking and discuss everything from school at Geneseo to hiking in The Adirondacks of New York State to living in North Carolina. We talk about our families, what we did before we hiked, how we came to hike on the trail, and more.

The act of hiking requires you to bare your soul. Your hiking partner sees you at your worst. They see you upset over a rainy day, angry from tripping over a rock, or frustrated about equipment malfunctions. They see you first thing in the morning, and they see you sweaty and stinky with dirt smeared everywhere after a long day on the trail.

They also see you at your best. They see you giving yourself to help someone and receiving help when you need it. They see your sheer enjoyment of living with nature, picking wild berries, and smelling the flowers as you pass by, or sharing your food with someone who accidentally dropped their pot of food on the muddy ground.

There is no lying out here, other than using a trail name. Everything out here is "authentically you". Your entire personality is on display while hiking. You'll find out quickly if the person you're hiking with is a morning person or a night person, whether they are quick to help others or shy away from responsibility. You'll find out if they are A or B personalities, planning every day with intricate mileage plans or hiking as far as they want each day and stopping. You quickly notice those who crave attention and those who try their best to melt into the background.

Little Bus is the type of guy who sings in the rain and is grateful for the water to drink and to help the flowers bloom. He's thankful for the sun for the same reason. He doesn't complain, speaks kindly of other people, and is optimistic every day. I keep looking for an excuse to stop this infatuation, but I can't find one.

About halfway to Pen Mar County Park, my left quad muscle begins to hurt. It's tender and sore, so I pop a bunch of Advil and move on. I'm sure it will go away soon. I slow down a little, and Little Bus gets ahead of me.

When I arrive in Pen Mar, Little Bus and Fireball immediately come up to me. Fireball has been staying with relatives in the area while she takes some time off to nurse some injuries, so she's driving hikers around. She offers to take Little Bus and me to a local pizza shop, so I drop my gear at the backpacker's area and jump in the car.

We run into a half-dozen hikers at the pizza shop and have fun getting to know each other. We gorge on pizza until our bellies swell with pepperoni and soda.

"C'mon, Trail Gimp, let's get back to our tents."

"Okay, I'm coming." I swivel around on my bench, but I can't lift my left leg. I stare at my thigh and will it to raise, but it doesn't budge. I have zero control over it. Confused, I put my hands under my thigh, lift my leg, and throw it over the bench. I swivel around the rest of the way, but I still can't stand up. "Little Bus, give me a hand, will you?" He grabs my hand and pulls me up. It's weird. I can't move my left leg at all. It's not painful; it just doesn't move.

We leave the pizza place, and I drag my left leg behind me. I feel like I'm in a zombie movie. With pizza.

We wake up late with zero incentive to move. We have leftover pizza for breakfast, never even considering the fact that it's been sitting out, unrefrigerated, for 12 hours. I have never enjoyed cold pizza in my life. If pizza comes hot, you're supposed to eat it that way. But when it comes to hiking the Appalachian Trail? Cold pizza for breakfast is the best! We spend some time talking to a forest ranger and finally leave town at 10:30 am, and I'm still dragging my leg behind me. Little Bus asks me about my leg and wonders why it won't move, but we are both clueless about the reasons.

Almost immediately, we find ourselves at the Mason-Dixon line. Since we are both initially from the North, we hoot and holler, and I do a one-legged dance to celebrate hiking from Georgia to "the North". We take obligatory photos at the sign and move on. It's fun to celebrate little things like that with someone.

It also means we're entering Pennsylvania, which is known for its rocks. Trail legend says that "Pennsylvania is where boots go to die." Other comical lore states that members of the Pennsylvania trail-maintaining clubs spend their spare time sharpening the rocks before the thru-hiker season. We aim to hike 15 miles today, and in those miles, we'll pass several shelters.

We take our time hiking and chatting, trying to figure out why my left leg doesn't move as it should, with no answers. We stop at every shelter we come to, eat and rest, sign in, and read the shelter registers. It's different not having to look for notes from Little Bus, and I've gotten ahead of some of my friends, so it's nice to be able to leave messages for them. Little Bus and I hike together as if we've known each other for years. Sometimes we talk about anything, and sometimes we walk in silence. Usually, Little Bus winds up ahead of me because I'm dragging my leg behind me. I'm popping plenty of Advil, so I don't feel all that sore, but it's tiring to hike this way.

We heard that Caledonia State Park, about 20 miles north of the Pennsylvania border, will have fireworks for Independence Day, so we plan to get there and celebrate the holiday with anybody in the park. However, once we arrive, someone tells us the fireworks are actually in a different park, and since it's beginning to rain, many of the picnickers pack up early and leave. We end up at the shelter and celebrate the Fourth among hiker friends.

Today marks a day for which I'm very excited. After researching the Appalachian Trail for years, I've heard about the exclusive half-gallon club at Pine Grove Furnace State Park, the halfway point of the trail. Technically, the halfway point moves yearly based on relocations and land acquisitions. But the state park has a camp store where you can buy half a gallon of ice cream. If a thru-hiker eats it all before it melts, they gain entry into the coveted half-gallon club, and the reward is a wooden spoon with "Member of the Half Gallon Club" written on it. I don't eat much breakfast this morning, saving room for that half gallon.

Thru-hikers regularly consume a pint of ice cream in town, so it's assumed that a half-gallon will be no problem. We arrive at the camp store and read the register from other hikers who leave advice for all the newbies. Some suggest not getting something like plain vanilla because your taste buds get too bored. Others suggest avoiding chocolate chip cookie dough because it is too filling. Little Bus disagrees with that theory and buys a half gallon of cookie dough ice cream, while I decide to go midway and get a half gallon of cookies and cream. I devour the first half of the container reasonably quickly. It's cold, it's a hot sunny day, and I love ice cream. I am enjoying my friends and the environment. However, about midway, I begin to slow down. My appetite wanes, and I still have more than a pint to finish. My spoonfuls get progressively smaller until finally, after an hour and six minutes, I force the last spoonful of cookies and cream down my throat. I groan out loud, and other hikers laugh at me because they finished theirs in about half the time. I get up to walk around and immediately fall to the ground, holding my swollen belly and groaning like I ate Thanksgiving dinner. Little Bus laughs at me, grabs my hand, and says, "Come on, let's get you up and walking around."

We are rewarded with our membership spoons, and I am so disappointed. I *knew* exactly what I'd be getting: a small wooden spoon, exactly like one in a Dixie Cup of ice cream, with a red stamp stating, "Member of the Half Gallon Club." But it just looks so *tiny, generic, and not at all remarkable*. It's hardly a worthy prize for the feat we just finished.

We walk around the park, stroll on the beach, and explore the historical aspects of the park. We decide to get bunks at the Ironmasters Mansion Hostel in the park. The caretaker tells us, "Unless your name is on it, this is a community kitchen. If you see something in the cabinets or the fridge, help yourself." We rummage around the fridge and find some leftover pasta for dinner, familiarize ourselves with the place, and play games while we do laundry. We see a life-size outdoor chess set and pretend to play as I rack my brain trying to remember what Nightgrumbler taught me about chess. I fail miserably, and we move pieces around to make them look good for photos.

The mansion was once part of the Underground Railroad System, so we explore the basement to see where slaves were hidden from slave hunters behind a false wall, to hide them as they made their way to Canada and freedom. It's a sad fact of American history. Little Bus and I are silent while imagining how the hidden slaves must have felt: the fear of being found, which would mean being returned to their master and then tortured or killed, and the uncertainty of escaping to an unknown place, all combined with the hope for a better future while relying on the kindness of strangers on their perilous journey. After a sobering living history lesson, we finally leave the basement and agree to go to sleep in our separate bunk rooms. We make a pact that whoever wakes up first must wake the other one up.

I roll over in my bunk when I hear, "Psst! Hey, Trail Gimp!"

I open one eye, glance at the door, and see Little Bus poking his face in. *He's awake already?* "Okay, I'm coming," I groggily answer back. "Give me just a minute."

I get up and limp into the kitchen, where Little Bus has already poured me a cup of coffee and a glass of orange juice. He's already making pancakes, and we have a leisurely breakfast on the porch. We haven't spoken about that kiss back in Harpers Ferry yet, and everything between us has been platonic since then.

We discuss plans for today and decide to head out after lunch, and we head back to our bunk rooms to take showers and get ready.

It's my first time taking an actual shower since I realized my leg doesn't work correctly. I'm in a tiny shower stall that is too small to bend in, and I can't pick up my leg to wash my foot. Balancing precariously on my right leg, I pick up my left leg with one hand while cleaning my leg and foot with my other hand. *How the heck will I finish my hike if I can't even pick up my leg?*

After dividing mail drops, packing our backpacks, and getting ready to hit the trail, we procrastinate while sitting on the porch. Little Bus announces, "I'm hungry again."

We head back into the kitchen, where I find ingredients to make a killer salad, while Little Bus finds noodles to cook with some leftover spaghetti sauce. We eat, procrastinate some more, clean the dishes, and finally head out for the trail while I hear the song *Daydream Believer* from the Monkees playing on an oldies station on an old radio in the kitchen. I limp down the path with a spring in my step, singing aloud, "Cheer up, sleepy Jean, Oh what can it mean, To a daydream believer, and a homecoming queeeeeen." I'm a little off-key, but I don't care. I'm happy.

Within a few minutes, we reach the sign marking the official halfway point of the trail, so we stop to sign in and read the register while we take pictures. We've hiked 1,090.5 miles thus far, according to the sign.

I think about the last thousand miles. I started on March 29, and now it's July 6. I've hiked by myself and with various people for varying lengths of time. I've visited friends and family I haven't seen in a long time. I've taken time off for injuries and my grandmother's funeral. I've accepted the hospitality and generosity of strangers. I wonder what I don't know about the coming months. But I know that hiking with Little Bus can get me through anything, and I'm looking forward to the next thousand miles.

We arrive in Boiling Springs, and I'm interested in comparing the springs here to the springs in Saratoga Springs. Here, the springs form a veritable river, producing over 20 million gallons of water a day. This spring differs from home, where dozens of springs are located throughout the city, but none flow at this rate. It's an interesting difference.

We find the regional Appalachian Trail Conference office, where we can drop our packs to explore the town and get lunch. When we sign into the register and hand it back to the staff member, he glances at it and says, "Trail Gimp? The Trail Gimp from 1996?"

Puzzled, I said, "Yep, that's me. I went home early in 96 because of injuries, but I started again on Springer Mountain on March 29."

"I'm Allgood! I met you in 96 a bunch of times."

I look at him and recognize him under his beard. His story was also chronicled in the book about the 1996 hikers.

We hug and recount our lives for the past two years. Allgood loves the trail so much that after he completed his hike two years ago, he got a job as a ridge runner for the Appalachian Trail Conference, and he's stationed here in Boiling Springs. His job is to hike back and forth on a designated section of the trail to ensure the trail and hikers are safe. It seems like the perfect job for a former thru-hiker.

Little Bus and I leave to get some lunch, resupply at the local grocery store, make phone calls to family and friends, and nap in the sun. We finally head back to the ATC offices after several hours. Just as we're about to hoist our packs, an employee volunteers to take our packs to the Scott Farm, where she lives with some other staff members. It's ten miles up the trail, and we need to pass the farm anyway, so it's not out of our way.

We agree, and Little Bus and I take off on the trail, walking and limping without the weight of our packs. We pick fresh berries along the way, smell the wildflowers, and enjoy a nearly flat, ten-mile walk in the woods and fields. I sing *Daydream Believer* aloud over and over because the darn song is stuck in my head. When we arrive at the Scott Farm, we can smell the rains coming, so we ask if we can camp on the covered porch, along with a half dozen other hikers already there. Granted permission, they offer us beer from their kegerator, and we have an impromptu porch party.

As we're getting ready for bed, Little Bus drops the bomb.

"Gimp, I just want to make sure you don't have any expectations about us hiking together."

"Expectations?"

"You know, romantic expectations. You know I've got a lot going on with graduate school, and since I don't know where I'm going to be after finishing the trail, I don't want you to have any expectations that I may not be able to meet. I like hiking with you, but I don't want anything to get in the way."

Expectations? What do I expect? I expect you to fall in love with me, hike to Maine with me and live happily ever after with me. But I can't say that, or I will scare him off for good.

"Little Bus, don't you worry about anything. Things are just fine the way they are," I lie. I am crushed, but I don't let on. I'd rather have his friendship than nothing at all. Maybe he will fall in love with me in due time.

I procrastinate in the morning because it's still raining. As I change into my hiking clothes, I scream bloody murder at finding a tick on the sole of my foot. It's half the size of a penny, so it must have been on my foot the entire night, sucking my blood the whole time. It's so engorged it looks like it will pop at any moment. I can handle snakes, mice, and other creatures, but ticks nauseate me, and I can't pull them off. I try to touch my foot, but I gag a few times. Little Bus laughs at me, grabs my foot, and simply pulls the dreadful creature from my foot as I look away, disgusted by the entire thing.

"C'mon Gimp," he laughs. "Let's go."

I hobble along, falling further behind Little Bus until I can no longer see him. My leg hurts. Walking is painful, and I'm still trying to deal with last night's blow to my heart. I'm not enjoying anything about today as I drag myself into Darlington shelter for a refill of Advil. Little Bus is just about to leave as I arrive, and although he offers to stay and keep me company, I see that he's already packed. "No, thanks, you're already packed up. I'll catch you at the next shelter."

Once he leaves, I eat, sign in and read the register, and before I get cold again, I hit the trail, limping as fast as I can to catch up. I arrive at the next shelter hoping to find Little Bus, but two hikers tell me he left about 15 minutes ago because he was getting cold. I quickly eat another snack, read the register, and move on. Although the rain has subsided, the temperature dropped, and I hurry along to keep myself warm.

I finally catch up to Little Bus, enjoying the view over Duncannon, and we begin to hike together, but the wet rocks slow me down, and I hobble precariously from rock to rock. I wince in pain every time I need to put pressure on my left leg. My hiking poles become de facto crutches as I make my way down the trail.

Once more, I catch up to Little Bus when he waits for me on the road. We walk into the town of Duncannon together. It's 6:00 pm when we pass the Doyle Hotel. The Doyle is another legendary trail experience, as most of the early thru-hiking pioneers stayed here. Curious about the loud music and noise, we enter the bar to find a dozen hikers hanging out, playing pool, eating wings, and drinking beer. For people who are hiking the Appalachian Trail and experiencing "nature," we are certainly spending a lot of time in civilization.

We drink beer, play pool, order dinner, drink more beer, and play more pool. We intended to go to the other hotel in town since I heard the accommodations here are pretty bad. However, some hikers tell us that the other hotel is booked, so we ask about getting a room.

I laugh and cringe as we make our way upstairs. The wallpaper is peeling and the ceiling plaster is coming down in various places. The once beautiful, curved wooden handrail extending several stories is missing some spindles, is wobbly in many areas, and is in danger of plummeting to the ground. I burst out laughing as we enter our room. The furniture is ancient, the wallpaper is old and peeling, and the ceiling is coming apart layer by layer. The double bed has seen better days, with a severe dip in the middle. The bedspread looks like someone's grandmother had these in her spare bedroom long ago, and the matching curtains might fall apart from dry rot if I try to open or close them to get to the window.

Trying to decide whether the room is actually safe to sleep in, Little Bus drops his pack on the floor and flops onto the bed, and when I see that it doesn't collapse, I do the same. We take turns in the hallway bathrooms, where there is a tub but no shower. It's nice to relax in a hot tub while soaking myself clean. Eventually, I clean up, and we head back downstairs for more pool and beer.

We run into Jim and Greg, two hikers that Little Bus knows and that I met way back in Damascus almost two months ago. It's funny the way hikers meet up with each other. We might hike near each other but not see each other for days or weeks. I might pass someone as they take a day off in town, or vice versa. The four of us stay up until nearly 1:00 am. Finally, we head upstairs, careful not to use the banister for fear of falling to the ground with it. After Little Bus' chat a few days ago, I'm careful about staying on "my side" of the bed, lest he thinks anything different.

My leg is still sore in the morning, and I want to take an additional day off, but Little Bus says he's planning on hiking out today. Maybe I can convince him otherwise, but I don't want to cross that line.

We do laundry, go to the grocery store and the post office, and then head back to The Doyle. Little Bus packs up his things and we head downstairs. I promised to play pool with him again, so we grab a beer and begin playing. Jim and Greg show up with a couple of other hikers, and another party breaks out before we realize it. Beer and food follow, and it's nearly 9:00 pm when Little Bus announces he's ready to leave and puts on his boots.

"You can't leave this late!" I say.

"Sure, I can hike out of town and at least get to the next shelter."

"Little Bus, that's crazy at this hour," Greg says. "You may as well stay the night and hike out early in the morning." I silently thank Greg for trying to talk some sense into him.

After lobbying from five hikers, Little Bus relents and removes his boots and pack. Since we're exhausted, we head up to sleep around 10:00 pm, intending to wake up early.

At 8:00 am, we wake up and head downstairs for breakfast. We call friends and family, play a few more games of pool, and drag ourselves away from the legendary Doyle just before noon, complete with stories for me to tell my kids someday.

On our way out of town, we stop to get ice cream and chat for a few minutes while devouring our cones. "I love all the flowers around this town," I say, commenting about the flower-lined streets and the care the homeowners take in making their properties so pretty.

"I love the flowers, too," Little Bus agrees. "One day, I'll plant flowers all over the yard for my future wife."

As we leave town, I point out my favorite flowers, just in case he plants those flowers for me.

The extra day off in town has done nothing to heal my leg. I limp up the trail, trying unsuccessfully to keep up with Little Bus. As usual, he gets ahead, and I hike by myself. After five miserable miles, I hobble into the Clarkes Ferry Shelter. My eyes are red and swollen, trying and failing to hold back my tears. I'm mad that I can't keep up with Little Bus. I'm furious that I'm injured. I've never been in this much agony before. And I can't go on.

"Little Bus, I need to stay here. I'm sorry," I say, nearly in tears.

"I know. I was hoping you would come skipping up the trail, and it breaks my heart to see you limping in here, obviously in so much pain."

I sit at the picnic table, and Little Bus and I chat for a little longer.

"Here," he says as he hands me his coveted deck of playing cards. "Maybe this will keep you busy while you rest and heal."

He hugs me, hoists his pack, and waves goodbye as he hikes up the trail. I hold my tears until he's out of sight, and when I'm finally alone, I can't stop the river of tears from flowing. I look up at the sky and cry, "God, Greg, Grandma, I don't know what you have planned for me, but it better be good."

CHAPTER FOURTEEN

MISSING

July 1998

I'm bored to death. I've played Solitaire at this shelter for 24 hours. I've played this game since my grandfather's Aunt Jo taught me how to play as a child. It's fun for a while, but nobody plays for a full day unless they can't physically do anything else and need to keep their mind from spinning out of control into the abyss. When will I be able to hike again?

Lemmondrop walks into the shelter today, and she's pretty sure I pulled my hip flexor muscle. She tells me to use my Lexan water bottle as a hot-water bottle, warm my muscle for 20 minutes, then massage it, and repeat. I have my stove set up so I can reheat the water occasionally. I warm, massage, and repeat all day long, in between strategically placing cards in their correct order and suits.

I pull out my guidebook and maps to figure out a plan. I can stay here for one more night, but then I must hike out tomorrow, or else I will run out of food. There are a ton of people hiking behind me, but they were out of my sight because I had tunnel vision for Little Bus. The one benefit of slowing down is that hikers whom I haven't seen in a while are coming in. Wayah gives me the rubber tips off his hiking poles so that I can put them on mine, and I won't slip on the rocks so much. Adam also comes in; a Marine I haven't seen since Pearisburg about six weeks ago. I'll try to be better friends with everyone going forward.

Soon the day is here, and I must hike on whether my leg agrees with me or not. I've been warming and massaging my leg like an obsessed pre-game athlete, so I hope it's ready. After just a few feet on the trail, I cry out loud and realize that my leg hasn't healed with one day of rest.

Every step makes me cringe aloud. I am still hiking at two miles per hour, but the pain in my leg is unbearable, and I scream to the world.

"WHY IS THIS HAPPENING TO ME? WHY CAN'T I HIKE LIKE A NORMAL PERSON? WHY DO YOU ALLOW ME TO HAVE ALL THESE INJURIES? WHAT THE HELL ARE YOU TRYING TO TEACH ME? TELL ME! GRANDMA? GREG? I WANT TO KNOW WHY I'M OUT HERE, ENDURING THIS AGONY!"

I don't get an answer. I can do one of two things. Fall down on the trail and stay here forever or keep moving. Really, there is no choice. So, I stagger up the trail.

I arrive at Route 225, stop, and consider hitching a ride into town. There aren't any cars on the road, and I'm too tired and frustrated to pull out my map to determine if the nearest town is to the left or the right. I feel sorry for myself for 30 minutes and then get up, dust myself off, and hobble toward the Peters Mountain Shelter, still three miles away.

I make it to the shelter in 90 minutes. This place is enormous; it has two levels, a few picnic tables, and can easily sleep 20 or more hikers. The only problem with the shelter is that the water source is about 500 feet down the mountain. I'll cross that bridge when I come to it. It's Sunday, July 12, and I've decided to stay here until I run out of food, which should be about Thursday. Then, I can hike six miles until I reach Route 325, and then perhaps call my parents and have them get me.

I make myself comfortable, and every day, hikers come in from Duncannon, and many leave me some extra food. I receive cans of tuna, packets of rice dinners, packs of tortillas, candy, and energy bars, and luckily when hikers head down the trail to get water, they take my bottles with them, so I haven't had to get to the water source yet. It looks like I'll be okay on food for a little longer than expected.

It's nice when hikers come in, so I have some company, but it gets boring in the morning and afternoon when everyone is hiking. On the upside, I've won all the versions of Solitaire, even the games that seem impossible to win. Nothing is impossible if given enough time.

There is a week-old newspaper here, but I've already read it cover-to-cover. I take short walks around the shelter to prevent my muscles from getting too cold. The privy, a trail word for outhouse, is about 150 feet away, and it sometimes takes me 10 minutes to walk that far. I try not to go to the bathroom too much to make those trips minimal.

Today is Tuesday, and although my original plan was to hike out Thursday, the receipt of extra food keeps me here longer than expected. Other hikers are giving me first aid supplies and painkillers like Arnica tablets and Advil. It appears that I can stay here a little longer without starving to death. I write a letter to my parents, explaining where I am, and give it to a hiker who will mail it in a few days when he passes a mailbox in Port Clinton, the next town we would get to on the trail.

A lot of hikers come into the shelter today, including Lobo and Pacemaker. I haven't seen Lobo since Harpers Ferry when he got off the trail to meet up with Pacemaker for a while. Pacemaker confirms my injury.

"Yep, Trail Gimp, that's your hip flexor that's injured. I pulled my hip flexor years ago when I was in gymnastics, and it took six months to heal! But I continued to compete, so that's why it took so long."

This leg might take six months to heal? Six months? I don't have that kind of time!

I wake up Thursday morning and still have plenty of food. It seems that word has gotten out to the thru-hikers that I am injured and stuck at this shelter, and most people are bringing me a little extra when they leave town. I've been here for five days and haven't needed to go down to the water source either. Hikers really do take care of each other. I'm writing a letter to Little Bus when I hear someone running on the trail, getting closer to the shelter.

I look up to see a girl, around high school age, wearing running attire and trail running shoes. She has blonde hair pulled back into a ponytail, and she's athletically trim with long, lean legs.

"Hi, I'm Katie. I live around here. I like to practice running on the trail for my track team. I heard you were up here and thought I'd bring you some snacks. Here are a few bags of peanuts for protein and a big bag of M&Ms just for fun. I hope this helps a little."

"Oh, thanks so much. That's so nice of you. I'm Trail Gimp, but my real name is April. I understand about running the trails. I used to run track in high school, and I was an assistant track coach when I taught school. Are you the one who brought that newspaper?" When she nodded, I added, "Oh, thank you. It's been helpful to read about the real world while I'm stuck here, trying to heal my leg a little."

"You're welcome. I'll plan to come back tomorrow or the day after. Aside from a newspaper, is there anything else you want?" I tell her that other hikers are taking care of me, but I thank her for asking.

"Okay, well, I'll bring you some good snacks anyway. I've got to get home, but let me take that trash out of here for you. I brought a bag for it." I fill the bag with whatever trash has accumulated, and she gives me another one to use. She leaves, telling me she'll see me in a day or two.

It's around 5:00 pm, and since I'm starting to get hungry, I look through my food bag, trying to figure out what to make for dinner from the random assortment of food I've received. I hear some noise outside the shelter, and a man with a huge backpack walks in and empties his pack by dropping two coolers on the picnic table and a large bag of groceries. "Are you Trail Gimp?"

Nodding, I answer, "Yes, I am."

"Well then, these are for you. I'm Dean. I ran into your friends Cool Rabbit and some others at Route 325, and they told me you were injured and stuck here. Well, no hiker is gonna starve on my watch, so I've brought you three or four days' worth of food, and a 12-pack of ice-cold Pepsi, including a bunch of ice. Here's my name and number, and if you need more food or anything else, you have someone call me. It doesn't take me long to hike in here."

I'm speechless. Somehow, I manage to say thank you and take his contact information. The local people who maintain the trail and take pride in helping fellow hikers are amazing.

It's Saturday. Katie returned yesterday with a newspaper and snacks as promised, so I spend a quiet morning reading the paper and catching up on what's happening in the real world. I heat some water to take a sponge bath and wash my hair since it's been an entire week since I've showered, and I feel pretty gross. After getting as clean as possible by bathing out of a pot, I spend the day writing letters to Little Bus and my friends in Charlotte. Waves of hikers are making their way through the area, and it's nice to see some familiar faces, like Growler, Wandering Bear, Hawkeye, Minnie Pearl, Tree Hugger, Got Milk, and The Family!

I love The Family, and their story, which I've picked up from trail registers over the past few months. Suzy is the mom. Her trail name is Suches 75. She attempted to hike the trail back in 1975 but quit when she got to Suches, Georgia, which is only 20 miles from the beginning of the trail. She always wanted to return to the trail, but with five home-schooled kids, a husband, and a farm, she never had the time. After hearing her stories of the trail, her kids decided to study extra long so they could take time off to hike together as a family while Dad stayed home to mind the farm. They range in age from 10 to 22 and are all amazing people. I can't imagine being 10 or 11 years old and thru-hiking the Appalachian Trail.

It's now Monday, my ninth day at this shelter. Technically, hikers aren't supposed to stay in a shelter for more than two days. It's trail etiquette to allow room for other hikers, and it prevents people from using them as homeless shelters. I keep practicing my hiking, walking up and down the trail for 30 minutes at a time, but I always end up wincing in pain and hobbling back for another dose of Advil and a hot water bottle.

As I'm making lunch, I hear some noise and a familiar voice exclaim, "Trail Gimp! What are you still doing here?"

I look up to see Allgood, my 1996 hiker friend I saw at the ATC headquarters in Boiling Springs. "Hi, Allgood! I'm okay. I have a pulled hip flexor muscle or ligament; I've heard it called both. Anyway, I've been staying here, trying to heal up. How did you know I was here?"

"The office in Boiling Springs heard that someone was living in this shelter, so I hiked up to see what was happening."

"Crap! I sent my parents a letter explaining my injuries, but they must not have received it yet."

I explain to Allgood how the other hikers and locals have been giving me food, so I'm not starving, just trying to buy some time to heal up.

"Okay, Trail Gimp. You know the rules for staying in shelters. How much time do you need? If you can't hike on your own, I'll need to call in a helicopter to evacuate you."

"Oh, Allgood, a helicopter? Really? That's crazy. Okay. Today is Monday, and I promise I'll leave on Wednesday. Can I have two days to prepare?"

"Two days. I'll give you two days. But I'm coming back to check on you. I'll call your parents and tell them you're okay, and that you'll call them when you get to a phone. Deal?"

"Deal. Thanks."

Wednesday arrives quickly. I pack everything and prepare for the next few days. I've memorized the upcoming sections of my guidebook this past week, anything to keep my mind off Little Bus. I don't know if I'll ever see him again, as I'm sure he's hiking big miles to catch up to Jingle and Desperado. Missing him is wearing me down, so mentally, I'm trying to let him go. I just can't figure out why I'm still alone. Almost everyone has their trail family by now. I'm friends with many people, but I don't have 'my people'. Nightgrumbler and Sugarfoot left; I can't keep up with Little Bus, so I wonder what's in my future.

My leg is sore and tired, but it's not painful. I hike at a snail's pace, about a mile and a half per hour. I stop to take a bath in an ice-cold stream, and after a long rest, I end up hiking and camping at the top of a mountain. I must have walked faster than I thought because I completely missed the spring. I'm now camping for the night with a total of 16 ounces of water.

I use four ounces to make dinner and another four for breakfast. I leave camp in the prime summer heat with one cup of water and eight miles to get to another water source. Of course, I immediately ration my water and scold myself for missing the spring, as I've done before. *Idiot!*

I've been hiking for two hours, and I scan the landscape with every step to look for water. I step over a small mud puddle but stop a few feet later. Was that puddle...*moving?* I retrace my steps and locate a small brown puddle, only three or four inches in diameter. I lean down to look closer, and the water appears to have a little flow. I take off my pack, get on my knees, pull a few leaves out of the way, and stare at it until I realize I'm at a tiny, unmarked spring. I scrape some mud out of the way to form a small pool and find the little area from which the water flows.

It's still a bonafide mud puddle, so I grab my water filter, add two coffee filters to the pre-filter for "extra" filtration, and begin to filter water. After a few minutes, I have a quart of fresh, crystal clear, icy cold water, which I guzzle almost all at once. It is easily some of the best water I've ever had. I filter two more quarts and write a note on a piece of paper that I attach to the nearest tree, writing, "Spring", with an arrow pointing to the little pool I created. Maybe that will help someone like me in the future.

I stop at the next shelter to sign in, read the register, and leave notes for anyone wondering where I am. There is a hostel ahead, and as much as I need to hike to get some miles in, I should get to a phone to call my parents. I run into George sitting at a picnic table. He's a hiker who came through the Peters Mountain Shelter a few days ago. He looks confused. George hiked from Georgia to Duncannon back in 1991 at the age of 70. Seven years later, he planned to hike the rest of the trail. Sadly, he admits that the demands are too much for his body to handle. He wants to go home, but he thinks he has missed the trail to the hostel. I tell him to follow me, and we walk into the hostel together. The owner, Ann, is happy to see me.

"I'm so glad you came by. I've been keeping an eye out for you."

"How did you know I'd be coming?"

"Everybody is looking for you! Apparently, when you didn't call your parents from Delaware Water Gap as expected, they called that Post Office and confirmed that you hadn't picked up your mail drop yet, and they knew you hadn't taken any money from your bank account. Not knowing what to do, they called the Pennsylvania State Police, who advised them to call the local Park Ranger, who told them to call the regional ATC in Boiling Springs. They told them you were long gone, as you went through town weeks ago. But then someone called your mom back to tell her you were injured. They gave her my phone number, and she called me here to see if you had come by yet." She hands me the phone and says, "Please, call your mother now."

Phone in hand, I take a deep breath and dial my worried mother. "Hey, Mom, I'm so sorry for not calling earlier. I sent you a letter to tell you I'd be taking some time off, but apparently, you haven't received it yet."

"Where the heck have you been? I've been worried sick. I was told you sprained your ankle or something. Are you okay? Do you need us to come to get you?"

"I'm fine now. I pulled my hip flexor muscle, and it hurt too much to continue hiking. I was only going to take a day or two, but everyone kept bringing me food, so I wasn't rushing to leave. I'm still hiking, slowly, but I'm okay now. Tell Dad there's no reason to worry." I continue to tell her about my plans to get to Port Clinton and Delaware Water Gap and that I would call when I get there.

I'm back on the trail, hiking my own hike. I'm alone, but I run into various friends. My leg can't decide whether it's okay or injured. Sometimes it doesn't give me any problems at all, but sometimes I cringe in pain whenever I move it. It's a deep, internal pain where my leg meets my hip. The rocks in Pennsylvania aren't helping; sometimes, I slip off a rock or accidentally kick one with my boot, causing a shock wave to reverberate through my leg into my hip. It usually ends with some four-letter words unintentionally being screamed to the universe.

I stop at a clearing to drink water and rest my leg for a few minutes. I look for the next white blaze to show me where the trail is, but I can't find it. I wander around in circles until I finally see a white blaze on a tree and begin to walk down the trail. The area looks familiar, but I follow the blazes anyway. After 10 minutes, I see a hiker named ZigZag, and he asks, "Trail Gimp, why are you hiking south?"

"South?"

"Yeah, you're hiking the wrong way."

Exasperated and frustrated at wasting time and energy, I turn around and continue. When I reach the clearing again, I'm still stumped as to where the trail goes, and ZigZag has already disappeared. The clearing is surrounded by trees, without a clear path coming or going through them. I see a pile of rocks in one area, but I don't see any white blazes on them. I waste more time wandering in circles, and I'm so angry I start screaming obscenities at the top of my lungs to the universe. I yell, scream, throw my hiking poles, and throw a giant temper tantrum.

"Gimp, what seems to be the problem?"

I look over my shoulder to see Purple, who had walked into my meltdown without me seeing him.

"I can't find the freakin' God Damn trail, and I've wasted an hour getting lost already! My leg is freakin' killing me, and I'm not sure how much I can take of this," my voice rising in anger again.

"Well, it's got to be here somewhere." He walks to the rocks and adds, "Here, the trail is this way."

I walk over to where he's standing, and there, right before my eyes, is a 2x6-inch white rectangle painted onto a rock, indicating the trail. If I had taken one step further, I would have seen it the first time I was looking.

Now I'm embarrassed. I'm 28 years old, and I just threw a giant temper tantrum because I couldn't find the trail, and Purple, who is 19 or 20, walks in on me and then shows me the way within seconds.

"Thanks, Purple. I appreciate your help. I guess I'm just having a bad day. Sorry about my temper tantrum," I say, feeling foolish and stupid.

"It's okay, Gimp. It happens to everyone. I hope you have a better day. I'll see you up the trail," and he takes off on his hike.

Lesson learned. Temper tantrums don't solve problems; they only prevent you from finding the solution.

I hit another legendary thru-hiker institution yesterday – I stayed at the Palmerton Jail. Legend has it that the local police department allowed hikers to stay in empty jail cells. Nowadays, they have bunks in the basement for thru-hikers, but it's a clean and safe place to stay, with hot showers.

Today, as I climb out of Lehigh Gap, I see a bunch of kids hiking, perhaps 10-12 years old, so I follow them up the cliffs. Their shirts indicate they are with the local YMCA. I'm climbing behind a kid named Mike, and he's falling further and further behind his group.

"This hiking sucks! I hate this. I'm never gonna catch up," he whines. He reminds me of some of my fourth-grade boys that just needed a little extra love and attention.

"What seems to be the problem?" I ask.

He looks at me as if he didn't expect anyone to answer him or care about what he said. "Nothing," he mutters.

"Well, I'll tell you what. I'm April." I can't use my trail name. I'm no longer in trail mode, I'm in teacher mode. And Trail Gimp isn't a teacher, April is. "I've been hiking slowly because my leg hurts. Why don't we hike together for a little while? We'll keep your group in sight, but I won't leave you alone, deal?"

"Okay."

"What's your name?"

"Mike."

"Well, Mike, can I ask you a question? Is that your backpack?"

"No, I borrowed it from someone," he says while looking away. "We're hiking overnight, and I don't have my own pack." He seems embarrassed at not having his own pack.

"I understand – hiking gear can get pretty expensive. That's smart of you to borrow it before spending the money on something you may or may not like. I noticed, though, that your pack is swinging around a bit. Can I help you adjust it, so it fits you better?"

"You can do that?"

I instruct Mike to take off his pack, adjust some straps, and help him put it back on while adjusting the straps more to fit him better. The pack fits his hips better, taking the weight off his shoulders, and it doesn't swing around anymore. "How's that? Feel a little better?"

"Yeah, that's much better. It feels lighter too. How did you do that?"

"Well, I've learned a lot about hiking and adjusting packs since I started my hike in Georgia a few months ago."

"You started in *Georgia? Georgia, the state?*"

"Yes sir, I'm thru-hiking the Appalachian Trail, and since I injured my leg, I've been limping, so I've fallen behind a bunch of my friends too... So, I know a little about how you feel. The important thing is just to keep going. So, let's go."

We walk up the trail, and when his counselor returns to find him, I introduce myself and tell him I don't mind hiking with Mike for a while. It turns out we are all hiking to the same shelter anyway.

Mike and I hike together for several hours until we reach the shelter. He joins his group with a big smile and, presumably, an enormous sense of accomplishment. Groups of campers aren't supposed to stay in the shelters, so they are tent camping while I set myself up in the lean-to. I run into Mike again while getting water at the spring, and he thanks me for the hundredth time for helping him today. He insists on carrying my water bottles and filter for me all the way back to the shelter.

After dinner, the YMCA group creates a small fire, and we sit around, talking about the trail and what we learn from hiking. I answer a hundred questions about the Appalachian Trail. When did you start? How many miles a day do you hike? What do you eat every day? Do you wear the same clothes every day? What did you do to your leg? Why are you limping? Why do you hike with poles? What do you do when it rains? Why are you walking to Maine when you can drive there instead? When do you think you'll finish?

It's nice to talk to the kids. I still love teaching, but not in a classroom setting, I guess. I hope I helped Mike in some way. He seems a little more confident than he was this morning. He's not complaining, and he's talking to his friends. He even smiles and laughs a little.

If I can help someone with my experience of limping for hundreds of miles, I guess it's worth it.

CHAPTER FIFTEEN

MAKING MILES

August 1998

The song "Daydream Believer" that I heard at the Iron Mansion's hostel is still stuck in my head, and it's finally driving me batty. I run into Delaware Water Gap for a night in a hostel, eat some great food, and eventually, I break down to buy a radio – I'll do almost anything right now to get that song out of my head. I'm just about to cross the border from Pennsylvania into New Jersey.

I stop at Super Walmart. After spending so much time on the trail and in small towns, my senses are overloaded. People are *everywhere*! Children are running and not listening to their screaming parents; the loudspeaker calls for price checks, additional cashiers, or people who have wandered away from their kids or parents. People weave in and out of line. This place even has a McDonald's in the back of the store. It's loud and obnoxious. I just want my tiny radio.

I'm not sure if the radio is helping or not. I didn't spend the extra few dollars for a digital display, so every few steps I take, it switches to a different radio station. One minute I'm bouncing along to Bon Jovi, and in a few steps, that cuts out, and I'm listening to some country crap. Either way, The Monkees are out of my head, so it's still a win.

I've looked at my guidebook and tallied my days on the trail. I've been on this trail for four months and have taken 33 zero-hiking days. That's over a month of no-hiking. Some of that was for my Grandmother's funeral, and some was from staying in the Peters Mountain Shelter, but still. According to my notes, I've hiked 1,271 miles, but I still have 890 miles to go and two and a half months to hike them. That's 356 miles per month or 12 miles per day. It doesn't seem like much since I've been hiking around 15 miles every day, but 12 miles per day is without any days off. I have to catch up and put in some miles to ensure I make it to the end of the trail, at Mount Katahdin, before October 15, the day Baxter State Park closes to the public.

The Rangers will still allow thru-hikers to enter the park and climb Katahdin, but only with permission, which depends on the weather. I've heard stories of hikers waiting for a week or more for good enough weather to finish their hike. If you try to summit without permission after the park closes, you will be billed for rescue efforts if you are stuck on the mountain for any reason. Helicopters can be crazy expensive, so I have my deadline, and I must hike. As much as I'm limping, I limp fast. I'm averaging about two and a half miles per hour, which is good with a leg that won't lift.

I'm not sure why I insist on limping and continuing in such pain. I've already quit my career and given up my apartment. If I stop hiking, I don't know what to do or where to go. And I don't have much money left. Finishing the trail will give me some sense of accomplishment, I hope. After all, there haven't been too many people that can say they've thru-hiked The Appalachian Trail, and only a fraction of them are women. Perhaps that will show everyone that I can accomplish *something*.

Today, I will get to Kathy's parent's house. She grew up not far from the trail in a small town called Central Valley in New York. Most people know it as the home of Woodbury Commons, a shopping center with over 250 designer outlets, located an hour north of New York City. Her parents still live here, so they invited me to stay with them. I find a pay phone on the side of the road, and once I call Mr. Morgan, he's here to pick me up within minutes. Mrs. Morgan hugs me and then throws me into the shower, taking all my clothes to wash and giving me some of Kathy's clothes for the interim. It's interesting being in Kathy's house without her or her brothers, but her parents treat me like one of their own kids, even going so far as to call the local rangers to make sure there are no fires that I needed to worry about. I've never heard of forest fires along the trail. Only a dad would call to make sure.

I call my parents to update them. They knew I'd call them from Kathy's house because I'm only a two-hour drive south of them. It turns out that they have a party to attend in New Jersey tomorrow, so they invite me to come along. I can meet them in a parking area on the Palisades Parkway, just off the trail.

In the morning, I leave my pack at Kathy's parents' house and slackpack through Harriman State Park, enjoying the flowers, trees, blue skies, and the freedom of walking without a pack. Miles fly by until I get to The Palisades Parkway. This is the most dangerous road crossing along the trail. You walk out of the woods and bump into a road with two lanes of traffic flying south. Although there is a 55 mph speed limit, let's face it, it's New York City traffic, and few people drive less than 80. I run as fast as I can to the median, which is densely covered in trees for about 50 feet, then get to the northbound lanes. Thankfully, I don't have to cross these today since I'm meeting my parents at a rest area only a few hundred yards away.

I turn left and walk the median until I see a parking lot and find my parents waiting patiently for me. They know I'm limping, but I think they are a bit shocked by *how much* I'm limping. They haven't seen me since Grandma's funeral, so I think they are a little shocked by my appearance. My hair has been in a ponytail for months, my clothes, although clean, have developed a gray-ish color, my arms and legs are scratched and bruised from bug bites and run-ins with tree limbs and rocks, and my big, bulky leather boots are worn and battered. Although I've lost some body fat, I've gained a lot of muscle. One woman I met at the Mohican Outdoor Center referred to my legs as "tree trunks," and although I'm sure she meant it as a compliment because of the muscle I've developed, going from "chicken legs" to "tree trunks" is a bit of a hit to my self-esteem.

"Oh, it's so good to see you, April!" Mom cries. "You look so tired. Are you okay?"

I take turns hugging my parents and answer, "Yes, I'm fine." *I've just walked over 1,300 miles. What did you expect me to look like?*

They drive me back to Kathy's house, and our parents talk while I shower and repack. Then, it's a huge dinner at a restaurant and a party. Most people wear dresses and suits, and I walk in wearing my cleanest shorts and camp sandals. It's what I have, and I'm okay with it.

Mom and Dad take me to a local outfitter to buy me a few things, ensuring I have enough food and plenty of supplies to keep me safe. I walk out with some fancy freeze-dried food, including ice cream, new socks, a platypus hydration system, waterproof solution and shoo-goo to repair my boots, and some other odds and ends. I'm excited about my Platypus. Instead of filling quarts of water and stopping to grab my bottle, unscrew the top, take a drink, and return the bottle to the pocket of my pack, I have a large bladder that I fill with filtered water. The bladder sits atop my backpack, and a hose hangs down near my mouth. When I need a drink, I just bite the valve, and water flows. When I've had enough, I stop biting. It's so simple, and I'm sure it will make me hike faster.

They also give me my new sleeping bag. Unfortunately, when Kathy took my winter sleeping bag home, she kept it in my car. Somebody broke into the car and stole it. Kathy was mortified and was afraid to tell me. It was a synthetic 20-degree bag, but had a down liner that added 20 degrees, effectively turning it into a zero-degree bag. I actually loved the liner more than the bag itself, so after some back-and-forth conversations with my parents and the outfitter at home, they bought me a Western Mountaineering 20-degree down bag. It's my new favorite thing in the world.

My parents drive me back to the Palisades Parkway, where I can pick up the trail again exactly where I left off. We have a lot of leftover cake from the party, and muffins from breakfast, so Mom decides to give it all to the hikers coming through. The only way we could think to surprise hikers was to put smaller pieces on individual plates, wrap them up with plastic wrap, and put them in plastic grocery bags and hang them at eye level from the trees, with a note on them that said, "for any hiker, from Trail Gimp's mom." Mom and Dad give me a hug, tell me to be careful, and thrust some money into my pocket. Just in case. I tell them I'll be fine, and I'll call them when I get to the next town.

I finally arrive at Bear Mountain State Park. I can see the skyline of New York City through the haze, and many people living there are in the park today. I swear, I've never seen so many people in one pool at one time. When I finally reach the zoo, I almost cry.

The trail meanders through the center of the zoo, so I finally get to see some animals that are elusive on the trail. But seeing a bobcat, three bears, two foxes, and other animals in cages breaks my heart. I want to unlock all their cages and set them free. I see children gawking at the bears, and I want to scream at them. Don't *you know that bears are beautiful wild creatures with fuzzy butts who are supposed to be scared of humans?* I saw one bear in the Shenandoah Mountains, but he ran away when he saw me. I saw his fuzzy bottom running into the woods to avoid detection. These animals don't belong in cages.

One of the things about speeding up a little is that I catch up to some people. I've met scores of hikers along this journey so far, and it's nice to chat with everyone and make new friends, even if it's just for a few days. Some friends tell me they are planning to spend the night at the Graymoor Friary, the home of the Franciscan Friars of the Atonement. They invite thru-hikers to spend the night in July and August. Check-in time is from 3-5 pm, and dinner is served at 5:30, but it already 3:56 pm and I still have 5.4 miles to get there. I hope they will accept me if I'm late.

I'm trying to hurry but I think I'm lost. I took a right onto an old road about 20 minutes ago, following some white blazes. I can't see many white blazes ahead of me, but I see them on the back side of the trees when I turn around. I know this is the trail. I keep going, and then I see the remnants of a white blaze, *scraped off* a tree. Damn it! The trail *used to go* this way, but must have been rerouted some time ago.

I turn around and walk back to that intersection, and yes, there, across the street, is a double white blaze, indicating a turn, and more white blazes painted on trees, indicating the trail. I have no idea how I missed that. I'm mad at myself, and worse, it cost me almost an hour of time. My legs hurt and I ran out of water on top of the mountain, but I manage to drag myself into Graymoor at about 7:00 pm. I wander around parking lots, trying to figure out which way to go, when I finally run into some hikers.

They show me the way, and I'm introduced to Friar Pius, who takes me in. I've missed dinner. Niteyes and Hopwood are going to find some food, so they offer to grab me some dinner. I throw $20 at them and head inside and go to my room. This place is not like any other hostel. I am expecting a bunk room, but no. I have my own room with utilitarian furniture, but I have *real sheets* on my twin bed. I feel like I am back in a college dorm. There is a long corridor of rooms, and shower rooms, bathrooms, and a laundry room are located at the end of the hallway. Monkhead is doing laundry and offers to throw my dirty clothes in with his. I just came from visiting Kathy's parents and mine, but I grab the opportunity to give him whatever clothes need washing. I run to the showers, change into clean clothes, and anxiously await dinner.

Niteyes and Hopwood finally show up, apparently after an escapade. They walked all the way to the deli, only to find it closed. They came back to Graymoor empty-handed, and Father Pius exclaimed, "Well, she can't go hungry! Let's go." He drove them into Peekskill, where they found an Italian restaurant, and they brought me back a chicken parmesan sub sandwich. I finally sit down to eat, and though the homemade sauce and melted cheese make it messy, it's the most delicious sub I've ever had. The tender chicken nearly melts in my mouth, and I grin with euphoria and joy. Life is good.

Breakfast is served in a giant dining room filled with round tables seating eight. The hikers sit together, and we discuss the joys and privileges of staying here. I've been here for all of 12 hours, and already, my mind and soul are improving. This is one of my favorite places ever, and I feel welcome here.

The friars don't charge a fee, but donations are accepted. I put some money into the donation bin, and I vow to send another donation once I'm home and working again. This was a surprising treat, and I feel like $20 isn't nearly enough.

It's comforting to be with a group of hikers again. I've caught up with a bubble, and it's almost like a party at the shelters every night. We're close to towns almost every night, so there is usually some town food we can eat instead of the same old tuna fish and noodles.

There are celebrations as we cross state lines as well. The trail in Virginia is about 500 miles long and takes roughly five to six weeks to traverse. Pennsylvania is only 233 miles, but still takes a few weeks because of the rocks. Alternatively, New Jersey, New York, Connecticut, and Massachusetts total 302 miles collectively. It finally feels like we're making miles.

I'm about to get comfortable at The Mt. Algo Lean-to as we enter Connecticut, and a bunch of friends drag me along, saying, "C'mon, let's go into town and grab a beer!"

It's Thursday in Kent, Connecticut, and there's already a veritable party at one of the local bars. We make ourselves comfortable, drinking beer and watching a local band belt out covers of classic rock music. I know I'm supposed to be hiking a wilderness trail, but we've entered New England, and we're really hiking through the woods instead of a "wilderness". I have a feeling we'll be visiting more towns more frequently in the next few weeks.

I call my mom to update her on my whereabouts, and she tells me that Little Bus has called her a few times to check up on me. Initially, he called because he heard that I was off the trail. He's glad to know I'm okay and still hiking. He called her once more when he was in North Adams,

Massachusetts, to update her on his maildrops so I could send him letters or postcards if I wanted. Mom invited him to stop at her house for a day to rest, but he never did. Too bad. I was hoping he'd fall in love with my family and then with me by default. I know I'm not hiking with him, and I have a lot of other hiker friends, but I think about Little Bus all the time. He leaves me some notes in the registers, and I see the messages that Desperado and Jingle leave for him, planning for him to catch up to them and planning possible summit dates. I need to stop thinking about him, but I don't know how yet.

Since we've entered New England, the distances between towns have shrunk. Instead of carrying four to six days' worth of food, I only need about three days, on average. Many farm stands are near the trail, and farmers often allow thru-hikers to pick a quart of blueberries or blackberries at no cost, so long as we respect their crop and clean up our mess. Additionally, stores and convenience stores are readily available, and often a random diner or restaurant along a road. It's a joy and surprise to walk along the road to find a restaurant and have someone else make a fabulous gourmet sandwich instead of the usual canned tuna fish on a dry bagel.

The problem with so many towns and restaurants is that I have difficulty *being* in the woods because towns are often so close and easily accessible. To make matters worse, once I enter Massachusetts, I feel like I'm "home". I'm now in areas where residents can watch the same news broadcasts I've grown up watching. Being so close to home makes me miss the comforts of home, so I call my mom and dad and ask them to pick us up. I've been hiking alongside a woman named Hawaii for a few weeks, and she comes home with me to rest for a day.

I considered myself home since I was in The Berkshires, a place often talked about on the news in the weather reports. Apparently, I'm further from home than I think because it takes my parents two hours to pick us up. They thought I was quitting and coming home; they are a bit shocked and annoyed when I tell them we just need a day off, and most of the Inns in the Berkshires are too expensive for thru-hikers to afford.

We spend a busy yet relaxing day at home, visiting my Grandmother's grave, cleaning all our gear, and planning the rest of our hike while my friends and relatives pop over to visit. The time off allows my leg to rest since I haven't had any days off in almost a month, and I'm still limping. Hawaii is resting and is thrilled to have a soft bed to sleep in. I had forgotten that it is the middle of the week, though, and since most people work, I need to find someone to drive us back to the trail in Massachusetts. My Aunt June is the only one not working and reluctantly agrees to make the trip.

Massachusetts is beautiful. I have my first experience with an Appalachian Mountain Club hut atop Mount Greylock at Bascom Lodge, where thru-hikers can spend a nominal amount of money to sleep on the attic floor or in bunks, or wherever they find space. Shelters are different than lodges. Shelters are basic wooden structures with a sleeping platform. Appalachian Mountain Club lodges or huts are *hotels*. Bascom Lodge is open to anyone and is relatively popular since one can drive to the summit, the highest point in the state. They offer hot and cold breakfast and lunch, and for those that plan ahead, dinners as well. There is a seating area with rustic but lovely furniture, akin to a small hotel lobby, a reading area with used books one can borrow, and a small gift shop with just about anything you need to purchase. It's warm and inviting, especially on a cold, drizzly night like tonight.

I'm looking forward to the hut system in the White Mountains of New Hampshire. The huts are fairly expensive to stay at, but they allow thru-hikers a work-for-stay so that you can get a nice, hot meal and a warm bed for an hour or two of work. The problem is that they only allow a certain number of hikers to do that, so you must get there early and leave a little later, after your chores.

At Mount Greylock, I feel like I've actually walked home because, after my failed hike in 1996, I came to this area to offer trail magic to hikers.

I'm also not far from where Luke, from Charlotte, lived before moving down south. I have an odd sense of feeling closer to him, just being in the area he lived before I met him. I still think of him and talk to him, but no more than any of my other friends in Charlotte. Usually, when I call Leah and Kathy, they pass the phone around so I can talk to anyone else with them. They all seem impressed that I've made it to New England. Perhaps they expected me to quit and come home, so my determination to finish is exciting for them.

I'm beginning to miss my friends a lot. I love the friends I'm making while hiking, but my body is getting sore. I hope I can make it another 500 or so miles to Katahdin. I'm in Manchester Center, Vermont, and I've been to this town countless times when I lived in New York. It's an interesting town because there are scores of fancy outlet stores. I've been in the Baccarat outlet many times, ogling over the gorgeous crystal stemware and dreaming about which pattern I might want in the future. I don't even think of entering the store today. Why would a hiker need fancy crystal stemware? I don't wish to have shop staff give me any dirty looks over a "you break it, you bought it" rule. I walk by the store but gaze longingly at the window displays.

Little Bus leaves me a note in the register atop Bromley Mountain. I get a thrill when I find a note from him. I know he just wants to be friends, but I'm pretty sure I can get him to love me if he knew the real me. But if I can't catch up to him, I guess it's a moot point.

I walk into The Inn at The Long Trail today and feel like I'm making progress. I've passed this place dozens of times in years past, often driving to Woodstock or Quechee, Vermont. I'd never been inside before, but the Irish bar's friendly bartender and warm atmosphere persuade us to stop for food and drink. We have another small gathering here of eight or nine hikers. Hawaii and I get a room for the night upstairs in the Inn. This place is better than The Doyle, though it could still use a remodel, updated to at least the last decade. It's also my dad's birthday, so I call home to chat with him and everyone else at the house for the party. Since I'm on a phone, I also call Kathy and Leah. I think I'm running up their phone bill by calling them collect all the time because they don't seem to be thrilled by "accepting the charges" anymore. I will have to give them some extra money when I finally finish and get back to Charlotte. Still, it's nice to chat with everyone and update them on my progress.

We leave in the morning and plan to meet at the second shelter, 18 miles away. It's a beautiful day with clear blue skies and ponds to admire when we pass. Once I hit the woods, I smell the fir trees and stick my face into the needles, inhaling the unmistakable scent of a Christmas tree. People call me a tree hugger, and they aren't wrong.

I have a few miles left before I get to the shelter to meet Hawaii and a bunch of others. I arrive at a sign that points to the Lookout Cabin. It's privately owned, but it's only about 100 meters up to the top of the mountain, and I heard the view was worth it. I climb the last few feet and gaze in wonder. Atop the mountain is a rustic cabin. It doesn't have any furniture; it's a shell meant for camping, but it has a tower that offers almost 360-degree views, and the view from the front of the cabin is beautiful in itself. There is a register here, and Tulie, another hiker, said she would have stayed here if she had enough water. I have a snack and regret the fact that I, too, must leave.

But why? Why must I leave? I have plenty of water. I remember a passage Evergreen had written in a register sometime back: "Don't let shelters rule your life." And I had been doing precisely that. I would plan my days hiking from shelter to shelter, not considering the location or scenery.

That's it—time for something different. I am going to stay.

The guidebook says that the cabin is off limits because it's locked, but the door is unlocked with a note that invites hikers to stay, as long as we respect the property and clean up after ourselves. Deal.

I set up my sleeping area, grab my food and go outside to cook dinner. I eat outside, admiring the Green Mountains before me, the Adirondacks to the West, and the White Mountains to the East. I look to the Adirondacks and wonder which ones I've climbed in years past, and then look to the Whites, imagining where in those mountains Little Bus might be. I imagine owning this little cabin as I watch the sunset while dreaming about my future.

Tonight is the first time I've camped alone in a long time. I miss my friends, but I relish the quiet and spend time writing in my journal, admiring the stars, and picking out my favorite constellations. This cabin is a perfect place. Reluctantly, I pull myself away from the view and turn my headlamp off to get some sleep.

I wake at dawn, and I see a sunrise I'm sure I'll never forget. The sun is flame-red, which turns the clouds and sky into various shades of pink and red. Mountain peaks stand tall amid a sea of fog collecting in the valleys. I savor the solitude of a quiet morning.

I know I will finish my thru-hike.

I'm standing on the bridge over the Connecticut River, which divides Norwich, Vermont, and Hanover, New Hampshire. Dartmouth College is located in Hanover, and I've read countless Appalachian Trail books and magazines that discuss Dartmouth and the Dartmouth Outing Club.

I always knew I would get here someday, but when hiking in Georgia, New Hampshire is so far away, you might as well be talking about the moon. I wonder if other hikers have this epiphany. Through all the hardship and doubt, injuries and emergencies, do other people have a moment when they *just know* they will finish? And now I'm here.

I'm here! I can't hide my excitement and jump and scream as much as I can with a gimpy leg. As much as I know I'm Trail Gimp, I know I'll complete my thru-hike at Katahdin in 454 miles.

CHAPTER SIXTEEN
APRIL, MEET TRAIL GIMP

September 1998

I'm excited about being in New Hampshire. I love seeing college campuses, and Dartmouth is one for the record books. The Ivy League college has beautiful architecture and plenty of open areas for students to gather. A few fraternity and sorority houses allow hikers to stay in their houses or on their covered porches for free or with a small donation. It's a safe place to sleep and drop your gear while exploring the small town. Many of the hikers I know stay here, but a few stay at the Hanover Inn.

I'm used to paying a few dollars to stay for the night. The Hanover Inn costs *more than 200 dollars per night!* It's an impressive, four-story brick hotel with all the amenities of a four-star hotel. I'm a little jealous of the luxury those hikers can afford, but I remind myself if I'm looking for luxury, I wouldn't be on The Appalachian Trail.

I stash my things at the Alpha Theta house and run into town to do errands, like buying food at the local grocer and checking out the local outfitter for gear I don't need and couldn't carry anyway. What would I do with a cool new fleece? Or an updated version of my water filter? All my stuff works perfectly fine. I stop at the post office to gather mail and smile when I'm handed a postcard from Little Bus and Jingle. They sent me a note from Mount Washington a week ago. I won't be there for another two weeks.

When I took two weeks off the trail in Pennsylvania, I met so many hikers, and now I'm catching up to some of them. It's comforting to hang out with hikers I've known for so long, some of them since Georgia, like Growler. We talk about how walking into Hanover has affected our mental status.

"I feel like I'm finally making progress," one hiker offers.

"I can't believe we've walked through 12 states. We only have New Hampshire and Maine left," says Wandering Bear.

"I finally know I'm going to finish," I said. "I wasn't sure before, but now, I know."

"Gimp, we all know that you'll finish," Growler adds. "We've learned that nothing is going to get you off this trail. You've been limping since when? North Carolina? You were limping at that farm in Erwin, Tennessee, and I don't think I've ever seen you without a limp since the beginning. You don't give up."

It's nice to know I have people encouraging me.

Two days after leaving Hanover, I'm trying to make 19 miles to the Atwell Hilton tonight. It's an old house owned by the National Park Service, but hikers can camp on the lawn. Dizzy B is a local trail angel and often brings water to the hikers.

I run into Wandering Bear on the trail and pause at the intersection of the side trail that leads to the Hexacuba Shelter. It's supposed to be a cool shelter designed by a physics major and built by the students of the Dartmouth Outing Club. I'm curious about its architecture and design. Mathematically, hex means six, and a cube has six sides, including a top and bottom, so would this shelter have six sides? I'm curious to know. But the real reason for my interest is to see if Little Bus left me another note.

Wandering Bear heads up the trail, telling me he's heading to the Atwell Hilton. He heard that Dizzy B sometimes brings beverages other than water. I glance toward the shelter, knowing I will get comfortable and probably stay the night if I get to the shelter. And I want to go to the Atwell Hilton.

That's it! I'm tired of spending extra time going to shelters to look for notes from Little Bus. He's almost done hiking the trail by now, and I'll probably never see him again. Get over it, Gimp. Move on.

I switch directions and head north on the AT. *Sayonara Little Bus! Catch you in another lifetime,* although mostly trying to convince myself that I mean it.

The Atwell Hilton is another glorified party. Dizzy B brings water, soda, and lots of beer, and we sit around the campfire, roasting marshmallows, swapping stories, and drinking just a little. It starts to rain, so Wandering Bear and I illegally camp in the house. I'm not sure if the building is condemned or just off-limits to hikers, and I semi-carefully weigh the consequences of sleeping in the rain or remaining dry but possibly being crushed to death by a building collapse. Figuring that the chances of a building collapse are remote, I opt to stay dry and throw my sleeping bag on the floor.

In the morning, Wandering Bear and I wake up early and leave the building, hoping to be out before any surprise inspections by the park service. Once more, we sit around the fire before he gets picked up by some friends, and I move north. I'm headed seven miles to Glencliffe today to meet up with Catherine. She and my late grandmother have known each other for decades, and our families have been friends throughout the years. I haven't seen them since I moved south, so when they heard I was hiking the trail, they *insisted* I stay with them for a night or two when I got to this area.

I see Catherine waiting for me near the post office, and she gives me a giant hug and ushers me into her car.

"Oh my goodness, that backpack of yours looks so heavy! How much does that thing weigh?" Catherine asks.

"Oh, I'm not sure. With my winter gear, maybe about 45 pounds?"

"Oh, there is no way I could survive. You young people can do anything," she laughs.

She takes me home, feeds me dinner, and suggests I take a long, relaxing bath. It's a simple luxury I have not had the time to enjoy recently, and I soak in a tub of bubbles until my skin is clean and wrinkly. I get to bed early and sleep for nearly 12 hours.

When I wake up, I realize I have the entire day to relax. My body likes the rest, and my leg thanks me for not carrying 45 pounds up and down rocks all day. I spend the day with Catherine's daughter Debbie, and her daughter, going out to lunch, watching movies, resupplying, and being spoiled and doted on by a substitute grandmother. I realize today is only my second day off in 957 miles since my time off in Pennsylvania.

I must continue hiking, and Catherine drops me off at the trail. It was nice to be spoiled. I hug Catherine goodbye and then head up the path for the long climb up Mount Moosilauke. At 4,802 feet, this is the first mountain to ascend above treeline, so I'm both nervous and excited. I haven't been above treeline since I hiked in the high peaks of the Adirondacks in New York before I moved down south. The trail is easier than I expected, but it's a long climb uphill. Usually, I like to spend a few minutes at the summit of mountains, resting and enjoying the scenery. Today though, it's only 40 degrees with sustained winds of about 30 mph. The clouds have come in, and I can only see a few feet in front of me. I hurry to the shelter to get warm.

I'm snug as a proverbial bug in my sleeping bag, along with eight other hikers. I'm finally able to meet Mountain Dew. He's been ahead of me on the trail, and I've read his journal entries. It's nice to put a face to the stories, finally. Hawaii is here, as is Victory Gallop, a hiker I've met a few times in the past two weeks. One of the guys here has a radio, and we're listening to some music, all quiet in our bags and watching the rain fall. I sent my radio home weeks ago; I got tired of hearing a new station every time I hiked another 50 feet. And it lightened my pack by about three ounces.

In the morning, it's still raining, ensuring it will be a crappy day. I plan to hike 15 miles to Lonesome Lake Hut, an ambitious and perhaps stupid goal. I must remember that I'm in the White Mountain National Forest now. These mountains are no joke; the weather can change quickly, it can snow any time of the year, and most hikers slow their pace as they navigate the rocky and difficult terrain.

I descend Mt. Moosilauke slowly, and I immediately wonder if my 15-mile goal is too lofty. I slip on wet rocks, grabbing tree branches to prevent myself from falling into the stream, now a raging torrent threatening to end my life if I so much as step near the edge. I step into a mud puddle and sink halfway to my knee. I am soaking wet from head to toe.

My knees burn, my feet ache, and my muscles are sore from hiking over and around boulders, trees, and roots. It's difficult to keep my balance, never knowing if a puddle will swallow my boots again. And all of this is in the first 30 minutes this morning. I get a reprieve at the road crossing in Kinsman Notch, only to immediately ascend the next mountain.

I'm in pain and I gasp for air, and I'm acutely aware that all the miles I've hiked have not prepared me for what I'm about to encounter this week. I trip over rocks and tree roots, slosh in puddles, and my stomach growls. I need to rest and eat, but the ground is full of puddles and too wet and muddy for me to sit on. I stop for a minute to catch my breath and immediately get cold. I can see my breath in the frosty air. This cold and wet weather is the kind that causes hypothermia. I *must keep moving; I have to stay warm.* Instead of resting, I thrust my hand into my backpack, pull out a dry bagel, and move on. I gnaw on my lunch and imagine the nice, hot meal I can cook once I arrive at the shelter.

I see the sign for the shelter after seven miserable hours. The smart thing to do is to abandon my plan and stay here. It's 3:40 pm, and the September daylight will soon fade to dusk. My hope of a warm, dry shelter slowly disappears; every step reveals another tent, indicating the shelter is probably full. General trail etiquette states that when it rains, the shelter is full when everyone is in it. But there are limits, and this one is clearly past its limit.

I collapse on the edge of the shelter and drop my pack on the ground. It's generally quiet – hikers in their tents stay to themselves, locked in their sanctuaries. Some people in the shelter are sleeping; some are reading, and others chat in low voices. Nobody discusses the weather. After hiking 1800 miles, nobody wants to hear anyone complain about the rain and cold.

I need food quickly, but with a crowded shelter and everything outside so wet, there's no room for me to set up my stove. Cooking is not an option, so I pull out another bagel. I collect and drink water from the rain dripping off the shelter roof. I want to squeeze out my spongy socks, but what's the point? I eat and relax for 30 minutes while contemplating my options. The other hikers tell me to stay.

"Trail Gimp, just set up your tent and stay safe. You'll get to the hut and dry out tomorrow."

"Don't even attempt to climb Kinsman in the rain. Stay put. Safe is better than dead."

Setting up a tent in the rain is less appealing than the hut six miles up the trail. It's 4:00 p.m., and I should be able to hike the distance before it becomes completely dark.

But it's raining, which will slow my progress a bit.

But I just ate and refueled my body.

But I don't want to slip on the wet rocks and get hurt.

Well, I've been limping for three months already, so it's not a big deal.

But it's getting colder, and I don't want to risk hypothermia.

But I don't want to set up my tent in the rain. And the hut will be warm and dry, and there will be hot food waiting for me.

The last argument is enough for me. I hoist my pack, bid farewell to the other hikers, and walk away from the shelter, their pleas for my sanity growing faint with every step.

Within minutes, I realize they might be right, but the lure of the hut won't allow me to turn back. The guidebook prepared me for Eliza Brook, a gently rolling stream, perhaps a few inches deep. I'm unprepared for the torrent of water reaching my knees, nearly toppling me over. My hiking poles help me balance, and I concentrate on moving one foot at a time, planting each boot squarely and evenly on a slippery and uneven bed of rocks, stone, and moss under a foot of rushing water before moving the next foot. Crossing a stream that should have taken ten seconds takes five minutes. I ignore this warning and continue to climb Kinsman Mountain.

The rocks are slick, the path steep, and I move slowly, stoically, each foot secure before moving the next, as if guided by an unseen force. I can't see the summit or the grandiose view. I see a few feet of rain and my breath as I climb up the narrow, precipitous trail.

I hear voices. Some hikers appear through the mist, descending, propelled by gravity. I move a few inches to let them pass, and they tell me I still have quite a way to reach the summit. How long have I been climbing? Fifteen minutes? An hour? Time is standing still. The other hikers complain of weary legs, aching knees, and heavy packs. For some reason, I notice nothing. My feet are warm, my legs solid, my lungs strong, my pack light. I climb, hand over hand, stepping slowly but surely. I hear my grandmother's voice. *"You have this, April. You'll be fine."* The hiking becomes easier, the slope less steep.

I'm suddenly at the South Peak, though it's gotten darker, and it's still raining. Another ascent, and I'm at the top of the North Peak. I hear my cousin's voice. *"Keep going, April. You'll be fine."*

Thirty minutes later, I arrive at a campsite. Common sense tells me to stay here and set up my tent. The hut is still two miles down the mountain. I consider the benefits and perils of staying or moving forward. *It's barely above freezing. The sun has set. But if I wanted to stay in my wet tent, I would have stayed at the last shelter. I've come too far to give up now.*

What time is it?

I make a deal with myself – if it's later than 7:15 pm, I need to stay and set up my tent. My watch reads 7:13 pm. Stay or go? It's taken three hours to hike four miles. I have two miles left.

Should I stay or go? Stay or go?

I hear the word "GO" and run down the trail. I slow when I reach the rocks. Oh, this is dangerous. *Oh shoot – this is steep, really, really steep. Be careful. Oh God, please don't fall. Please be careful.*

I descend slowly, holding onto every wet, slippery rock. My hip flexor is still not fully healed, and my leg begins to shake from the exertion. I shake with every step. Yet, somehow, I don't feel it. No pain. I'm wet but warm. My knees should ache, but they don't. I find strength I didn't know I had.

The trail is completely dark except for the dim light of my headlamp. Step down, step down again, one more time. Repeat. I don't know how long I'm descending. How long is this mountain? What time is it? I hear my grandmother's voice again. *"Soon, April, you'll be there. A few more steps. Be patient."* I trust in something I know nothing about. I keep moving. Downhill. Slowly. The trail becomes less steep, and then, like a mirage, I see a light in the distance. It's there, and then it's not. What is that? *Am I finally going crazy?* The light is a beacon that pulls me forward. I feel warm and strong. I move on, propelled by that unseen force. It's not a choice. I just move.

I emerge from the woods to a clearing, realizing the light is the hut. I walk toward the door and hear, "Trail Gimp, is that you? It's so late. Get in here before you freeze to death!" Victory Gallop welcomes me in through the back door. A croo member, someone who lives and works at the hut, brings me to a room with warm blankets and a dry bed, where I collapse from sheer exhaustion. I'm warm. I'm safe. I'm grateful. It's 9:40 p.m. I've taken 13 hours to hike 15 miles today.

I change my clothes and head back to the main room. Dinner is long over, but I can use the kitchen to make food, and the dining room has a cozy wood stove and several tables to plop down to eat. Other hikers tell me how foolish it was to hike this section of trail in one day, especially since I've been injured for so long. But I don't feel like I made a choice. After Eliza Brook, I never felt the cold, the rain, my pounding heart, or the aches in my knees and legs. Nothing. I wonder if perhaps someone was guiding me today, holding my hand and keeping me safe. Maybe Aunt Jo or other relatives who have passed on? My Grandmother and Greg, for sure.

I head back to my room, snuggle under warm woolen blankets, and thank my angels for keeping me safe. I fall asleep instantly.

Victory Gallop giggles when I see him in the morning. "I can't believe you made it into the hut so late last night!"

"It was a miserable day on the trail. I could only repeat 'get to the hut' over and over again," I said.

"How did you manage Kinsman in that horrible rain with your leg?"

"Honestly, I don't remember it. It may sound weird, but I don't think I was in control. I heard my cousin's and grandmother's voices a few times, telling me to continue slowly and that I would be safe. I didn't feel the cold. I wasn't out of breath. My legs and feet didn't hurt. It was the weirdest thing – I can't put it into words."

"I understand. Sometimes the universe speaks in different ways. I'm sure your relatives were looking out for you from the other side."

The calendar demands that I leave the sanctuary of the hut. If I want to get to Maine, I must push on. On the way down the mountain, I have to rock-hop across a river, proving that my leg still has some additional healing to do. I can't land on my left leg since the jolt from landing reverberates up and through my hip, but I have difficulty pushing off from that leg to land on my right leg. How can I rock-hop across rivers if I can't jump?

I suffer through it, slipping more than a few times and cursing just as often, and I wonder if it would have been easier to just slog through the river and get wet. Everything in my pack is still wet, so I hike into North Woodstock when I hit the road. I immediately walk to the laundromat to wash and dry everything I own and let out a big sigh of relief once I have dry clothes again. I run into more than a dozen hikers in town, most of them smart enough to get off the trail yesterday in that awful weather and enjoy a day in town. According to everyone I speak to, I've just about caught up to most people who came through the Pennsylvania shelter.

I hike halfway up the ridge and camp at a small area designated for tents, then continue to hike the Franconia Range in the morning. I've been nervous about this section of trail for years; the mountains are all above 4,000 feet in elevation, and most are above treeline, so hikers are exposed to the weather for most of the range. The views are amazing, and I can see mountains all across New Hampshire. The Presidential Range spreads out in front of me. It looks like I can run from mountain top to mountain top in a few minutes, but I know this section will take several days.

I hike above the treeline, admiring the views, and then descend again into the trees and rocks of another mountain. Progress is slow. I spend hours scrambling up and down rocky trails below treeline, then remove my pack, put my fleece and rain jacket on, and since I don't have gloves, I throw a pair of expedition-weight Smartwool socks over my freezing fingers. Once out of the elements, I get too warm, remove my pack and rain gear, put my backpack back on, and continue. Repeat all day.

I pull myself up to the top of Mount Garfield, and at 4488 feet, is one of the most challenging climbs I've done so far. I emerge to see Gumby and Grasshopper, Niteyes, Birdman, and one other hiker I've never met.

"Hi, everyone!" I exclaim between gasping for breaths.

"Trail Gimp! How did you get here? My goodness, which parts of the trail did you skip to get here?" asked Niteyes.

"Skip? I didn't skip any parts."

"You had to have skipped some miles to catch up."

"No, I just kept hiking slowly. I've only taken two days off since I've last seen you."

I don't think they believe me. No matter. I remove my backpack to eat a snack and enjoy the awesome view. I get cold again, and I hit the trail and book it to Galehead Hut. I hope to get a work-for-stay option, as spending $50 or more every night will be painful for my wallet. As an expert cleaner, I'm allowed to help clean dishes after dinner and the bathrooms in the morning before I leave. It's a fair deal.

As I leave the hut, I have some urgency in my step, as my parents are meeting me down at Crawford Notch for the night. It's still 15 arduous miles away, but I can't wait to see them. I love my parents, and I especially love that they are bringing my replacement boots since mine are falling apart. I have duct tape wrapped around my boots, preventing my soles from falling off.

I had planned to meet them on Mount Washington, but hiking plans don't always work out perfectly. Dad is a bit of a science nerd like me, and he's looking forward to getting to Mount Washington. I know he needs to plan it for the weekend when he's not working, so mom and dad are actually on Mount Washington today, and they'll drive around and pick me up before dinner.

I stop at Zealand Falls hut for lunch, grab a few snacks that don't have the word "granola" or "bagel" in the title, and head back down the trail. I reach Crawford Notch, and since my parents aren't here yet, I use the free time to catch up with my journal writing. Mom and Dad drive into the parking lot as I finish my final sentence.

I walk over to hug them and throw my pack into the car. Phew; I'm done carrying that for a day. They whisk me off to a restaurant down the road, where I stuff myself with luxuries like french onion soup and baked stuffed shrimp. It's a far cry from the Lipton noodles and tuna fish that are daily staples in my diet.

After dinner, Mom says, "I'm sorry, April, I love you, but you stink. We're heading to a laundromat to wash everything you have." And with that, we find ourselves in a little place where she takes everything except my rain gear and throws it into the washing machine on *hot*, and then, before I can stop her, she adds *fabric softener* to the load.

"Mom! You can't wash some of these things in hot water, and fabric softeners will attract bugs and animals. That stuff is awful!"

"Well, we need to do *something* to remove that smell!"

I know there is a slight smell of sweat embedded in the fabric of my clothes, but it's really not that bad. I can't stand it when she exaggerates like that.

My clothes are clean, dry, and scented, which makes me gag, but mom is happy that they smell "a little better." They take me back to the hotel room, where we get comfortable and ready for bed. As I'm cuddling up under my blankets, I hear my mom sniffing the air like a German Shepard.

Sniff. Sniff sniff. Sniff, sniff, sniff.

"What is that *smell*?" She sniffs her way across the room until she reaches my backpack.

"Oh, no, this is NOT staying in the room with us. This is gross!" She takes my backpack and puts it outside the room into the hallway.

"MOM! You can't leave my pack out there! Someone might take it."

"April, trust me, NOBODY is going to take a pack that smells like that. But I can NOT sleep in a room with something that smells that bad. You're lucky I don't make *you* sleep in the hallway."

I sigh, pray that nobody takes it, and fall asleep.

CHAPTER SEVENTEEN

CONQUERING FEAR

September 1998

Mom and Dad drive me back to the trail after a hearty breakfast, and I stare out the window at some cliffs. "I'm glad I don't have to hike up *those!*" My goal is Mizpah Hut, only six miles up the trail, but the guidebook says the trail is relatively steep and to adjust mileage accordingly. If I can get to Mizpah Hut early enough, I hope to get another work-for-stay option.

I begin climbing, and as I look back over Crawford Notch, I realize I am on those appalling cliffs I saw from the car. They looked vertical from down below, and although they are steep, there is a slight grade to them, so I don't feel like I'm going to fall off a cliff.

I reach the summit earlier than expected, so I sit down, eat a snack, and guzzle water. I begin hiking again, following the white blazes, and realize I'm only halfway up the mountain. The trail follows a completely different direction than I thought. Ugh!

I climb, hand over hand, scrambling for the next place to put my hands to help me balance and pull myself up. My hiking poles are getting in the way, so I collapse them and hang them from my backpack, which only irritates me more as they clang against my legs.

Who the hell located the trail up this section of cliffs? I swear the trail designers are masochists. Why would they do this? Suddenly, I'm stuck on a rock. I can't find a place to put my hand to pull myself up. I don't see any place I can put my foot and climb a little. I see one tiny flat section to the left, a few feet away, but my left leg doesn't have the strength to get there.

I look around for white blazes and see a few to the left, about fifteen feet away. *How did I get off the trail?* I see places where climbing would be easier, but I am stuck here. I can't move over there because I can't *reach* anything.

I'm stuck.

I start to breathe faster, and I can feel my pulse in my clenched hands. What happens if I fall off this cliff?

That's kind of a stupid question, don't you think?

What happens if I try to jump up to that handhold and miss?

You will fall and probably die.

It's that simple. I take some more deep breaths to calm myself down and contemplate my position. I'm a few thousand feet in the air, clinging to rocks, and I can't move. I have a 50-pound pack pulling me backward toward certain death if I let go of this rock. I try once more to reach a stone above my head to pull myself up and get closer to the white blazes, but I panic, afraid I won't be able to reach it and get comfortable once more on the rock.

I've been stuck here for 20 minutes. Instead of getting upset, I think. *Come on, April, think! You have a few choices.*

Right. I can go back down the trail and go home. This option is unappealing after hiking 1800 miles already.

I can let go, fall off the mountain, and plummet to my death. This option is very unappealing.

Or, I can find a way up the trail. Somehow.

As I'm deciding what to do, I think of Earl Shaffer. He is the first to complete a thru-hike and is hiking the trail this year again on the 50th anniversary of that hike. I saw him in Hot Springs, and the man is *ahead* of me. How did he make it up this trail at 79 years old?

Trail Gimp finally emerges. *Fine. If Earl Shaffer can climb these cliffs, so can I.*

I look for that rock that I was too afraid to reach. I reach up with my right hand, pray, and with every ounce of strength I can muster, I push my body with my left leg and jump up to grab that rock with my right hand. My right hand and leg are momentarily off the mountain, and I pray to every relative I have in heaven. *Oh please, Greg, keep me safe. Please, Grandma, make sure I don't die. Please, oh please, oh please.*

My hand reaches that rock while my foot naturally finds a place to land.

Oh my God. Thank you. Thank you, God, for not letting me fall. Thank you, thank you, thank you.

Slowly, and by praying a lot, I manage to reach the top of the Webster Cliffs.

I drop my pack at the top, grab a snack, and thank everyone for keeping me safe. I rest for half an hour to calm my heart and allow my legs to stop shaking. *I'm safe.* I can't believe I made it up those cliffs. I can't believe I didn't die. How many other hikers have the same feeling along the trail? I only saw the hind end of a bear in the Shenandoah National Park. What would I have done if it charged me? Have other hikers experienced that? I remember back in 1996 when I camped with The Accident Waiting to Happen, Squirrel, and Drew at the base of Siler Bald in North Carolina in a thunder and lightening storm. We were terrified we would get struck by lightening or have a tree fall on us. I was so grateful in the morning, *and relieved*, to be safe. The fear is real and the relief is real. I wonder how many more times it might happen in the next 340 miles.

Finally, I'm up and heading for Mizpah Hut. Luckily, I arrive in time to receive a work-for-stay exchange, and I offer to clean the bathrooms in the morning since I'm great at that, and it's the job that nobody wants.

After dinner, I go outside to enjoy the stars and talk to some other hikers. The remote location, without any light pollution, enables me to see more stars and constellations than I've ever seen. I feel like I can reach out and touch them.

The hikers I'm talking to aren't thru-hikers but are out for a few days.

"Where are you headed?" they ask me.

"Katahdin."

"You're trying to get to Mount Katahdin from here?" another asks.

"Yeah, I'm thru-hiking and will finish at Mount Katahdin next month."

"Oh, you're never going to make it, especially walking around with a limp like that. The trail is too hard, and you've only got a month to get there. Why don't you just go home and finish next year?"

"Yes, exactly, I have an entire month. I've been limping since Georgia, for the most part, and I know what I can and can't do. I'll make it," I retort.

"Well, I think that's a stupid decision. I've hiked that section before, and I know how hard it is. Do yourself a favor and go home."

"Well, I'll certainly take that under advisement. Now, I'm going to head to bed; I have a long day tomorrow. Goodnight."

What a bunch of assholes. Now the only thing they've done is piss me off and make me more determined than ever to get to Katahdin. I'll show them. Jerks.

I wake up early to eat and clean the bathrooms and knowing it will be a busy day, I leave the hut and hike the ridge, heading to Mount Washington. Then, I run into the following sign:

Well, that sounds inviting. The trail to Mount Washington is full of rocks and stones, mainly granite. There is some high-altitude vegetation to the sides of the path, and the rocks on the trail are worn from thousands of hikers climbing them over the years. I can see for miles with the clear skies. I don't think I could have asked for a better day to climb Mount Washington.

Slowly, step by step, I reach the summit. A tourist takes my picture for me, and I run inside to grab some food from the cafeteria.

An old-fashioned cog railway transports tourists and supplies to the summit several times per day. Since it's a beautiful day, tourists are everywhere. There are lines in the cafeteria, lines in the weather museum, and lines to get pictures in idyllic places. I meander through the crowds, sending Kathy and friends a postcard from the post office in the building. Today is September 14. Little Bus was here on August 27, more than two weeks ago, when I was not even halfway through Vermont.

I rest for a few hours and move on because I still have six miles left to get to Madison Springs Hut. Staying at the hut is a crapshoot because two days ago, the hut closed to the public for the season. A croo member from Mizpah told us that Madison might have some work-for-stay options because they are cleaning up from the season and may need some help.

I run into some friends on the way to the hut. The cog train passes before us, and though it's a thru-hiker tradition to "moon" the train if it passes you, I opt to keep my clothing intact and push forward. Some of the other hikers follow tradition, turn around and drop their drawers, to the horror of some passengers and the amusement of others.

The trail is not difficult, following a relatively flat and slightly downhill path to the hut's front door. Thankfully, the croo open the doors to thru-hikers, allowing us to stay at no cost in exchange for helping with inventory.

By the time evening rolls around, 18 of us volunteer for inventory duty, and because they had already cleaned the bunk rooms, we lay our sleeping bags in the main dining area like a giant slumber party. We inventory all the kitchen utensils and supplies. What would have taken the croo a few days to inventory has taken all of us less than two hours.

The morning brings rain and clouds. The croo turns on the radio to get updates from the weather observatory located on Mount Washington:

"38 degrees with visibility of ten feet." We erupt into laughter at ten feet of visibility. Yesterday while I was at the summit, it was a balmy 50 degrees with 90-mile views. We were so lucky.

I leave Madison Springs Hut early, and the trail crosses giant rocks and boulders. On a nice day, this might be fun. Today, it's a death trap. My poles slip on the rocks and get stuck in crevices between them. The rocks are wet, and my boots continually slip. My leg has gotten worse over the past week with the rocky terrain, and I hike slowly, trying to prevent myself from falling and breaking a leg. Growler passes me. Wandering Bear and Hawkeye pass me. Skiddah, Jackrabbit, Flint, Gumby, Grasshopper, Niteyes, and 30 Seconds all walk by me.

The rain turns to sleet, and the rocks become more dangerous. I'm hiking downhill now, so gravity is pulling me, and I am scared to death I will slip and tumble down the mountainside.

Almost eight treacherous miles later, I drag myself into the Pinkham Notch Visitor Center. I throw my pack on the ground, get food from the visitor center, and sulk.

Today just sucked. It's cold, and although the rain and sleet have stopped, the staff tells me there may be thunderstorms tonight. Most of the hikers from last night are here as well, and since the price for a room is a tad pricey, many have their tents set up in a designated area near the center. I follow their lead and set up my tent.

"Hey," a croo members says. "A bunch of us are going down the road to a bar to see a band play. Do any of you want to come along? We can drive you back here afterward if you're interested."

I'm exhausted and grumpy, but perhaps a night on the town is just what I need to cheer up. Seven of us clamber into two cars along with the hut croo, and they drive us to a local Inn with a bar. We eat, drink, and dance to the band until one in the morning, and we finally head back to our tents.

A night out is just what I needed. I had fun, I let loose, and I'm hiking the trail to have fun and meet people. I hang out with some friends at a campfire and chat with them for a few more hours. I collapse in my tent at 4:00 am.

For some unknown reason, I wake a few hours later at 7:15, so I take the opportunity to head to the breakfast buffet. I leave around 9:30 with a slight hangover and begin climbing Wildcat Mountian. The only good thing about this difficult hike is the weather; it's beautiful. Sunny skies allow endless views. It's mid-September, and the deciduous trees have just started to change colors. The maples are turning red, oak trees are turning orange, and birch trees are turning yellow. The colorful mix with the evergreens is a sight to behold. Other than that, I would highly suggest that everyone NOT attempt one of the most infamously difficult climbs on three hours of sleep with a hangover. Progress is slow.

I intended to get to the Imp shelter tonight, but it's getting dark, and I hiked a tad slower than expected. I'm about to reach the summit of North Carter Mountain, and I stop when I see the easterly views all the way to the ocean. I sit down, pick out the lights of Portsmouth, and stare off into the great black space that I assume is the ocean, about 90 miles away. On the mountainside behind me, I see the lights and summit of Mount Washington perfectly positioned between two spruce trees. It's an incredible view.

Screw the campsite. I'm camping here on a slab of rock.

The trail is only a few feet wide, but I'm positive nobody will pass by at this late hour. I set up my stove to cook a hot dinner, then use my tent as a bivy sack over my sleeping bag for extra warmth since the trail isn't wide enough to set up my tent. I sleep as far to the right as possible, snug against some rocks, and put my pack on my left side as a wedge to prevent myself from rolling a thousand feet off the mountain. I alternate gazing at the lights of Mount Washington with the lights in the valley until I can't keep my eyes open anymore.

I wake early to a glorious sunrise, a giant yellow orb illuminating the distant ocean and every tree in the valley and up into the mountains. Growler, Hawkeye, Grasshopper, and Gumby eventually pass me, commenting on the gorgeous yet slightly dangerous choice of campsite. I finish hiking down the trail and celebrate a little when I reach Gorham. I survived the Whites! I can't believe I made it through the Whites, limping the way I have been.

I spend a day at a hostel called The Barn, resupply and do laundry, and then I begin The Mahoosuc Range. The guidebook says the Mahoosucs are more complicated than they appear, but I'm pretty sure nothing can top those White

Mountains. I camp at Gentian Pond Shelter with Victory Gallop and O'Tim and head out in the morning. I have an excited little bounce in my step, as today is our last day in New Hampshire. I should be in Maine by lunchtime.

The guidebook is correct – the Mahoosucs suck. The trail is cruel. There isn't one flat section of trail for miles. I slip on rocks, trip over tree roots, and slog through mud. I am out of breath, and my leg is shaking from exertion, even after hiking 1900 miles. The rocks are wet, the mud sticks to my boots, and I slip on the moss that coats every rock and fallen tree limb on the trail. I yell and scream about how much pain I'm in and how this trail sucks.

I climb up a huge rock, then slip and fall on my butt. My water bottles fall out of my pack, tumbling to the bottom on the other side, and I follow them, sliding and ripping my shorts while my hiking poles twist and strangle my wrists. I land with a thud at the bottom of the boulder. I pull myself up, find my water bottles, and stagger a few feet until I see a clearing. I throw my pack down, sit down to sulk, and look up to see a sign:

Yeah? Fuck You, Maine!

CHAPTER EIGHTEEN

THE BEGINNING OF THE END

September-October, 1998

I sit at the New Hampshire – Maine border to have lunch, and just as I'm about to leave, I hear a thud, followed by some loud cursing, then a sound I assume to be a water bottle careening to the base of that giant rock, and then Niteyes tumbles into the exact spot where I landed. He is followed by 30 Seconds, Grasshopper, and Gumby, all slipping down that rock in some form or fashion.

We collectively complain about the terrain and finally head out to begin the state of Maine. We have 281 miles to go!

I'm nearing the Mahoosuc Notch, which I've been both excited for and dreading for years. The Mahoosuc Notch is at the base of two mountains. Rocks and boulders have fallen to the bottom through the millennia, piling up on one another. The Appalachian Trail traverses this mile-long section, going over, under, around, and sometimes, through the chaotic maze of house-sized boulders and car-sized rocks, with a few trees thrown in for good measure. It's an obstacle course of epic proportions.

Once I reach the beginning, I scream aloud to the world, "TRAIL GIMP IS IN THE NOTCH!" I hike through the first section, unexpectedly enjoying the challenge. I catch up to Niteyes, 30 Seconds, Gumby and Grasshopper, Longdrop, and another couple who camped with us last night. We are now eight people going through the notch at one time.

Hiking with others is much easier than going through this alone. We push each other, pull backpacks through crevices when we crawl under boulders in tight spaces, and lift or pull each other over boulders. Surprisingly, this doesn't hurt my leg. I need to swing between boulders occasionally, so I use my arms more than my legs sometimes. Someone before us placed full-sized, wrapped candy bars in the cracks between the rocks, free to anyone willing to take the time to fish them out, so I feel like a winner with a few candy bars in my pockets. It's also cold in the notch, with ice in some crevices year-round, as the sunshine can't penetrate this far down.

It takes two hours and four minutes to emerge victorious from the most difficult and notorious mile of the entire Appalachian Trail.

I've hiked some rugged terrain the past few days, and I'm running out of supplies, so I take an unscheduled stop in Andover. A local guy happens to be driving by as Growler, Wandering Bear, Hawkeye, and I emerge from the woods, and he takes us into town. I remember a couple I met in North Carolina – Honey and Bear. They were hiking the trail initially with the express point of promoting their new hostel in Andover. I hunt down the information they gave me over five months ago, and as soon as I talk to Bear, he comes out to pick me up.

Bear is retired, and he and his wife, Honey, love to hike. Bear is not quite 6 feet tall, with gray hair and a short beard and mustache to match. He wears jeans and boots, and usually wears a knit cap and a fleece jacket. He has a twinkle in his eye that makes you wonder what he is up to. Honey is about 5-9, a few inches taller than me. She has short, wavy blonde hair and always smiles and laughs. She wears sweatshirts and shorts, revealing strong legs. I don't know if she is of Norwegian descent, but she looks like she could fit right in with my family. She reminds me of several of my aunts.

They recently decided to add a hostel to their house called The Cabin. They are still building the bunk room, so for now, hikers share spare bedrooms or sleep wherever they can. I'm comfortable with Bear immediately. He's a kindred spirit, and I feel like I've known him for years. We arrive at his house, and Honey greets me like I'm her own daughter.

They see me limping and ask about my story. I give them an abbreviated version, and they say, "Oh, no, we have room, and you're sleeping in a real bed, not a bunk room or the floor." They show me to a bedroom and instruct me to put my things there. "We just upgraded our bathroom, and we have a jacuzzi! I bet a nice, hot jacuzzi will make that leg of yours feel better! But don't tell everyone; we don't allow all hikers to use our private bathroom."

I don't know if they are blowing smoke up my butt or if I am unique, but they sound sincere. I soak for over an hour, allowing dirt embedded in my kneecaps and palms to find freedom. I haven't been this clean since I stayed at Catherine's house two weeks ago! Honey and Bear have a collection of clean clothing in all different sizes, allowing hikers to wear something clean while washing every bit of their clothing. My clothes go into the washer, and Honey shows me the phone, so I can call my parents.

After a hearty dinner, I collapse into my bed.

I wake up in the morning to coffee, juice, eggs, bacon, sausage, toast, and fruit on the table. Bear says, "Help yourself, Trail Gimp. Hey, do you want to slackpack today? I'm bringing a couple of guys up to East B Hill Road. I can drop you off there, and you can slackpack south, then I can pick you up at Grafton Notch when you finish if you want to spend another night here."

It's the best idea I've heard in a while.

I eat and hurry to get dressed. Hiking without a pack is easier on my leg, so I walk for the day, thoroughly enjoying the scenery and weather. Today is September 22, and it is full autumn in Maine. The trees are a mix of reds, yellows, and oranges, with evergreens scattered throughout. The air has a crisp, clean smell, and I feel *free*. I feel like I'm out for a casual walk today, taking my time meandering along the trail without a care in the world.

Back at The Cabin, I make myself at home. Fric and Frac are hikers I've bumped into several times, and they are making dinner for all the hikers tonight. More hikers come to The Cabin, and we sit around talking for hours.

Once again, Bear offers to slackpack me, but with a twist. Skiddah and Jackrabbit join me, and Bear hands us the keys to the truck. "Here you go – how about you guys drop Trail Gimp off at South Arm Road, and she'll hike south while you two leave the car and start hiking from East B Hill Road. When you meet up with each other, hand the keys to Trail Gimp, and she'll get the truck and drive up to pick you up where she started. How's that?"

It's not a new truck, but I can't believe Bear is giving us the keys. The hiking community is like that.

I spend four glorious nights at The Cabin, calling friends and family every night and slackpacking for 10-15 miles every day. Although I'm still hiking, I'm not carrying my 45-pound pack, so my legs get a little reprieve for a few days. I walk faster without my pack, so I spend less time hiking and more time relaxing, which both mind and body need. There are other hikers who join us over four days, including Earl Shaffer, for one memorable night. He borrows Jackrabbit's guitar and entertains us for hours, playing and singing, reciting his poetry, and talking about the trail. I feel much better when I hear he's not thrilled about how difficult the trail has gotten.

When Earl first hiked, the trail traversed many forest service roads and private property from Georgia to Maine. As The Appalachian Trail Conference found more money, it gradually purchased land, rerouting the trail as necessary to create a permanent route. Accordingly, the trail wasn't as arduous back then, as far as climbing over the highest peaks for the sake of climbing the highest mountains. He feels the trail is far too difficult. He's 79 years old. I wonder if he would have felt the same if this had been the trail when he was 29.

I leave The Cabin and walk through the country, admiring its beauty. Maine is unlike anything I've seen before. I think it might be my favorite state on the trail. They say Minnesota is the land of 10,000 lakes. I believe Maine might be the land of a million lakes.

Lakes and ponds with names like Mooselookmeguntic, Horns Pond, and Flagstaff dot the landscape. Spruce and fir trees are everywhere, always giving the trail a Christmassy scent. The maple, oak, birch, and other trees are all ablaze in their peak colors. A typical view consists of colored leafy trees, evergreens like pine, spruce, or fir trees, some part of a lake or stream, and always some rocks. Rocks are everywhere; not quite like in Pennsylvania, where the trail is littered with thousands of rocks, but instead, house-sized boulders that form the summits of mountains.

I trip over rocks and tree roots because I always look around in awe of the beauty surrounding me. I'm lucky to be here. I am walking through this majestic land, counting my lucky stars. And I thank my angels in heaven for getting me this far.

I'm nearing the Kennebec River, a famed waterway along The Appalachian Trail. Maine is not a place for sissies. The Maine Appalachian Trail Club doesn't bother with frivolities like bridges across streams. No siree, if you're going to hike the Appalachian Trail in Maine, you better believe your feet will get wet. You will be trudging through icy rivers and streams, and the first thing you will do upon reaching a shelter is to remove your wet boots and socks to put on warm, dry socks. It's a fact.

However, the Kennebec is different. The Kennebec is a major river in Maine. Historically, logging industries floated logs down the river to get them to the paper mills and factories. In the early years, hikers crossing the river might have hundreds or thousands of tree trunks coming at them. Although the logging industry no longer float the logs downstream, they still have a dam upriver, which the state uses to control the flow of the river whenever they need additional power. The extra water flows downstream at random times, so the current can change anytime without notice. Many hikers have lost their backpacks, and a few have lost their lives trying to reach the other side.

To end these tragedies, the Appalachian Trail Club instituted a ferry system, where someone with a canoe ferries hikers across the river at no charge. They even painted a white blaze on the canoe to show people "this is the trail" because so many hikers considered taking the ferry "cheating."

I want to ford the river myself, as the early pioneers did. Growler and Wandering Bear have had many conversations with me, trying to change my mind, but I remain steadfast in my desire to walk to the other side.

I arrive at the Kennebec within a few minutes of Growler, Hawkeye, and Wandering Bear. I take one glance at The Kennebec and cry, "Oh, hell no!"

Seeing a 400-foot wide river, four to six feet deep, with my own eyes is *very, very different* from seeing a few pictures and reading about it. Although that woman I met several hundred miles ago referred to my legs as tree trunks, I know the river would wipe me out the minute I step foot in that thing. I can't wait to jump into that canoe.

I climb into the front seat of the canoe, and the shuttle man hands me a paddle. Hawkeye climbs into the middle, and the shuttle man is in the rear. We shove off into the river, and I begin to paddle, looking at the water in front of me. I paddle and paddle, looking up to see the other bank. To my dismay, our destination is floating upriver. Looking around to get my bearings, I realize that my 'paddling' isn't helping in the least. The strong current is pushing us downstream, and I need to dig in and use every ounce of energy I have to help get us across the river and back upstream against the current. I feel like an idiot.

We make our way across the river, unload our packs, and sit along the banks to wait for the other hikers to cross. The shuttle runs at certain times throughout the day; this is the last time slot. Many hikers plan their days around the ferry schedule.

After Growler and Wandering Bear make it across, we head to the Caratunk General Store to buy snacks and ice cream. I've seen pictures of hikers sitting on the porch of this small-town general store, and I feel like I've finally accomplished something as I do the same. I can't believe I've almost achieved this dream I've had for years.

Crossing the Kennebec is exciting for a few other reasons. It means we crossed the 2,000-mile mark, so we have 150 miles left to hike. And to a lesser extent, it's exciting that I'm now on the last page of the guidebook. I hike 15-20 miles every day and walk into Monson with Growler, Grasshopper, and Gumby.

Monson is significant because it's the last town I'll reach on the Appalachian Trail. I need to resupply here to hike the "100-mile wilderness". We walk to Shaw's Boarding House, another legendary trail institution. The Shaws have invited hikers for over 20 years; many have stayed here and written about their experience. I find a bunk and say hello to over a dozen hikers hanging out in the common room. They invite me to join them, but the local diner is calling my name, and I run for dinner instead.

I am an odd hiker. Of course, I eat cheeseburgers, fries, ice cream, and other junk food in towns. After all, a hiker needs the calories to burn. But the thing I miss the most out on the trail? Fresh salads. I love salads, and other hikers always give me a funny look when I order a salad before anything else.

I sleep well at the hostel and get a ride out of town with Mountain Dew and a few other hikers. As we're in the back of the pickup truck, driving down the road at seventy miles per hour, I see my sunflower bandana get whipped away by the wind and tossed out of the truck's bed, floating into the great beyond. It's only a bandana, but it makes me sad. That blue bandana filled with bright yellow sunflowers has been with me since I first stepped foot on the trail in Georgia. It's my washcloth, sweat rag, potholder, towel, eyeglass cleaner, and anything I need it to be. In the 2,000 miles I've hiked, the bandana has faded from wear and the sun, and now it's gone. I guess a part of me wants to stay in Maine.

When the driver drops us at the trail, my thoughts return to hiking. My bandana is gone, but I need to move on. Up the trail, I walk into the 100-mile wilderness. There is no civilization for 100 miles until we reach Abol Bridge Campground and Baxter State Park, the home of Katahdin. Hikers need to be prepared with at least seven days' worth of food heading north, and for thru-hikers heading south who are just starting their journey to Georgia, it's recommended that they carry ten days' worth of food.

My pack is heavier than it's been in a while, loaded with extra food, gas for my stove, and all the cold weather gear I've been carrying. The trail isn't incredibly difficult anymore, but it's October third. I am in northern Maine, the weather is getting colder, and the sunlight is fading faster every day. It's not yet a race to get to Katahdin, but it's getting urgent.

I hike with Mountain Dew for a while, and we discuss The Cabin and how great Honey and Bear are. He is more of a purist than I am, and he makes fun of others for slackpacking for a few days instead of carrying their packs the entire way.

"Well, I'll tell you what, Dew. I've been limping for most of this trail, and my body has had it. My body told me to quit a long time ago. But I can't. I'm determined to finish this hike I started. And if hiking for three days without a pack enables my leg to heal a little and allows me to finish my hike, that's fine with me, and you have no business judging me for it," I say, my face beginning to turn red and holding in my anger before it spews out of my mouth. I slow down a little and allow him to get ahead of me.

I have about a mile left to get to Wilson Valley Lean-to tonight. The sun has set, but the full moon illuminates the landscape as if it's still the middle of the day. The only thing standing in my way right now, at 7:10 pm, is a very large stream. The "stream" is a stream only in Maine – a bonafide river in any other state. It's perhaps 50 feet to the other side and appears to be a foot or so deep.

It's getting late and cold, and I don't want to have wet boots that won't dry, so I do the only smart thing there is to do – I remove my boots and socks and put my Teva sandals on. I prepare for the cold water and step in, expecting to walk across the river in a minute or two.

Instead, the worn rubber soles of my sandals immediately slip on wet rocks, and I land on my butt in the river before I can even blink. I pull myself up and retreat to the bank. Looking around for a shorter crossing, I eye some boulders, maybe 50 or 100 yards upriver. I hike upriver and look around.

I can rock-hop across this!

I jump onto the first boulder, steady myself, and continue to jump, each time landing precariously on wet sandals and balancing my 50-pound backpack, hoping not to fall into the river. Halfway across the river, I realize that the next boulder is entirely too far for me to jump. I look around for another way, but I don't see anything.

I can't see the bottom of the stream up here, so I put my hiking pole into the river to feel for the bottom. The rushing water immediately rips the pole from my hands, but thankfully, I'm wearing the attached wristband. I pull my pole out of the stream and realize that the stream took the rubber tip. *Better the rubber tip than the entire pole, I suppose.*

I steady myself on the rock, trying desperately to find a way out of this situation. It never occurred to me that the amount of water downstream, at a foot deep, would be condensed and rushing through only a few feet of available space between rocks. I feel stupid. *You idiot! Why didn't you think about the amount of water flowing through this? You took physics as an elective in college for crying out loud. You're smarter than this!*

I move about the top of the rock, and in one fell swoop, I am in the stream facing upriver, and the water is lapping at my chest, pushing me and my backpack down and back into the boulder. The volume and force of the water prevent me from standing. Although the moon is still shining, it's later and darker. The stream is no longer an inviting crystal-clear obstacle; it's a cold, black abyss.

Don't panic, Gimp. Don't panic. Breathe. How do I get out of this? There is nobody around to help me. I am on my own.

I take a big, deep breath, and with all my energy, push forward enough to free my pack. With weight redistributed, I can fully stand up, and I use my poles as two legs of a tripod to balance my body.

Well, I'm wet at this point. My camera, which is hanging around my neck, is now waterlogged. I'm pretty sure any film in it is damaged, and the camera is probably useless. But the bigger picture is to get out of this stream.

Using my hiking poles, I slowly make my way toward the bank in rushing, hip-high water. Once I reach the bank, I walk downstream until I meet the Appalachian Trail, where I sit down, remove my stupid sandals, and put my boots back on. Amazingly, my boots stayed dry because they were at the top of my pack. My feet are dry, but the rest of me is wet. I hurry up the trail to the shelter, almost a mile away, hoping to create body heat and prevent hypothermia.

Soon, I hear a vast wind sweep through the woods, almost like a tornado. I begin to panic once again and then laugh out loud. I crossed some railroad tracks a little while ago. People always say that a tornado sounds almost like a freight train. Wouldn't the opposite be true as well?

Finally, I drag myself into the Wilson Valley Lean-to, where Mountain Dew has already made a campfire.

"Trail Gimp! What are you doing here this late?" he asks.

"Cold…" I stammer. "Wet… fell in stream," I add quickly, with chattering teeth. I drop my pack next to the fire and warm my hands over the hot flames.

"You crossed the stream *at night? By yourself?* That's so stupid! Why didn't you camp on the side of the river until the morning? You could have killed yourself!"

I can't exactly tell him I came to the lean-to because he was here. I've run into him for a few weeks now. I think he's interesting, and I want to get to know him a little more. Not in a Little Bus kind of way, but more of a friendship. He seems angry at the world, and I've always wanted to see if I could lend an unbiased ear, someone he could talk to.

Instead, he gives me a lecture.

"I know Dew, you aren't telling me anything I haven't already scolded myself for. It's over and done with. Let it be." My happy mood disappears, and I unload my backpack to make dinner and warm up. I'm happy that my sleeping bag and clothing are dry since they are packed in waterproof stuff sacks. I change into warm, dry clothes and begin making dinner near the fire.

"Thank you for making this fire. It's very helpful right now."

"If you weren't stupid enough to cross the river at night, you wouldn't need it," Mountain Dew retorts.

Fine, be like that. Jerk.

I make my dinner, eat in silence, and say goodnight to a few hikers I hadn't noticed in the back of the shelter. Got Milk is quiet, taking a vow of silence for the 100-mile wilderness.

I know a lot of hikers take this vow, as the 100-mile wilderness is almost sacred – the last section of the trail, finishing a trek we started so long ago. I know myself – there's no way I can *not talk* for a week. I respect those that can.

Except now. Dew is mad at me for being stupid, and frankly, so am I.

I crawl into my sleeping bag and hope for a new day tomorrow.

It's October 6, and the weather is beginning to catch up to the calendar. Or, perhaps, ahead of it. It was cold yesterday but more frigid this morning, and according to my thermometer/compass/keychain, it's approximately 25 degrees. I put hot water in my water bottles to use as heaters last night, keeping me toasty when I slept, but now, they are cold. I also put my clothes in my sleeping bag to prevent them from freezing. However, mummy bags are tight by design, so there is little chance of changing in one.

I learned long ago that male hikers recognize when a female is about to change, so the guys turn their heads while I change. There is nothing fun about taking off warm clothing to put on damp and cold clothing in freezing temperatures. I cringe as I remove warm pants and pull on dank, smelly leggings, and I audibly wince when I pull off my warm shirt to put on my very sweaty and dirty sports bra and shirt. The icing on the cake is pulling off my warm camp socks and pushing my feet into similarly smelly and damp socks.

Once dressed, I sit in my sleeping bag to get warm again while I cook breakfast and make coffee. And now it's time. It's time to take my nice warm feet, thrust them into frozen leather boots, and attempt to tie frozen laces. There is no use in complaining. We are all in the same boat and past the point of tolerating anyone's complaints. Don't want to be here? Then go home.

I head out on the trail with a few people, and I hike slowly since my boots are frozen, and it's difficult to walk properly. Snow and ice crunch beneath my feet as I walk, and I still can't believe I'm hiking in northern Maine in the cold. I stop after an hour as my boots thaw and loosen up, and I remove my pack to re-tie my boots. I look through the trees, and finally, I see glimpses of Mount Katahdin. The goal. The ending point of my journey.

I continue to climb Whitecap Mountain, enjoying the views of the wilderness and crystal-clear skies. I reach the summit and check out the solar-powered pollution monitor for a few minutes. It's too cold to stay very long. I begin my descent, look into the wilderness, and stop short. There, right in front of me, is Mount Katahdin, in all her glory. I can almost reach out and touch her. Of course, she's still 70 trail miles away, but I can't believe I'm almost there.

Whitecap Mountain is the tallest peak along the Appalachian Trail in the 100-mile wilderness. The ground slopes down to the valley, covered in fall foliage and dotted with ponds, and extends 70 trail miles to the base of majestic Mt. Katahdin. This is the closest and best view of the finish line I've ever seen in person. I stand there for a moment, staring at her incredible beauty. The top half of the mountain in covered in light snow, the bottom half shrouded in evergreens. It looks like I can jump off this mountain and be there by tonight. But I know it will take another three to four days. My goal is to summit on October 10.

I shiver from a chill and break away from the mesmerizing view. I stop for lunch at Logan Brook lean-to and say hello to some section hikers.

"Are you Trail Gimp, by any chance?" one of the hikers asks.

Surprised, I answer, "Indeed, I am. Have we met?"

"I'm Crazy Train! We met when we hiked in 1996!"

"Crazy Train! Of course, I remember! You cut your hair and your beard!"

He introduces me to his girlfriend and explains that they are hiking the 100-mile wilderness this year.

"I'm glad you're back on the trail since you got off early in '96. Good for you," Crazy Train says.

We share some great stories while relaxing for lunch. But as always, it's time to push on. I still have ten miles to go today. I've been hiking nearly 20-mile days for a while now. The trail is usually less steep, and the brisk air forces me to walk longer and faster to stay warm.

As I pass by Mountain View Pond, I hear a noise, and a gigantic bull moose is sauntering in the pond, about 50 yards away. His rack is so huge I could use it as a lounge chair. I've heard moose in the woods before, but I haven't been this close to one. I watch him for a few minutes, and then as I move on, a pileated woodpecker flies by my head and starts pecking at a tree. I can't believe the size of this woodpecker. He's about 18 inches long, and the red spot on his head is unmistakable. It's the first one I've seen up close; a beautiful and striking bird.

At Crawford Pond, I contemplate setting up my tent on the sand to enjoy the beauty. In Maine, ponds can be a few feet in diameter or something I would refer to as a lake. This is the latter. It has crystal-clear water and is as serene as can be.

No, I must move on. If I want to finish on October 10th, I've got to get to the shelter.

I walk on, enjoying my stroll in the woods, a mostly flat and dry section of the trail. Suddenly, I realize, *I am not limping!* I don't know when my leg healed, but I'm walking properly again. My leg doesn't hurt at all. *And Pacemaker said it would take six months to heal. It only took me three!*

I finally arrive at the shelter and collapse into it. I'm still hiking slower than everyone else who arrived earlier, including a crazy few people that tried swimming in the natural swimming hole out front. It's nearly dark, and it's entirely too cold to go swimming, in my opinion. It might be nice in mid-summer, though.

The shelter register indicates that tomorrow might be filled with trail magic. We will see!

Indeed, today is trail magic. Some former thru-hikers come to Lower Mary-Jo Lake to set up a thru-hiker feed station. I stay for two hours, munching on burgers, chips and dip, roasted bananas and chocolate chips, cookies, and coffee. The lake is picture-perfect, and I chat with other hikers from previous years. I heard Blue Moon went home, and I'm sad for her. I knew she had a close friend at home who was sick, and she hoped that her friend would stay healthy until she finished her hike. Her friend is not doing well, and Blue Moon abandoned her hike to go home to see her while she still can.

It's an incredible act of friendship. Blue Moon has hiked over 2,000 miles, and just as she sees the finish line, she leaves to be with her dying friend. I hope I'm lucky enough to have friends like that.

The sun is warming things up, and I hike for the rest of the day in a short-sleeved shirt and pull my pants up to my knees. The trail is still typical Maine, filled with rocks, tree roots and mud – so much mud. There are a few bog bridges to walk upon, but more are needed. I see a large tree across the trail ahead of me. It's too big to jump over, and walking around means scurrying through the woods off-trail. I stop to think and then simply hug the tree, throw my right leg over it, and follow with my left. I don't see the other side, but I feel the crunch as my right foot slams into and then slips off a branch, landing with a thud and a twist on the ground below. *Aaagghh! Are you kidding me?*

I can't believe it. My left leg just freakin healed, and now I twist my ankle? It's not broken, and with nothing else I can do, I limp on.

I reach Nahmakanta Lake and stop short to admire the scenery. The lake is large enough to have small waves lap at the soft, sandy beach. I remove my pack to sit, appreciate the beauty, and weigh my options.

I'm supposed to hike another two and a half miles to get to the shelter. I told all the guys that I would be there. But this view is mesmerizing. The clear lake, surrounded by wilderness without a dwelling in sight, begs me to stay.

I can't turn this down. There is another hiker here, someone I don't know, in a tent on the beach. I set my tent up as well, several yards away from him. I'm about to make dinner as he heads my way.

"Hi, I have some extra hot water if you'd like it – that way, you don't have to set up your stove if you don't want to."

"Oh, thanks, that's so nice of you. I'd appreciate that," I said as I hold my pot out for him to dump the water into. It's nice to have some hot food quickly. We talk for a while and sit by the lake, but I soon feel like he's getting too friendly. He might just be a nice guy interested in my hike, but he's asking too many questions about me, how far I've hiked, where I live, and what I do for a living. Most of my answers are lies. I'm not entirely comfortable anymore. The eerie cries of loons on the lake don't help at all.

"Well, thanks for hanging out and for the hot water. I've got a long day tomorrow, so I'm going to get to bed."

"Where are you headed tomorrow?" he asks.

"I'm not sure. I'm supposed to meet up with all the guys I was supposed to meet tonight. So, I need to find them first." This is a lie, but I figure mentioning "all the guys" would help deter this guy's interest.

I retreat to my tent, emerging only long enough to brush my teeth. I seriously consider leaving to get to the shelter, where, I assume, all the guys have gone. I'm pretty sure there are eight or ten hikers there. But it's too dark, and my neighbor seems quiet in his tent. I'm sure I'm overreacting, but I set my watch alarm early so I can get out before my neighbor wakes up, just in case.

It's drizzling when I wake up, so I go back to bed, but I'm still hiking by 7:00 am. I get to the shelter to have breakfast, and it's good I didn't get here last night. If everyone who signed the register is any indication, it would have been a full house.

Following a maze of rocks and tree roots and stumbling through swampy trails, I finally arrive at Rainbow Stream Lean-to for lunch. This shelter was featured in a National Geographic article years ago, one of the articles that piqued my interest in hiking this trail. After exploring the area and eating, I'm packing up to move on when my neighbor from last night walks in.

I say hello to be polite, and when another hiker asks where he's headed, he answers, "Oh, about seven miles north of here."

That's where I'm going. Is he going there because he thinks that's where I'll be? I don't say anything and secretly hope he won't make it that far.

I take off, enjoying the scenery and thinking that my hiking days will soon end. I enjoy the freedom from bosses while I still can, and I continue walking.

It's getting late, and I'm afraid I don't have the energy to make it to Hurd Brook Lean-to, so I poke around for an appropriate campsite. I find a small, level site behind some tall grasses near the south end of Rainbow Lake. I think it's a perfect place to set up my small tent, and since it's nearly dark, if that guy passes me, hopefully, he won't see my tent.

The loons on the lake freak me out. Their calls are long and eerie, and they cry into the night. I finally fall asleep, with no sign of that guy. Either he passed by without seeing me, or he didn't get this far.

I wake up early. I'm only 22 miles from Mount Katahdin. The finish is right before my eyes, taunting me as I climb up Rainbow Ledges. The steady climb is not difficult, considering I've hiked over 2,000 miles to get here. At the top, I see another view of Mount Katahdin, closer than I've ever been. I take a quick break at Hurd Brook Lean-to. The excitement is palpable, and I hurry to get to Abol Bridge Campground to have a junk fest at the camp store.

As the trail exits the trees, I finish the 100-mile wilderness, just like that. I see a can of Diet Pepsi that Redrock left four days earlier with a note: "for any hiker emerging from the wilderness." With the recent weather, the soda is still cold. It's a nice, unexpected treat.

I see Abol Bridge ahead of me and hurry, expecting to see Mountain Dew, Got Milk, Victory Gallop, or anyone else, and I'm dismayed when I get there and don't see anyone. I run inside the camp store, buy as much junk food as my finances allow, and devour a microwaved sandwich, candy bars, chips, and another soda while sitting outside and enjoying the views.

Outta Chocolate shows up, and I finally get a chance to thank him for the candy bars he left me back in Pennsylvania. Then a van shows up, and The Family pops out, one by one, like a car full of clowns, including Blackjack, whom I first met back in North Carolina.

The father from The Family offers to take my pack up to Daicey Pond Campground, so Suches 75, The Artist, and I take off up the trail, slackpacking and enjoying freedom and camaraderie.

Suches 75 and The Artist take a break, and I continue, enjoying the final few miles of trail before the campground and the last shelter, reserved for thru-hikers before they climb Mount Katahdin.

I stop at Big Niagara Falls and Little Niagara Falls, enjoying the scenery and the calming sensation that natural waterfalls provide. There are several layers of falls, cascading over rocks and cliffs, each thunderous and powerful, splattering me with water if I get too close. I can feel the trail coming to an end, and the electricity in my feet is evident, pushing me faster. I'm so excited that I pick up my pace and eagerly walk toward Daicey Pond. As I get closer, I see two people leaning against a rock, appearing to wait for someone. A few feet more, and I realize they are waiting for me!

I see Carolyn, my dad's cousin who lives in Maine, and Mr. Schneider, my childhood best friend's father – the one who took me on my first hike as a Girl Scout.

"What are you two doing here?" I ask after hugging them.

"Your parents came up yesterday, and I decided to tag along," Carolyn says. "Where's your backpack?"

Mr. Schneider, who still lives around the corner from my parents, adds, "Your mom has been keeping me updated on your hike, and I've hiked Katahdin once, a few years ago. I asked your mom if I could come up here and maybe hike the last few miles with you."

"That would be great!" I respond. "A friend of mine took my pack at Abol Bridge, and he's bringing it to Daicey Pond Campground, so I've been slackpacking these last seven miles. I'll pick it up in a little while."

We walk to the parking lot, where I find my parents, hug them, and catch up with everyone. I find The Family and retrieve my pack.

"April," my mom says. "We're heading back to the hotel in Millinocket. Mr. Schneider will come out in the morning to hike. Do you want to come with us? Or do you want to camp here?"

Oooh, that's a dilemma.

I'm finally here at Daicey Pond campground, where I know a lot of thru-hikers are spending the night. Should I spend my last night on the trail with them? Or should I climb into the car with my parents, have a filling, hot meal, sit in a hot tub to soothe my achy muscles, and sleep in a real bed?

Hot tub! Hot tub! Hot tub!

There isn't much of an argument. Mr. Schneider and I decide to slackpack to Katahdin Springs Campground, two and a half miles away, to make tomorrow's hike easier.

We meet my parents there, and then I pile into their car and head to town. I feel a little guilty as I'm eating a wonderful dinner in comfort, soaking in a hot tub, and finally taking a hot shower and sleeping in clean sheets, as my hiker friends are huddled together in the cold, eating whatever is left in their food bags. It's technically my last night on the trail, and I'm not even on the trail. I'm not sure if I made a good or bad decision.

CHAPTER NINETEEN

MOUNT KATAHDIN

October 10, 1998

I wake up at 4:00 in the morning to eat and dress before I meet Mr. Schneider at the elevators at 5:00. It's October 10th, the final Saturday before Baxter State Park closes to the public, and we expect the park to be busy. Mr. Schneider wants to get in line early so we aren't denied entry behind any day hikers. There isn't necessarily a cap on the number of hikers on the mountain, but there is only a certain number of parking spots, and when they are filled, they don't allow any more cars.

He's right; a dozen cars are already waiting when we arrive, but they give us our passes, and we park the car, beginning our hike at 7:17 am. I see Victory Gallop in the parking lot, and he's hiking today with Jeanne, his fiancée, who came to pick him up from the trail.

The mountain is a nice climb, nothing too tricky initially, and we stop for a quick break after two hours to eat and watch the wildlife. Mr. Schneider is an avid outdoorsman, and it's nice to hike alongside him, sharing stories of the trail and different places we've been. But it's still a little weird because I haven't seen him in years, and combining memories of home while hiking the trail is a combination I'm not used to.

Generally, the trail and my home life are two separate entities involving two separate people. At home, I'm April. Here on the trail, I'm Trail Gimp. It's almost like two separate lives are converging at once, and I don't know how to handle it. Nevertheless, I hike.

I still can't believe I'm hiking Mt. Katahdin. Right now, it feels like any other mountain. But today is different and I know it. Today is the last day. And I'm with Mr. Schneider and not my hiking buddies.

We begin hand-over-hand climbing, moving over rocks and boulders and using ladders that have been nailed into the mountain. We catch up to Victory Gallop, which brings me back to reality. I am on the trail. I am still Trail Gimp. Everything is the same as it's been for the last six months or so. The rocks are challenging, but I enjoy climbing. Victory Gallop cries, "This is like The Mahoosuc Notch gone vertical!" I laugh because it's so true. I'm having a good time, thoroughly enjoying the obstacles, made easier by the fact that I'm not wearing a 45-pound backpack. My parents brought up my old daypack, so I have some water and snacks, a small camcorder, and my celebratory bottle of Moët, my favorite champagne.

We can only see a few feet in front of us. It's cloudy and misty, and it drizzles every once in a while. It would be cold for most people, but I have so much adrenaline running through me that I'm not cold, even though I'm only wearing a light jacket. It's not the ideal weather to climb Katahdin, but it's the end of a 2,000-mile journey, so I'll take anything now. We reach the tablelands, a mile-long plateau, and it's a welcome relief after climbing 3,000 feet already.

The Tablelands are fairly level, strewn with rocks, and at approximately 4,000 feet in elevation, are devoid of most plant life. It looks like a moonscape, with small rocks littering the landscape, and a flattened path in front of us, worn down from the thousands of hikers who have come before me. The frosty air only adds to the mystique. The summit is still a mile away, barely visible through the mist.

We walk on, breathing easier because of the nearly-level trail. I know I'm near the end. I'm grateful I've made it this far. I've spent six and a half months walking from Georgia, limping most of the way. I've depended on the hospitality of strangers. I've dug deep within myself and found strength and tenacity I didn't know I had. But what am I going to do once I reach that long-sought-after sign proclaiming I've reached the summit of Mount Katahdin? What do others do?

Some hikers turn around and hike back to Georgia, attempting what's known as a yo-yo. But I can't do that. I'm done. My body needs a break. I need to rest. I have no idea what I will do in the coming months, but I know I'll be okay. Somehow.

The elevation increases a little. Through the mist, I search for the sign. Is that it? No, that's a person. Mr. Schneider and I continue to walk. Where is it? How long have we been hiking? My eyes scan the landscape before me, searching for the sign I've seen in dozens of books and articles – the sign indicating the summit of Mount Katahdin, which means "Greatest Mountain."

While searching, I hear voices. The voices of other hikers, some before us and some behind us. It's hard to see who they are, and the voices carry with the wind. It's hard to tell how far ahead or behind someone is when you can't see them and can only hear partial sentences. It's a strange day. I'm with others, but sometimes feel like I'm alone.

Is that it? Wait! That's the sign! That's the summit of Mt. Katahdin! There – in front of me, is the end of my journey.

I stop for a minute and fumble for the mini-camcorder my sister lent me. I turn it on and as we near the sign, I record us hiking to the summit, hurrying with the last energy I have. As I reach the finish line, I can't take my eyes off the famous wooden sign. Basic backcountry-brown, with large white lettering proclaiming KATAHDIN, Baxter Peak, Elevation 5267 feet, Northern Terminus of the Appalachian Trail. The rest of the lettering is half worn but indicates trail mileage to certain places in Baxter Park and 2,135 miles to Springer Mountain in Georgia. It's an old sign. I know the mileage is more than that. I know I've just walked 2,160.7 miles.

I take my turn and kiss the famous sign, as most thru-hikers do. I'm here! I can't believe I'm at the infamous Mt. Katahdin sign! It's taken us three hours and 45 minutes to reach the summit, but it's taken me six months and 12 days to get here, including two weeks of time off twice.

Mr. Schneider takes my picture at the summit, arms outreached in sheer delight and accomplishment, and once again, I have that feeling of empowerment. I did this! I made it, and I pop the bottle of champagne to celebrate. The cold, sweet bubbles are a startling contrast from the water I'm used to drinking, and I'm giddy with excitement. But I need to be careful. I still need to get back down to the base of the mountain.

There isn't much to see here, as the clouds cover the views. The summit is full of day hikers coming from various trails, and I share my champagne with the many thru-hikers making their way up from The Appalachian Trail.

Before long, we're celebrating at the summit with Got Milk, DragonFly, Victory Gallop, his fiancée Jeanne, Fric, O'Tim, Mountain Dew, and Scooby. We've finished our hikes. Where we go from here is anyone's guess.

There are 40-mile-per-hour winds up here with some drizzles, and we begin to get cold. We decide to head down, saying, "It would be nice to see what it looks like from up here."

Just as we turn to leave, a gust of wind blows up from the valley, pushing the clouds out of the way. We see the entire Knife-edge trail, The Tablelands, and for a brief moment, all the way down into the valley. We stand immobilized as we see ponds in the distance and exquisite cloud formations on the summit from the mist blowing by. We are mystified and enamored by the beauty, and then, not a minute later, the fog is back, blocking all views.

I take that as a gift from my heavenly relatives and head down the mountain.

Descending is almost more difficult than climbing, as I'm fighting against gravity. It would be a shame to hike 2,180 miles with a limp only to break my leg, or worse, on the way down. We hike together as a group.

Some slow down to enjoy the last few moments on Katahdin, while others, like me, hurry to meet family.

Mom and Dad meet us about a quarter mile from the end of the trail, and we walk together to the Ranger station.

I'm finished! I completed The Appalachian Trail! I finally achieved something I put my mind to. I'm not a failure, after all. I've limped for more than a thousand miles. I've walked through 14 states. I've met people from all walks of life. I've depended on them. I became friends with them. And I've even loved some of them. I've hiked through dehydration, injury, heat exhaustion, and freezing temperatures. I've laughed a lot, and I've cried even more. I've carried my clothes, food, stove, fuel, water filter, and more on my back for 2,000 miles. I did it. And I know that if I can do all that, I can do anything now. I don't know what to do when I get home, but I'll figure it out. One day at a time.

Mom runs to her car and returns with a platter, revealing the celebratory cake she made. We share it with Fric and Mountain Dew at a picnic table and bring the rest into the ranger station to share with everyone else finishing today. I hug Mountain Dew and Fric to say goodbye and assume I'll see them and others in the tiny town of Millinocket. Mountain Dew and I have spent a lot of time together in Maine, and we actually became pretty good friends, despite the lecture he gave me at the beginning of the 100-mile wilderness. I will miss him a lot, but hopefully, I'll see him in town.

I gather my things, say goodbye to Mount Katahdin, indeed the "Greatest Mountain", and pile into the car.

I've finished my hike, but my journey is just beginning.

EPILOGUE

Some hikers realize how much they love the simple life and have no desire to rejoin society or the rat race as they've done in the past. Some plan to hike the Pacific Crest Trail, The Continental Divide Trail, or both. These are two other National Scenic Trails stretching from the US-Mexican border to the US-Canadian border. Some hikers immediately turn around and begin hiking back to Springer Mountain in Georgia (or Mt. Katahdin in Maine), turning their thru-hike into a yo-yo hike. Some hikers get jobs as Forest Rangers, and others work for The Appalachian Trail Conference. A few, like me, consider the Appalachian Trail a one-and-done type of thing. When someone asks me about my next long-distance hike, I say, "Next time I go cross country, I'm going in an RV."

After my hike, I stayed with my parents for a few weeks to figure out what I wanted to do with my life and to reintegrate into society. One would think that there wouldn't be a problem getting used to the creature comforts of real life, but it's a real adjustment for many folks.

Most people were surprised at my appetite. I was no longer hiking, but I had very little body fat when I finished, and I still burned thousands of calories a day, which required a lot of food. It's hard to curb your food intake when you've been eating as many calories as possible.

I had difficulty waiting to use the restroom until one was available. I was used to going whenever necessary, and hunting down an appropriate public restroom was sometimes frustrating. Thru-hikers don't really talk about this, but it's a real issue.

Cars travel fast. I was used to walking everywhere at a rate of two-three miles per hour. A ten-mile hike could take three to four hours. A ten-mile drive takes minutes in comparison. Hikers generally don't drive much during a thru-hike, so it takes a little while to readjust to speed and traffic.

I developed an appreciation for simple things like electricity and running water. Hot water is easy to make when one doesn't need to put a stove together first. Using more than one pot when necessary is more helpful than I could have imagined on the trail.

I appreciate clean clothes every day and going to a restaurant or grocery store when I'm hungry.

The appreciation extends to society. The trail taught me that there are helpful people everywhere, willing to help out others. Of course, there are a few grumpy people in the world, but the vast majority of folks are kind-hearted and giving creatures.

While still at my parents' house, Weatherwoman came to visit me for a weekend. Matt, one of my high school friends, called me and invited us out, and he introduced me to his friend Brian, and we immediately hit it off. We ended up having a few dates, but after nearly three weeks at home, it was time to head back to North Carolina.

Since I had given up my apartment, I moved onto the couch in Kathy and Leah's apartment. I found a job I loved in uptown Charlotte and saved my money for an eventual apartment.

I took day trips on the weekends, usually to the North Carolina mountains, and hiked the small sections of trail that I missed here and there. I visited Nightgrumbler and Sugarfoot, who had indeed gotten back to their lives. Their dreams of completing a thru-hike of the Appalachian Trail have either dissolved completely or been placed into the category of "someday."

My friends claim I was quieter when I returned. I listened more before speaking, didn't jump to conclusions, and didn't try to solve anyone's problems. I no longer needed to make funny comments to make people laugh. I could sit in silence for long periods without talking, which some people didn't understand. I loved hanging out with my friends, but I also loved the quiet times, hanging out by the pool, and reading. Trail Gimp stayed with me, and though I was still me, I lost the parts of myself I didn't like and incorporated the elements of Trail Gimp I loved. I was a "new" me.

Little Bus finished the trail while I was staying at The Cabin with Honey and Bear. He and I got in touch, and he came to visit me in North Carolina. We realized we would make great friends but not a great couple. He was figuring out his life, and I was figuring out mine. He had spent years developing his career, and now that he was there, he wasn't sure that's what he wanted to do for the rest of his life. It was a situation I had just been through, and I could understand his predicament.

I went home for Thanksgiving and Christmas and had more dates with Brian. After several back-and-forth visits and gigantic phone bills, I decided to move home. I loved my life in Charlotte; I loved my job and responsibilities, but in the end, true love called, and eventually, Brian and I married. I've always found it funny that if I hadn't hiked the trail when I did, I wouldn't have been hanging out with my friend, Matt, and he'd never have introduced me to his friend. I guess I had to hike those 2,000 miles to find him.

As years go by, I think of certain situations on the trail and the lessons I learned from them.

1. **Take the first step.** Ideas and dreams are great, but hoping for them won't make them happen. If I wanted to get to Maine, I had to walk those steps. People could carry my pack, but nobody could walk those miles for me. The first step is hard. It can be crazy scary. Anything you want to do – lose weight, get a new job, get into or out of a relationship, take that trip – requires action. Do one thing

to set that goal in motion. Then, do the second thing. Dreams require action; otherwise, they remain only dreams.

2. **Don't be afraid.** Fear kills dreams and ambitions. The world can be a scary place. We can be hit by a bus tomorrow. Does that mean we must live in our homes forever, to stay "safe?" Living requires some kind of risk. We never know what will happen, so plan accordingly, but don't be afraid to live in the moment. I'll never forget being in Hot Springs on my first hike when someone asked, "Hey, does anyone want to go to Trail Days?" Without fear, I piled into a car with people I barely knew and had a great time. Don't be afraid to get out of your comfort zone to explore and enjoy life.

3. **Listen to your Gut Instinct and Inner Voice.** There is a difference between taking a calculated risk and a dangerous risk, and that is your gut instinct. If something feels wrong, it probably is. If something inside you screams, "get out," "leave," or "have fun," listen to it. I ran into a few people along my hike who made me uncomfortable. My gut instinct told me to leave, so I did. Was I wrong? I'll never know, but I'd rather be safe than a headline. Likewise, taking that unexpected trip to Trail Days in 1996 was great for me.

4. **Think big, positive, and take a chance at something great.** If you're going to think about something, make it positive. Something happens in your brain when you think positively. I had no idea when I started my hike in 1998 if I would finish, but I told myself I would. If I didn't think I'd make it to Maine, I'd have gotten off the trail earlier, perhaps in Hot Springs when Nightgrumbler left the trail or in Tennessee, hiking in so much pain. If that didn't make me leave, Pennsylvania would have. But I knew that if I were going to get to Maine, I'd have to overcome all these obstacles, one by one. I had to think I would make it; otherwise, quitting was an easy alternative.

In 1998, less than 25 percent of the people who started a thru-hike finished it. People drop off the trail for various reasons. Most go home because of injuries, but many go home because the trail is more physically and mentally demanding than they imagined. It takes a lot to wake up in freezing weather, change into cold, dirty clothes, and thrust your feet into frozen boots, all while smiling. Others leave because they are lonely and miss friends and loved ones. Others, like Sugarfoot and Blue Moon, went home because their priorities changed. I wanted to prove to myself that I could muster through the pain and loneliness, persevere through the cold and rain, and become one of the few that made it to Maine. Like Henry Ford said, "Whether you think you can or think you can't, you're right."

5. **Chances are, someone has gone through what you are going through. They survived, and so will you.** Climbing the Webster Cliffs out of Crawford Notch drilled this into my head. Twenty minutes is a long time to cling to rocks, not knowing how to get up or down. I was stuck and made excuses. But knowing that a 79-year-old man climbed those cliffs just days before me made me realize that if he could do it, I could do it too. Quite possibly, whatever life throws at you, someone has survived it too.

6. **Temper tantrums and self-pity don't solve problems.** I'll never forget throwing that temper tantrum when Purple walked in to see me yelling and screaming profanities at the world. I was embarrassed and felt like a child. The only thing the temper tantrum did was use up my energy. If I had bothered to think clearly and look around, I would have seen that white blaze on the rock and continued on my merry way. Temper tantrums and self-pity don't solve anything – they inhibit problem-solving. When you're angry, take a deep breath, figure out the problem, and find a way toward a solution. There is always a solution, sometimes hidden in plain sight. Feeling sorry for yourself doesn't change a thing.

7. **Recognize your wants versus needs**. I am great at getting what I need – shelter, food, and clothing. I need a reality check when it comes to something I *want*. I stopped at a friend's new house for a tour, and she showed me her giant closet, about the size of my bedroom. I counted 27 pairs of jeans folded on the shelves, not including any dirty laundry elsewhere. Hiking the trail, I had one fleece jacket that kept me warm and two sets of clothes. Even now, I don't need 27 pairs of jeans. It's okay for her, but I don't see the point. After ten years in our house, I wanted something a little bigger, with a pool. We finally found my dream house; it had a massive inground pool and plenty of room for friends and family. I wrestled with the cost, though. Did I *need* this house? Of course not; we nearly paid off our current home, and we could be debt free. But I loved that bigger house; I imagined our family parties around the pool and in the large living and dining areas. We eventually bought the bigger house, but there are plenty of other things we didn't buy, just because we didn't need them.

8. **Be proud of your accomplishments, not ashamed of your failures.** Everybody excels at some things and fails at others. It's okay not to be perfect in every aspect of your life. It's okay to try something and fail. Be proud of trying things, and celebrate your accomplishments, no matter how small you think they are. While resting in Pennsylvania, walking to and from the outhouse was a huge accomplishment, despite other people hiking 20 miles a day. When I left, I was hiking one mile per hour. Still, I celebrated leaving the shelter and continuing my hike. It turns out that I am a good teacher, but working in a classroom in a public school was not my ideal job. I've learned that I like to make my own rules and that following rules just because "that's the way we do things" doesn't make sense to me. I ended up creating my own business, and I've done well for the past 24 years, despite "failing" in my previous career. With the advent of Facebook, I spoke to a friend from

college, who was surprised at my job title – President and owner. He asked, "You're not teaching?" I had forgotten that he had known me only as an education major and substitute teacher. "Oh, gosh no," and I continued to explain how I went from a substitute teacher to moving to North Carolina to hiking the Appalachian Trail to starting my own business. I was no longer ashamed of my short stint at teaching but was proud of what I had accomplished since then. Learn the lessons from any failures, and celebrate your accomplishments.

9. **Slow down and enjoy life.** In the infamous words of *Ferris Bueller*, "Life moves pretty fast. If you don't stop and look around once in a while, you could miss it." I often saw hikers run past me on the trail, always trying to get to the next shelter, make another 25 miles, or get somewhere in a hurry. That's fine for them. My goal was to live and enjoy the trail, which included stopping to smell the flowers, slowing down to pick wild berries, and sitting down to enjoy incredible scenery and beauty. Yes, it was fun to night-hike a few times and to experience the trail in different lights, but I know I missed out on a few things I would have seen during the day. Life is busy. Stop to have a drink or a meal with a friend you haven't seen in a while. Allow your kids a few minutes to use the curb as a balance beam while walking. Enjoy the ducks in the pond. Watch the birds. See the fireflies in the evenings. There are myriad ways to stop and enjoy life if you only take a moment to see the joy in front of you. Find your joy.

10. **Have confidence and find your Power:** Hiking the Appalachian Trail gave me the confidence to do anything. I felt empowered to do everything I wanted to do. If I could walk over 2,000 miles through the mountains, through rain and ice and mud and injury, I had the fortitude to try anything at all. I wanted to invest in real estate, so I found someone who had done that and asked them to teach me. I wanted to start my own business, so I thought about what I wanted

in a boss and became that leader. I had always wanted straight teeth, and when I had some extra money, I put braces on my teeth. I was 43 years old. I thought people would giggle when they saw me, but I only received kindness and encouragement from my peers. Have the confidence to do what you want. You may fail, but you may surprise yourself, so don't compare yourself to others. You are powerful. Use it.

In 2000, I returned to Maine to hike Mount Katahdin again, this time in better weather. I stopped at The Cabin in Maine for a night to say hi to Honey and Bear. I noticed a framed drawing mounted prominently on the wall. I saw the unmistakable whale tail from Moby Dick. In lieu of payment for staying at The Cabin, he created a picture that he sent to Honey and Bear. It's a montage of colored drawings depicting scenes where a hiker is hiking up and down mountains, then with a few raindrops, and again with the hiker setting up his tent as more rain falls from the sky. The final picture shows the hiker peering out from his tent in a deluge, only to see animals lined up two by two, waiting to get in.

I loved the picture so much that I asked for a copy, and Bear handed me an 11x14 print, ready to go. I framed it and put it in my office, where I still see it every day.

I returned to The Cabin in 2006 during a vacation to introduce them to my husband and infant daughter, whose middle name is Laurel, named for Laurel Falls in Tennessee, one of my favorite places along the entire Appalachian Trail. It was great to spend more time with Honey and Bear and to let them see my progression from dirty, injured hiker to married mom and business owner. Sadly, Bear passed away in 2018, though I've heard that Honey still operates the hostel.

The Appalachian Trail is different today than it was in 1998. The Appalachian Trail Conference has changed its name and mission to The Appalachian Trail Conservancy, and has rerouted the trail, following easements and buying property to locate it in a permanent location.

In 1998, the trail was 2,160.7 miles long. Few hikers carried heavy cell phones, and most sent them home when they realized cell towers were few and far between. In 2022, the trail is now 2,194.3 miles. Everyone carries a cell phone, using apps on their phone instead of physical maps and guidebooks. When I hiked, a few hikers carried Walkmans, swapping cassettes with others or leaving one or finding one in shelters. Nowadays, phones supply unlimited music and people hike with earbuds.

Gear is different as well. Titanium pots and microfilters, lightweight fabrics, and hammocks allow hikers to cut their weight to fractions of what we carried. Few people wear heavy boots, as trail runners have become sturdier and more technical. It's not uncommon to see hikers carrying less than thirty pounds, including food and water.

The book *A Walk in The Woods*, written by Bill Bryson about his 1996 hike, was released in 1998. This book was a huge factor in creating interest in The Appalachian Trail, and the ATC reported a 45% increase in the number of thru-hikers after the release of his book. There were an estimated 1700 people who started Springer Mountain in 1998, and roughly 400 finished. (Not all thru-hikers register or confirm their hike, thus, the estimated numbers.) In 2018, 4,282 people registered for a thru-hike beginning either in Georgia or Maine, and 839 people reported completing a thru-hike.

The outbreak of the worldwide Covid pandemic convinced people they could work from anywhere, and people left chaotic cities en masse to enjoy the calm of the mountains. The significant increase in hikers along the Appalachian Trail has caused some problems. There is often overcrowding at shelters, which brings more wildlife, including bears. No longer do hikers hang their provisions from tuna fish cans; in many places, bear canisters are necessary to keep food safe. The trails have eroded faster because of the increase in foot traffic, and trail maintenance clubs work hard to maintain the integrity of the trail, ensuring it will keep for future generations.

Some of the beloved hostels have changed hands or closed with the retirement or death of the owner. Lennie and Gary retired and no longer run The Blueberry Patch in Georgia. The Nantahala Outdoor Center is still operating, though Horace Holden passed away in 2019. Woodshole Hostel in Pearisburg is still operating, though Tillie, the original owner, passed away in 2007. Rusty has been looking to retire and sell his property, though I can't find a definitive answer if any sale has occurred. The Doyle Hotel in Pennsylvania was sold in 2021, and the new owner made extensive changes and rehabilitated the property, bringing it back to its former glory. Graymoor Friary stopped allowing thru-hikers to stay, citing the huge cost and the change in a business plan. The grounds are open every day to the public, and they now offer retreats, conferences, and other events throughout the year.

Many hikers return to the Appalachian Trail to provide comfort for other hikers; trail magic is frequent, and more hostels opened along the trail in the past 25 years. There is an ongoing debate among former thru-hikers about the comforts afforded to hikers now.

Have too many comforts ruined the trail? Are hikers expecting trail magic every day, which nullifies the very meaning of trail magic? Because everyone has phones, are hikers glued to their phones instead of creating the camaraderie that ties them together? Are hikers wandering the woods alone, listening to their music, oblivious to the beauty surrounding them? Are they talking to friends and family every day, playing games on their phones at shelters, and always looking for the next place to charge their phones?

Or are they talking to fellow hikers, walking with joy, informing friends and family of their whereabouts when they get to town, and creating a community of hikers every year?

The decision is still out, but I think the trail is what a hiker makes of it.

In 2002, I was driving to work, a 30-minute commute down the highway. I found myself at a standstill in rush-hour traffic. I was irritated at the extra time it would take to get to work. I used to get out early to avoid the traffic, but I recently started my own part-time business and slept later in the mornings.

Brian and I had recently bought a house, working extra hours to make money to transform it into our home, purchasing paint and furniture, buying newer cars, and putting money away for retirement. But as I sat in my car, not moving at all and quite angry, it hit me like a lead weight. *I was in the middle of the rat race – the Rat Race –* the three most horrible words in the English language.

Did I not learn *anything* from the Appalachian Trail? Take away my membership to The Appalachian Trail Conference! Banish me from all activities related to the Trail! Let the Appalachian Long Distance Hiking Association reject me! Burn my backpack and the rest of my gear!

How could I have let this happen? How could I hike down Katahdin and land in a *cubicle*? How could I drive to work for over half an hour *each way*? Wasn't I supposed to be hiking The Pacific Crest Trail? Wasn't I supposed to become a forest ranger? How could I look my trail friends in the face? That part was simple because I was *too busy to see* my trail friends!

I had become an Appalachian Trail *failure!*

I chastised myself the entire ride to work. But one tiny part of me kept screaming back to all those comments, and the answer was simple: "Yes, but I actually *like* my job!" I loved going to work every day. I loved helping to solve problems. And I loved the little business that I was starting. I had great satisfaction every day, knowing I worked my hardest and did my best every single day.

And I loved my house. It was ours. My husband and I worked on it and turned it into our home.

And then I decided it was okay. So what if I was in the rat race? The goal of The Appalachian Trail is not to get you to walk out of society and live in the mountains forever. The goal is to find acceptance in your life, whatever that may be for you.

It's been 25 years since I hiked The Appalachian Trail in 1998. With the advent of Facebook, I've been in touch with some trail friends from both my 1996 and 1998 hikes. We remember the good times, and it makes us nostalgic for the romance of the trail. People have always asked me if

I would hike the trail again. Yes, in a heartbeat. But then I think of all the other long-distance trails out there. Maybe I want to hike the Pacific Crest Trail? Or maybe one of the trails in Europe, like the Camino de Santiago. But then reality hits. I hear a nagging voice deep down inside that says, "Remember – if you want to go cross country, do it in an RV."

The answer is: I don't know. I'm happy with life as it is right now. I don't know the future, so I'll never say never.

One thing I know for sure is that hiking The Appalachian Trail changes you in ways people can't predict. We become connected to the trail and all the other people who have hiked or will hike it in the future. We are all different, but we become a community of like-minded people. The trail becomes part of us. Every day, I think of my hike. Whether it's talking to someone I met back then, or remembering a particular situation I find myself in again, like complaining about the cold or dealing with the rain, I remember my trail.

The trail provides different things for different people. For some, the trail is a physical test of strength. For others, it's a way to explore. And yet, for others, it's a way to find themselves, giving them direction and hope when they once felt lost. And isn't that the meaning and purpose of life? To find your gift and share it with the world?

You don't need to hike the Appalachian Trail to find your purpose. You just need to remember the goal, to find your purpose and share it with others. But I needed the trail. I needed to hike. I needed direction. And I found that direction by following the white blazes.

The Appalachian Trail is a part of me. It always will be. It made me who I am today.

After all, I am Trail Gimp.

www.ingramcontent.com/pod-product-compliance
Lightning Source LLC
Chambersburg PA
CBHW020319010526
44107CB00054B/1904